PLAGUES & POXES

THE IMPACT
OF HUMAN HISTORY
ON EPIDEMIC DISEASE

PLAGUES & POXES

THE IMPACT
OF HUMAN HISTORY
ON EPIDEMIC DISEASE

Alfred Jay Bollet, M.D.

NEW YORK

Demos Medical Publishing, Inc.
386 Park Avenue South, New York, NY 10016, USA
Visit our website at www.demosmedpub.com

Library of Congress Cataloging-in-Publication Data
Bollet, Alfred J.
  Plagues & poxes : the impact of human history on epidemic disease /
Alfred Jay Bollet.— 2nd ed.
    p. ; cm.
Includes bibliographical references.
  ISBN 1-888799-79-X
  1. Epidemiology—History.
  [DNLM: 1. Disease Outbreaks—history. 2. Communicable
Diseases—history. 3. Epidemiology—history. WA 11.1 B691p 2004] I.
Title: Plagues and poxes. II. Title.
  RA649.B65 2004
  614.4'9—dc21
                                        2003011450
Made in the United States of America

TO AUDREY

"We've known so much of happiness,
We've had our cup of joy,
And memory is one gift of God
That death cannot destroy."

From "Should You Go First," by AK Rowswell, in Poems that Live Forever, ed. by Hazel Felleman, Garden City, NY, Doubleday, 1965.

ACKNOWLEDGMENTS

I would like to thank the publisher of Demos Medical Publishing, Dr. Diana M. Schneider, for her assistance and interest in this work. She has been an enormous help both as advisor and editor.

CONTENTS

PREFACE

The first edition of *Plagues and Poxes* concentrated on the recurrent appearances and disappearances of new diseases in various parts of the world, and the impact of those diseases on history, especially political and military history. Since its appearance so many new diseases of great importance have appeared that the point of the book is no longer news or surprising. Examples include AIDS, of course, the most important and devastating of the new diseases, but Lyme disease, a new devastating form of asthma, a new form of viral encephalitis, West Nile virus, and a new form of viral hepatitis, hepatitis C, has come to the fore and is now the most serious form of that disease. So many new diseases have appeared that we have books and papers on "Emerging Diseases" and, more specifically, emerging viruses. At the same time, established but relatively new diseases have waned in frequency, most notably peptic ulcers, cancer of the stomach, and rheumatic fever, and deaths from heart disease have decreased considerably. But a new phenomenon has come to the forefront of public consciousness—intentionally caused disease, or bioterrorism. Thinking about the history of disease, these new concerns have brought to mind the fact that historical phenomena—military, political, and technological—have impacted the occurrence and severity of disease for as far back as history goes. This new edition shifted the emphasis to the impact of history on disease, rather than the reverse.

Historical developments have always been causal factors in the production of disease, at least since the first agriculturalists domesticated previously wild animals and caught their diseases. Measles, smallpox, and a variety of bacterial diseases are examples. Knowledge of the deadly nature and contagiousness of disease has lead to military efforts to induce disease in enemies, especially during sieges; bubonic plague and syphilis are major examples dating back to the fourteenth and sixteenth centuries.

On the other hand, knowledge of how diseases are spread has led to useful and sometimes successful efforts to control outbreaks of disease, beginning with quarantine for bubonic plague and, most notably, the successful containment of an outbreak of a serious severe respiratory disease in 2003 (SARS).

Knowledge of the factors that have been of importance in the international spread of major epidemic diseases in the past, both infectious and non-infectious, is worth reviewing in detail, and that is the subject of this new, revised edition of *Plagues and Poxes*.

UNINTENTIONAL CAUSES

OF EPIDEMIC DISEASES

THE IMPACT OF
HUMAN HISTORY
ON DISEASE

MANY OF THE WORST DISEASES OF THE PAST — INFECTIONS such as typhoid fever, smallpox, and plague—have now become rare, at least in developed countries. In contrast, noninfectious diseases, such as cancer and coronary heart disease, have replaced them as major epidemic causes of death. It is usually human actions, including warfare, commercial travel, social adaptations, and dietary modifications, that precipitate the rise and fall of diseases.

Some infectious diseases that have caused the most devastating mass mortality in human history can trace their origin and mode of spread to human activity and behavior. Many other diseases, both infectious and noninfectious, have been caused and spread by technological changes that benefited society as a whole, but had serious side effects that resulted in epidemic disease. For example, changes in food technology, mainly the availability of new foods or new means of processing old foods, have inadvertently brought on massive outbreaks of disease. Beriberi and pellagra are prime examples of this phenomenon. In both instances, new technology made more food available and thus supported a much larger population; at the same time, because micronutrients and the conse-

1

quences of lack of them were not yet known, they induced nutritional deficiency diseases.

Such phenomena are avoidable, and those diseases caused by human actions are preventable. We have seen a most important example of this in recent times in the decreased incidence of coronary heart disease that resulted from changes in smoking and dietary habits in the United States and Western Europe. A clear knowledge of how and why epidemic diseases appear and spread is important in curbing the damage they do. (Although chemical pollution of the environment threatens to cause severe epidemic diseases, thus far only localized outbreaks of illnesses have been caused by air or water pollution. A discussion of the threat posed by these phenomena requires a separate volume and will not be covered here.)

Plagues and Poxes concentrates on the history of major outbreaks of both infectious and noninfectious disease caused by human action through the ages. Prime historical examples of how human action resulted in epidemics of infectious diseases include the search for gold in the New World, which spread smallpox and measles among previously unexposed Native American populations; the corresponding introduction of syphilis into the Old World by European adventurers; and the importation of African slaves into the Western hemisphere, which introduced devastating new diseases such as malaria and yellow fever. Such interchange of disease still occurs, with the AIDS epidemic probably the most important example in recent decades. An analysis of the historic spread of these diseases may be useful in preventing new epidemics.

Most of the diseases discussed in the following chapters are side effects—the consequences of human actions that unintentionally caused them. Today, however, we are faced with concern for the intentional spread of disease through acts of bioterrorism. Several chapters are thus devoted to the history and knowledge of those diseases that are thought to be potential candidates for bioterrorism.

ORIGINS OF SOME INFECTIOUS DISEASES. Before agriculture, humans lived in small hunter-gatherer tribes. A high infant mortality rate probably kept the population small, although evidence suggests that intentional measures, such as infanticide, lengthening the birth interval through prolonged lactation-amenorrhea, sexual abstinence, or abortion, were also used to keep tribal size down to levels that the food supply could support. Most clans or tribes were nomadic, following the seasonal patterns of availability of game and vegetation. Based on bone and skeletal analyses, paleontologic evidence shows that hunter-gatherers (at least the ones who survived to adulthood) were healthy people, maybe even healthier than populations that developed after the introduction of agriculture.[1]

The development of agriculture resulted in a considerable increase in the human population in those areas that adopted the new techniques. With agriculture came a more settled existence that led to larger population units and more complex social structures, including administrative or political systems involving kings, bureaucrats, and taxes. Large clusters of humans thus gave rise to true civilizations in which some people were able to devote their efforts to administrative or artistic skills instead of to simply obtaining food. Unfortunately, these larger and more condensed population groups also gave rise to "crowd diseases." Large groups of people allowed the spread and perpetuation of infectious diseases agents because susceptible, nonimmune people kept appearing in sufficient numbers to keep a disease from dying out.

The domestication of animals occurred along with organized agriculture. This resulted in larger numbers and greater varieties of animals living in close proximity to humans. Some of the diseases of these animals now could affect humans, or perhaps become genetically modified to become epidemic human diseases. The genetic structure of the relevant organisms provides clues that the animal diseases listed in Table 1-1 are closely related to human diseases. Other diseases may belong on this list, the most important being AIDS, which may be a simian disease that has spread to humans.

Another disease that might be discussed is typhus. However, although a great deal has been written about typhus in history, in many outbreaks it is hard to establish that the diseases being described before the mid-nineteenth century were in fact typhus. For example, typhoid fever was not distinguished as a separate entity distinct from typhus until the 1830s, and was named for its clinical resemblance to typhus. After that time typhus was less and less commonly diagnosed and typhoid became more and more a dominant disease and cause of death. There is a lot of evidence that typhus became common after the beginning of the sixteenth century, especially among armies, and that it was spread

Table 1-1. Human Diseases and Their Animal Counterparts

Human disease	Genetically related animal disease
Measles	Rinderpest of cattle
Tuberculosis	Tuberculosis of cattle
Smallpox	Pox viruses of domestic animals, including cowpox
Influenza	Influenza in pigs, ducks, and chickens
Whooping cough	Similar disease in pigs and dogs
Falciparum* malaria	Malaria in birds (perhaps chickens and ducks)

* The most severe form of malaria, which causes high rates of mortality in humans.

primarily by the troops during wars.[2] It became a constant threat to prisoners in jails (where it was often called "jail fever"), to people crowded on ships ("ship fever"), and when troops were gathered together for training ("camp fever"). During the American Civil War there were virtually no cases of typhus diagnosed despite optimal conditions for its spread. Soldiers existed in crowded living conditions and virtually all the soldiers and officer on both sides were heavily infested with lice; in addition, many of the soldiers were recent immigrants from European areas where typhus was common. But typhoid was the major killer disease while typhus—well known to Civil War doctors—was very rare. In view of the voluminous literature on typhus and doubts as to the accuracy of the diagnoses before the mid-nineteenth century, I have omitted coverage of that disease.

EPIDEMICS OF NONINFECTIOUS DISEASES. Histories of epidemic disease concentrate on those infectious diseases that caused famous outbreaks and affected the course of historic events, but great epidemics of noninfectious diseases occurred as well. These epidemics were possibly less dramatic because of their gradual onsets. However, many were as devastating as many infectious diseases in terms of numbers of deaths they caused. The most notable examples are the nutritional deficiency diseases, scurvy being the most famous from the standpoint of its effect on history. However, the concept of a deficiency of a specific, individual nutrient as a cause of disease was not understood before the early twentieth century. From the late eighteenth century onward, it was believed that disease was caused by the *presence* of something abnormal; how then, could it be due to the *absence* of something? Once the concept of micronutrient deficiency was understood, measures to limit the occurrence of these diseases began. Modern scientific methods soon identified deficient nutritional components, isolated them, and synthesized them so that supplements could be made available in adequate quantities to combat these dietary diseases.

The first deficiency diseases appeared when early human populations settled into farming communities, and the wide variety of foods enjoyed by nomadic hunter-gatherer groups was no longer available. Through paleopathology—the study of ancient remains—we can safely guess that the first epidemic nutritional deficiency disease was probably iron-deficiency anemia. In long-standing iron-deficiency anemia, bones, especially those of the skull, show changes caused by an increase in the size and number of blood forming spaces filled by the bone marrow, along with a corresponding enlargement of the marrow as it tries to compensate for the lack of iron by making more red blood cells. Such bony changes, called *porotic hyperostosis*, are seen in modern humans with long-standing anemia, especially those caused by genetic deficiency syndromes that begin in childhood. Although data is limited, a higher frequency of such changes has been found in the skulls and bones of early agricultural societies compared to the bones of hunter-gatherer groups. These findings most likely point to a lack of dietary iron, a vital nutrient present mainly in red meat but mostly absent in vegetables. As agriculture led to a more settled, less nomadic existence, the human diet changed from one of primarily meat, in the form of game, to vegetables and grains. This inevitably led to iron deficiency.

Although the domestication of animals provided new sources of meat, paleopathologic evidence of iron deficiency shows that these supplies were often inadequate for the burgeoning population. To compound the problem, settled agricultural societies are more prone to parasitic infections spread by the fecal contamination of water supplies; many of these parasites cause intestinal blood loss, thus aggravating the problem of anemia. Iron deficiency is most severe in individuals who need iron most—growing children and menstruating women.

Iron deficiency causes functional impairment, including weakness, lassitude, and a general lack of energy. Other enzymes in the body require iron in addition to hemoglobin, and the effects of iron deficiency are widespread in the body, as shown by the clinical observation that treatment of such patients with iron results usually in marked symptomatic improvement before the hemoglobin level begins to rise.

Changes in the availability and nature of specific foods continued to affect both the size of population groups and the health of these groups throughout history. For example, when New World maize (corn) was introduced to Europe, the greater caloric yield per acre resulted in a considerable population increase in areas that grew it, especially Spain and Italy. Potatoes introduced into Ireland from the New World resulted in a great increase in population there.

In Ireland during the 1840s and 1850s, severe famine resulted from the loss of the potato crops to a fungal infestation, coupled with British laws that required the export of food that was raised. The population of Ireland had risen from about 2 million to about 4 million after the potato was introduced. Deaths from famine (with scurvy diagnosed in a high proportion of the people), coupled with emigration, resulted in the population decreasing back to 2 million within a decade.

The effect of maize on population growth was similar to that of the potato, but the reason for the epidemic disease that followed was quite different. In both cases, the problem was the fragile nutritional state that results when any single vegetable crop is the main source of food. However, in the case of maize, an epidemic of pellagra resulted from the almost exclusive use of maize as a staple food. The epidemic was severe in southern Europe late in the eighteenth century and continued to be so at least through the nineteenth century; pellagra appeared in the United States late in the nineteenth century, causing millions of cases and hundreds of thousands of deaths. The cause of pellagra is not famine, but a deficiency in the amino acid lysine. A change in the method of milling corn resulted in the loss of the marginal amounts of lysine it contains, and the diet of those people dependent on cornmeal as their main staple was now deficient in this amino acid.

A similar epidemic of a nutritional disease occurred in the Far East late in the nineteenth century. Populations dependent on rice as their main source of calories and protein developed a new disease, beriberi, when the method of milling the rice was changed by new food processing technology that removed the nutritious outer layers of the rice kernel in the process of "polishing" it. Although the total quantity of food available increased as spoilage was diminished, diets that previously maintained health became deficient. As another example, rickets—a Vitamin D deficiency disease—became epidemic when children no longer received enough sunlight because of the crowded urban conditions and heavy smoke cover in cities during the burgeoning Industrial Age.

A BRIEF HISTORY OF BIOLOGICAL WARFARE.   Biological warfare is not a new phenomenon. Although war has always helped to spread disease, attempts have been made to intentionally cause epidemic disease almost since the dawn of recorded history. For example, since antiquity, wells and other water sources for armies and civilian populations under attack have been purposely contaminated with animal or human cadavers as well as with excrement. Among the earliest recorded examples of the use of agents thought to cause disease in battle are the actions of Scythian archers, who used arrows dipped in blood, manure, or fluids from decomposing bodies when trying to stop the invading Assyrians in the seventh century BCE.

Spontaneous diarrhea and dysentery have always been the scourge of armies in the field, vastly impairing the effectiveness of soldiers. In the fighting among the Greeks in the sixth century BCE, Solon of Athens had water supplies poisoned with hellebore, a purgative. During the American Civil War when diarrhea was ubiquitous—Walt Whitman said the war was "about nine hundred and ninety-nine parts diarrhea to one part glory"—a tradition arose not to shoot a man "while he is attending to the urgent call of nature" and was honored by both sides throughout the war.

As described in the chapter on bubonic plague, human cadavers were used in the fourteenth century in an attempt to spread disease during the outbreak of plague called the "Black Death." The epidemic began in an area of Russia, near the Crimea, during the siege of Kaffa (now Feodossia in the Ukraine). The besieging Tartars were dying in large numbers of a disease that caused the appearance of buboes in the groin, the classic lesion of bubonic plague. The Tartars attempted to spread the disease that was killing their soldiers by catapulting cadavers into the city with their hurling machines. Although the fleas that transmit plague may leave cadavers to seek living hosts on which to feed, the corpses catapulted over the walls of Kaffa probably were not carrying competent plague vectors. It is more likely that the disease appeared in the city because rats could move into and out despite the siege, bringing their fleas and plague bacilli with them. Soon, there was so much plague in the city that it was uninhabitable. It was abandoned, and the inhabitants boarded ships and retreated to their home port in Genoa, stopping at several other Mediterranean ports along the way. Plague was widely spread in this fashion.

Smallpox devastated the Native American populations when it was accidentally introduced by the Conquistadors. The Spaniards were immune to it because they had been exposed earlier in life. Smallpox also has been spread deliberately as a weapon of biowarfare. During the French and Indian War (1754–1763), Sir Jeffrey Amherst, commander of British forces in North America, suggested that smallpox be intentionally spread to "reduce" Native American tribes hostile to the British. During the fighting around Fort Pitt (now Pittsburgh), Captain Ecuyer, one of Amherst's subordinates, gave blankets and a handkerchief from patients in the smallpox hospital to the Native Americans and recorded in his journal, "I hope it will have the desired effect." *Fomites,* objects used by sick people that can harbor and potentially transmit disease agents, are not an efficient method of spreading smallpox, since the disease is spread primarily by airborne respiratory droplets. However, an epidemic of smallpox did occur among Native American tribes in the Ohio River Valley. Other contacts between Native Americans and Europeans might have been responsible, since smallpox had been affecting the Native Americans for more than 200 years, but the records reveal this act as a deliberate attempt to spread disease during war.

An important example of biowarfare in the Western Hemisphere was the use of curare by South American natives. Curare was made in a variety of ways, using extracts of the active principle from the bark of a variety of trees, with various plant additives and sometimes snake venom or venomous ants included. The mixture was boiled in water for about two days, then strained and evaporated to become a viscid paste. The potency of the paste was tested, for example, by pricking a frog with a stick dipped in the curare preparation and counting the number of leaps it would take before it collapsed and died. Darts dipped in the curare were then fired accurately through blowguns made of hollow grass stems such as bamboo. Since curare was scarce and difficult to prepare it was rarely used in tribal warfare—it was too valuable as a weapon for hunting. After being stuck by an arrow tip with curare on it, birds would die in one to two minutes, small mammals in up to ten minutes, larger mammals in up to 20 minutes, and the prey could be tracked until it died. The active agent in curare blocks the transmission of nerve impulses to the receptors in muscle fibers, paralyzing the muscles. Studies of its nature and actions led to improved understanding of the nature of the neuromuscular junction and the development of potent pharmaceutical agents with properties similar to those of curare. These drugs are used during major surgery to obtain good muscle relaxation, although the patient must breathe mechanically. In a sense, biological warfare can have its positive side!

Biological warfare made its greatest strides during the twentieth century. During World War I, the use of poison gases by the Germans on the Western Front is well known. Several agents were used, including chlorine and mustard gas, causing large numbers of deaths and horrific painful distress in survivors. The Allies countered with similar agents, but on a lesser scale.

Also during World War I, the Germans undertook covert biological warfare operations in neutral countries that traded with the Allies. Animal feed contaminated with anthrax and glanders (*Pseudomonas [Burkholdaria] mallei*) was used to infect Romanian sheep being raised for export to Russia. In 1916, cultures of these two organisms were confiscated from the German legation in Romania. Allegedly, the organism for glanders was also used by German saboteurs operating in Mesopotamia to inoculate 4,500 mules used in British operations against the Turks, and in France, saboteurs infected French cavalry horses. Argentinean livestock intended for export to Allied countries also were infected with anthrax and glanders, resulting in the death of more than 200 mules in 1917 and 1918. In the United States, during the early years of World War I, Germans attempted to contaminate animal feed and to infect horses intended for export.

Such biowarfare was banned by the 1925 Geneva Protocol for the "Prohibition of the Use in War of Asphyxiating, Poisonous, or other Gases, and of Bacteriological Methods of Warfare." The treaty prohibited the use of biological weapons, but did not proscribe basic research, production, or possession of biological weapons, and many of the countries that ratified the protocol stipulated that they retained the right of retaliation. A number of these countries, including Belgium, Canada, France, Great Britain, Italy, the Netherlands, Poland, and the Soviet Union—all parties to the Geneva protocol, began basic research programs to develop biological weapons after World War I. The United States did not ratify the Geneva protocol until 1975.

Between 1932 and 1945, the Japanese conducted an extensive program to study biological weapons, which they tested on Chinese prisoners. At a site near the town of Pingfan in Northeastern China, close to the city of Harbin, a program was set up that included about 150 buildings, five satellite camps, and a staff of more than 3,000 scientists and technicians. Additional units were located at Mukden, Changchen, and Nanking. Observations were made on prisoners infected with pathogens, including *Bacillus anthracis* which causes anthrax; *Neisseria meningitides*, the cause of cerebrospinal meningitis; various species of *Shigella* and *Salmonella*, which cause dysentery; *Vibrio cholera*, the agent of cholera; and *Yersinia pestis*, the cause of bubonic plague. At least 10,000 Chinese prisoners died as a direct result of these experimental infections or were executed after experimentation.

In addition, the Japanese also mounted biological attacks on at least eleven Chinese cities. The attacks include contamination of water supplies and food items with cultures of the organisms that cause anthrax, cholera, and dysentery. Cultures were sprayed directly into homes from sources on the ground or sprayed on urban areas from aircraft. The Japanese purposely tried to start an epidemic of bubonic plague by breeding fleas in a laboratory and allowing them to feed on plague-infected rats. The infected fleas were then released from aircraft over Chinese cities. As many as 15 million plague-fed fleas were released per attack when flea bombs with small amounts of explosive were released over Ningpo, in October 1940. The Chinese noticed that the Japanese planes came in very low and that the ground was white with jumping, snowlike particles, after the bombs fell. Cases of plague appeared in the town, and panic spread. About 500 deaths resulted, and a local shortage of coffins made it necessary for survivors to bury victims two to a coffin.

Some attempts by the Japanese to spread diseases among the Chinese backfired. In 1941, a biological attack on Changteh reportedly sickened the assaulting Japanese troops, causing approximately 10,000 casualties and 1,700 deaths among them, mostly due to cholera. Field trials were terminated in 1942, although basic research continued in the laboratories at Pingfan until the end of the war.

In Germany during World War II, Hitler reportedly issued orders prohibiting biological weapons development. Nevertheless, high-ranking Nazi party officials supported German scientists who performed such research. While no German battlefield attacks with biological weapons ever materialized, prisoners in Nazi concentration camps were forcibly infected with two species of *Rickettsia*, the organisms that cause typhus; hepatitis A virus; and several species of malaria. They were then treated with investigational vaccines and drugs. The only known use of biological warfare by Germany was the pollution with sewage of a large reservoir in northwestern Bohemia in May 1945, near the end of the war in Europe. (Unconfirmed reports state that the Germans considered releasing live, plague-infected rats from submarines so that they would swim to shore and spread the disease in Britain. They decided it wouldn't work.)

In an ironic twist, the combination of a vaccine and a serologic test was used as a biological defense against the Nazi program of exportation and extermination of civilians. The German army carefully avoided civilian areas known to be infected with epidemic typhus by testing the inhabitants for serum antibodies that indicated the presence or prior exposure to the disease (the Weil-Felix reaction). Consequently, physicians in one area of occupied Poland injected people with killed organisms (Proteus OX-19) that can produce a positive Weil-Felix test. Thus, they induced false positive tests for typhus, and those residents of the area who had positive tests were not deported to concentration camps.

The Allies developed biological weapons during World War II. Weaponized spores of anthrax were used in studies conducted on Gruinard Island near the coast of Scotland. As a result, the island remained heavily contaminated with viable anthrax spores, and no humans or livestock could use it safely until it was decontaminated in 1986.

The United States established a research and development facility at Camp (later Fort) Detrick in Maryland, as well as at several other sites. Experiments were conducted to study the organisms of anthrax and brucellosis (*Brucella suis*). During World War II, 5,000 bombs filled with anthrax spores were produced at a pilot plant; these bombs were destroyed after the war. The program was expanded during the Korean War (1950-1953), when a large-scale production facility with strong biosafety measures was constructed at Pine Bluff, Arkansas. A program to develop countermeasures to protect troops from biological attack was begun in 1953. Vaccines and antisera were studied, as were other therapeutic agents.

Voluntary human experiments at Fort Detrick were performed in a large aerosolization chamber known as the "eight ball." Volunteers were exposed to tularemia and to *Coxiellia burnetti*, the organism of Q fever, the only rickettsial disease that does not require an insect vector. Q fever is transmitted by inhalation and causes a flu–like syndrome and pneumonia.

Other studies were done with essentially harmless agents that could simulate dangerous microbes, including various fungi and several species of bacteria. Such simulants were released by aerosolization over New York City, San Francisco, and other cities between 1949 and 1968, so that the spread and survival of the biological agents could be studied. Despite the low pathogenicity of these agents, concerns about public health hazards led to these studies being discontinued.

During the Korean War, the Soviet Union, China, and North Korea accused the United States of using biological warfare against North Korean and Chinese soldiers. The United States denied the accusation and requested an impartial investigation, but neither China nor North Korea would cooperate with requests by the International Committee of the Red Cross and the World Health Organization to investigate. The episode demonstrated the propaganda value of biological warfare allegations even though no basis for the charges existed. Other accusations were made—including some by the Soviets, that U.S. tests of biological weapons resulted in a plague epidemic among Canadian Eskimos and an epidemic of cholera in southeastern China. The United States also was accused of covert release of dengue fever virus in Cuba.

Similar accusations against Soviet forces, made by the United States, were also widely regarded as erroneous. These accusations stated that yellow rain (aerosolized trichothecene mycotoxins derived from fungi of the genus *Fusarium*) was used in Laos, Kampuchea, and Afghanistan. Supporting evidence was not uncovered, and this particular species of Fusarium is so widely present in the environment that the tiny amounts found in these surveys were probably naturally occurring.

In 1972, a convention was adopted on "The Prohibition of the Development, Production, and Stockpiling of Bacteriological (Biological) and Toxin Weapons and Their Destruction." The United States implemented a policy never to use biological weapons, including toxins, under any circumstances whatsoever, except for research efforts directed exclusively to the development of defensive measures, diagnostic tests, vaccines, and the treatment of potential biological weapons attacks. Stockpiles of pathogens and the entire biological arsenal were destroyed between May 1971 and February 1973. One factor in the willingness of the United States to terminate an offensive biological weapons program was thought to be the availability of nuclear weapons for similar purposes. However, biological weapons are of much lower cost, a great deal easier to produce and disseminate secretly, and can give comparable—or even greater— mortality than nuclear agents. For this reason, they have become the weapon of choice for terrorists.

A biological agent was used for covert assassinations during the 1970s. Ricin, the lethal toxin derived from the ubiquitous castor bean, was weaponized by the Secret Service of the Soviet Union and deployed by the Bulgarian Secret Service. Metallic pellets 1.7 mm in diameter were cross-drilled, filled with ricin, and then sealed with wax that would melt at body temperature. The pellets were discharged from spring-powered weapons disguised as umbrellas. In 1978, such weapons were used to assassinate Georgie Markov, a Bulgarian defector living in

London, and in an unsuccessful attack on another Bulgarian defector, Vladimir Kostov. Similar weapons may have been used in at least six other assassinations.

In April 1979, an epidemic of anthrax occurred among people who lived or worked in a narrow zone downwind and within four kilometers of the Soviet military microbiology facility in Sverdlovsk (now Katerinberg) Russia. In addition, livestock as far as 50 km along an extension of the downwind epidemic zone died of anthrax. Although at the time the Soviets denied that this epidemic was caused by the release of agents from their biological weapons program, in 1992, President Boris Yeltsin admitted that the epidemic had been caused by the accidental release of anthrax spores. At least seventy-seven human cases and sixty-six deaths occurred from inhalation of anthrax, the largest documented epidemic of inhalational anthrax known to history.

During the 1970s and 1980s, the Soviet Biopreparat organization worked on biological weapons. It operated at least six research laboratories and five production facilities and employed 55,000 scientists and technicians.

At the time of the Gulf War, in 1991, at least 150,000 U.S. troops received toxoid vaccine against anthrax and 8,000 received a botulinum toxoid vaccine, both FDA approved for investigational use. In addition, 30 million 500 mg oral doses of ciprofloxacin were stockpiled in the Gulf area, enough to provide a one-month course of antibiotic prophylaxis for the 500,000 U.S. troops in the area in the event that anthrax spores were used as a biological weapon.

After the war, Iraqi officials admitted to having had an offensive biological weapons program that included basic research on anthrax, rotavirus, camelpox virus, aflatoxin, botulinum toxin, mycotoxins, and an anticrop agent called wheat cover rust. However, no such weapons were employed during the war, and claims that the Iraqi government has since destroyed these biological agents and nerve gases are being investigated as this is being written.

A BRIEF HISTORY OF BIOTERRORISM. The biological threat posed by non-state-sponsored terrorists was demonstrated in late September 1984, when the Rajneeshee cult intentionally contaminated salad bars in Oregon restaurants with a bacterial agent that causes dysentery, *Salmonella typhimurium*. The incident resulted in 751 cases of gastroenteritis and 45 hospitalizations. Despite extensive investigation of this outbreak, the origin of the epidemic as a deliberate biological attack was not confirmed until a cult member admitted to it the following year.

In March 1995, a Japanese cult called Aum Shinrikyo attacked civilians on a Tokyo subway using sarin, a poisonous nerve gas; twelve people were killed and about 5,000 sickened. The cult conducted research on anthrax, botulinum, and

Q fever; when seized by police, their arsenal allegedly contained an aerosolized form of botulinum toxin and drone aircraft equipped with spray tanks. The cult reportedly launched three other biological attacks in Japan, using anthrax and botulinum toxin that, fortunately, failed due to inadequate microbiological technique, deficient aerosol-generating equipment, or internal sabotage. Botulism spores are ubiquitous, and cult members obtained them from soil collected in northern Japan. In 1992, the cult also sent members to Zaire to obtain Ebola virus for weapons development.[3]

Bioterrorist attacks, funded or aided by rogue governments, are even more likely than biological warfare conducted by governments. Given the enormous potency of the agents known and the likelihood that such attacks will occur in the future, the history and status of these epidemic diseases is covered in this new edition of *Plagues and Poxes*.

ADDITIONAL READING

Ampel NM. Plagues— what's past is present: thoughts on the origin and history of new infectious diseases *Rev Infect Dis* 1991;13:658.

Cartwright FF. *Disease and History, The Influence of Disease in Shaping History.* New York: Crowell, 1972.

Creighton C. *A History of Epidemics in Britain.* London: Cass, 1965.

Crosby AW. *Ecological Imperialism, The Biological Expansion of Europe.* Cambridge, UK: Cambridge Univ Press, 1986.

Crosby AW. *Germs, Seeds & Animals: Studies in Ecological History.* Armonk, NY: M.E. Sharpe, 1994.

Diamond JM. *Guns, Germs, and Steel: The Fates of Human Societies.* New York: W.W. Norton & Co, 1997.

Ewald PW. *Evolution of Infectious Disease.* New York: Oxford Univ Press, 1994.

Garrison HFH. *An Introduction to the History of Medicine.* 4th ed. Philadelphia: W. B. Saunders Co, 1913.

Hoy S. *Chasing Dirt, The Pursuit of Cleanliness.* New York: Oxford Univ Press, 1995.

Kiple KF. *The Cambridge World History of Human Disease.* Cambridge, NY: Cambridge Univ Press, 1993.

Lederberg J. Viruses and Humankind: Intracellular symbiosis and evolutionary competition. In: Morse SS. *Emerging Viruses.* New York: Oxford Univ Press, 1993.

Mahy BW, Brown CC. Emerging zoonoses: crossing the species barrier. *Rev Sci and Technol* 2000;19:33.

McNeill WH. Patterns of disease emergence in history. In: Morse SS, ed. *Emerging Viruses.* New York: Oxford Univ Press, 1993.

Morse SS. Examining the origins of emerging viruses. In: Morse SS, ed. *Emerging Viruses.* New York: Oxford Univ Press, 1993.

Prinzing F. *Epidemics Resulting from Wars.* Oxford, Clarendon Press, 1916.

Rogers N. *Dirt and Disease, Polio Before FDR.* New Brunswick, NJ: Rutgers Univ Press, 1992.

Tomes N. *The Gospel of Germs: Men, Women, and the Microbe in American Life.* Cambridge, MA: Harvard Univ Press, 1998.

Walker DH, Barbour AG, et al. Emerging bacterial zoonotic and vector-borne diseases. Ecological and epidemiological factors. JAMA 1998;275:463.

Wills, C. *Yellow Fever, Black Goddess, The Coevolution of People and Plagues.* Reading, MA: Addison Wesley, 1996.

Zinsser H. *Rats, Lice and History.* New York: Bantam Books, 1934.

1 Richard H. Steckel, Jerome C. Rose, *The Backbone of History.* New York, Cambridge Univ. Press, 2002

2 Hans Zinsser, *Rats Lice and History.* New York, Bantam Books, 1935.

3 GW Christopher et al. Biological warfare: a historical perspective, JAMA 1997; 278: 412 – 417

PART ONE

Infectious Diseases

CHAPTER 1

BUBONIC PLAGUE

THE PROTOTYPE
OF PANDEMIC DISASTERS

ALL EPIDEMICS OF DEADLY DISEASES IN HUMAN HISTORY have been called *plagues* to stress how devastating these outbreaks are. However, whenever actual bubonic plague appears, panic develops, quarantine measures are instituted, and people flee the area. Although primarily a disease of rats and other small mammals, and their fleas, bubonic plague is spread from place to place by human commerce and travel, an excellent route for the migration of the animal vectors of the disease.

Formally known as *bubonic plague* because of the enlarged, painful, abscessed lymph nodes, or *buboes*, it produces, bubonic plague was also called the Black Death during a devastating pandemic in the mid-fourteenth century. The name most likely arose because patients with severe disease develop septicemia, a widespread contamination of the blood system. This, in turn, leads to a syndrome formally known as disseminated intravascular coagulation (DIC), in which multiple hemorrhages and patches of gangrene develop in the skin, turning large areas of the body black.

Like most other epidemic infectious diseases, war has played an important role in the spread of plague and, as early as 1347, plague was successfully employed as a form of biological warfare. As recently as World War II, the Japanese used airplanes to spread infected fleas over several Chinese cities, as discussed earlier.

Plague does not readily spread directly from person to person; its transmission depends on small animal hosts, especially rats and their fleas. Hungry fleas feed on infected rats and, when these rats die, the fleas may move on to a human host. Plague can be spread directly from person to person when it causes pneumonia and, although the same organisms that cause the bubonic form of the disease can cause pneumonia, severe lung disease does not occur frequently enough to rely on airborne pathogens to purposely spread the disease.

The septicemia that occurs in extremely sick plague patients can spread the disease without the help of rats. A flea directly feeding on the contaminated blood of a septicemic patient could pick up sufficient numbers of organisms to infect another person with its bite.

Sporadic cases of plague still occur in the United States, primarily in the Southwest, where small wild mammals and their fleas serve as a reservoir for the disease. When a couple from a rural area near Santa Fe, New Mexico arrived in New York early in 2003 they were unknowingly incubating bubonic plague. Their hospitalization led to alarming news reports. The husband barely survived after developing septicemic disease with DIC and gangrenous changes in his legs that required bilateral below-the-knee amputations. No further cases occurred, however, and public concern (and news media interest) quickly waned. The two cases that startled New Yorkers were no surprise to people of the Southwest, where a few cases occur almost every year.

BUBONIC PLAGUE IN HISTORY. Bubonic plague has caused major epidemics since ancient times, with huge mortality rates. Some historians suspect that the Plague of Athens, described by Thucidides during the Peloponnesian War (in the fifth century BCE, with outbreaks occurring in 430, 429, and 427), was actually bubonic plague. Epidemiologists disagree; Thucidides does not describe buboes, and mortality among doctors was the highest of all groups, suggesting human-to-human spread (contagion). Such spread does not occur unless the plague victim has developed pneumonia (pneumonic plague), and this form of infection usually primarily affects family members.

Thucidides reported that when human remains were left lying unburied because of the number of deaths, scavengers avoided them or, if they did taste the flesh died soon afterward. Such spread of bubonic plague could occur if the deceased person had infected fleas still on his body, but it has not been described in other epidemics that were more likely plague. Thucidides also mentioned that second attacks occurred, a very unlikely occurrence in plague, which gives its victims immunity; however, he points out that the second attacks were never fatal, suggesting some degree of increased resistance to the infection.

The disease reportedly spread to Athens from Egypt; Athens was a busy commercial city with a nearby port, whereas its enemy, Sparta, was inland, which might explain why it was spared the epidemic. The extremely high mortality in Athens, which claimed Pericles and his two sons among its victims, crippled its defenses. Sparta eventually won the Peloponnesian War, thus ending the Golden Age of Athens. (One author wrote that more ink has been spilt trying to explain this fateful plague than blood spilt during the war itself.)

In its early years, Rome was attacked by many severe epidemics of uncertain nature. Plague has been suggested as an explanation for many of them, but no descriptions of cases suggest that disease. The Antonine Plague of 164–180 CE, described by Galen, was spread rapidly by the return to Rome of infected soldiers in 166. Marcus Aurelius died of it. Galen's description is not recognizable to us, and some authors think this epidemic was more likely smallpox than plague; others favor typhus. In 251–266, the Plague of Cyprian, or the Aurelian Plague, in which half the population of Alexandria perished, also seems more likely to have been smallpox than plague. This epidemic also affected the invading Goths, who often gathered into crowds.

Many severe epidemics that occurred in the interval between the Justinian Plague of 542 and the Black Death of the fourteenth century have been labeled bubonic plague, but this identification is questionable. The high mortality rate of some of these epidemics suggests plague, but more persuasive evidence is lacking. The evidence for the Plague of Justinian having been bubonic plague is more convincing. Procopius clearly describes buboes during that epidemic. He also wrote, "There was a pestilence, by which the whole human race came near to be annihilated ... And this disease always took its start from the coast and from there went up into the interior." He added that, "at Pelusium [on the Mediterranean coast near the present-day entrance to the Suez canal, the plague] then moved to Alexandria and reached Constantinople in 542." Notably, the historical record of many devastating epidemics affecting the ancient world includes observations of the disease beginning in Egypt, or in Ethiopia and spreading to Egypt, then traveling down the Nile to cities in the delta and to other ports in the Mediterranean. Spread by human movements, and specifically by commerce, is a prominent feature of these and later epidemics.

THE BLACK DEATH. The most famous pandemic of bubonic plague was the Black Death of the mid-fourteenth century. The history of its appearance and spread illustrates how human activities, especially commerce, can cause the dissemination of a devastating disease, even one that primarily affects an animal species. The history of the Black Death and how it was spread is a model for the spread of many major epidemic diseases, since bubonic plague goes where travelers go. And, it is a history that starts with an attempt at biological warfare.

The story of the Black Death begins in 1338–1339, in the vicinity of Lake Issyk-Kul, in southern Russia near the Crimea, where a cemetery contains an unusual number of burials. Inscriptions state that the deaths were due to the plague. The disease spread from there along the main caravan routes from the Far East toward Western Europe and the Middle East. Even before the great pandemic traveled from the Crimea to the Mediterranean and other parts of the world, there is evidence of plague in southern Russia. For example, in 1346, outbreaks of plague accompanied traders along the Silk Road in Astrakhan (at the mouth of the Volga River) and Sarai (farther up the Volga). Records reveal the presence of the disease at caravan stations on the lower Volga River and, in 1347–1348, Ibn Battata, an Arab traveler and scholar returning along the Spice Route from India, reported hearing about the plague when he reached Aleppo in northern Syria. He noted that it had not been seen there before that year.

In this area of Central Asia, marmots were trapped for their fur, which was then sold to various traders who transshipped them along these caravan routes. Hunters and trappers always were happy to find sick or dying animals that they could catch easily, and around this time many untrapped marmots were found dead; trappers skinned these animals and sent the furs to be shipped to buyers in the West. Bales of marmot fur probably contained living fleas that became very hungry without a live animal on which to feed. Reports of illness in trappers were ignored. The furs reached Astrakhan and Sarai first and, when the bales were opened, the hungry fleas jumped out.

The area north of the Crimea, in what is now Russia, the Ukraine, and Rumania, was controlled by Mongols, descendants of the Golden Horde of Genghis Khan. The Russians called these people Tartars. The ports of the Crimea were used by rival Genoese and Venetian traders, who each allied themselves with rival Khans. The Tartar prince Janiberg Khan, who ruled the area known as Western Kipchak, became allied with Venice in 1340. His forces attacked the Genoese and their allies near the ports of the Crimea, forced them behind the walls of the fortified city of Kaffa (now Feodossia in the Ukraine), and besieged them there.

Gabriel De Mussis (1280–1356) left an account of the progress of the plague from the Crimea to his home in Piacenza in 1348. He described how, among the besieging forces of the Khan, "infinite numbers of Tartars and Saracens suddenly fell dead of an inexplicable disease...." They developed buboes in the groin and "putrid fever," and many died. "Tartars, fatigued by such a plague and pestiferous disease, ... observing themselves dying without hope ... ordered cadavers placed on their hurling machines and thrown into the city of Kaffa, so that by means of these intolerable passengers the defenders died widely. Thus there were projected mountains of dead.... And soon all the air was infected and the water poisoned, corrupt and putrefied, and such a great odor increased...." Thus we have a record of an early form of intentional biological warfare.

Because fleas leave cadavers to parasitize living hosts, it has been suggested that the corpses catapulted over the walls of Kaffa may not have been carrying competent plague vectors. Rats were not catapulted, but the city must have had its own supply. The cadavers may still have had infected fleas on them (either human or rat fleas, or both) and could thus have spread the disease inside the besieged city, or the infection could have been spread by rats migrating into and out of the city despite the siege. Either way, sickness made Kaffa uninhabitable during the winter of 1347–1348. The survivors fled to their boats and returned to the Mediterranean, spreading plague as they went, probably assisted by the ships' rats. Plague first appeared at Constantinople, the exit from the Black Sea and the capital of the Byzantine Empire; then it appeared in the Mediterranean ports of Egypt and the Near East.

When the Genoese ships from Kaffa arrived at Constantinople, crewmen were lying dead at the oars. Similar reports emanated from other port cities. Byzantine Emperor John VI [Ioannes VI Contacuzenus (1292?–1383)] wrote a history of his empire from 1320–1356 (he abdicated in 1352), stressing the Black Death "which ... attacked almost all the sea coasts of the world ... and all the islands, ... and spread throughout almost the entire world." He reported outbreaks on the Greek Islands of the Aegean and along the coast of Anatolia. In all, about sixteen galleys brought plague into Italian ports in 1348. Three made it to Genoa. One carried Venetians to their home port.

Twelve ships from the Crimea reached Messina in Sicily. When the citizens of Messina realized that ships were bringing plague, they drove them out of the ports. One ship went to Marseilles and carried the disease westward from there to Barcelona; the plague then spread throughout Spain and Portugal.

The Genoese realized that the ships from Kaffa brought plague with them and drove them away, but it was too late. The routes of the ships and of the refugees fleeing the affected cities illustrate how people spread the disease. It spread throughout Italy, northward into to Switzerland and Bavaria, and east to the Balkans. From Marseilles it spread by ship along the Mediterranean coast and up the Rhone River to Avignon, then the seat of the papacy. Because there were too many bodies to bury, Pope Clement VI (1300–1368) consecrated the river, so that dead bodies might be dumped in it. Plague also spread along the Mediterranean coast from Marseilles to Toulon and either down the Garonne River or by ship to Bordeaux. In August 1348, boats from Bordeaux carrying claret to Great Britain brought the disease there.

There is a record of a wool-carrying ship with full crew that left London bound for Bergen, Norway, in May 1349. Some days after leaving, the ship was found drifting off the coast of Norway with the entire crew dead. The disease then appeared in Norway and spread by ship to the rest of Scandinavia and to Germany; it reached Poland in 1351.

Plague reached into the depths of Russia in 1351 or 1352, not by spreading north from the region around the Crimea where the outbreak began, but via Sweden and Poland, because that was the direction in which trade flowed. The disease followed the trade routes and thus came back to Russia by ship via the Mediterranean, the Atlantic, and the Baltic Sea.

Boccaccio (1313–1375), whose father died of plague in 1348, described the disease in some detail. He mentioned buboes appearing in the groin and armpits, and added that, "the mere touching of the clothes or of whatever other thing had been touched or used of the sick appeared of itself to communicate the malady to the toucher." Air was "tainted by the scent of dead bodies" and people went about "carrying in their hands, some flowers, some odoriferous herbs, and other some divers kind of species, which they set to their noses." This practice, intended to ward off poisonous miasmas and disgusting, sickening odors, continued as a preventive measure until near the end of the nineteenth century. According to some sources, it is the origin of the practice of sending flowers to funerals.

Plague may have reached the Mesopotamian area independently of the Crimean ships, via caravans from Samarkand, in Turkestan, that traveled the southern route, south of the Caspian Sea, along the silk and spice routes, reaching Baghdad, Damascus, and then the Mediterranean coast. Ships carrying silks, slaves, and furs to Alexandria brought plague as early as 1347. From there it spread to Cairo, Gaza, and Beirut.

Inhabitants of seaports realized the danger of the plague and drove ships away, trying to institute a form of quarantine, but it was too little and too late. By the spring of 1348, Black Death was well established in Italy. *Quarantine,* derived from the Italian word for *forty,* lasted forty days, a period long enough for any incipient disease to become manifest and run its course. Quarantine became a standard practice whenever plague or any other feared disease appeared until well into the twentieth century. Facilities were established outside city walls for travelers to spend their period of quarantine before being allowed to enter the city. On land, quarantine was primarily designed to keep people outside the city, but infected rats and their fleas could still escape and infect a city. Keeping ships away from a port was more effective, but usually incomplete. There were few pockets of freedom from the Black Death.

It is estimated that the Black Death killed 25 million people during the years 1348–1350, a loss of one-third of the population of Europe and the Middle East. It has also been estimated that no less than 70 percent of those who contracted the disease died. In France, towns lost an estimated 50 percent and rural areas 30 percent of their inhabitants. The Black Death was followed by widespread famine because of insufficient labor to raise food. Malnutrition resulted in deaths from a variety of other diseases, probably including smallpox and typhus. "Sweating sickness" hit Britain at this time, with considerable mortality, but its nature is uncertain.

Severe epidemics of plague continued to occur in parts of Europe after the mid-fourteenth century. An outbreak began in Germany in 1356. As late as 1630–1631, 1.5 million people are thought to have died of plague in Italy, largely in Lombardy. In 1709, epidemic plague killed 300,000 people in Prussia. In 1720–1722, a severe epidemic in France affected Marseilles and Toulon, where 50 percent of the entire population died; in other cities, including Avignon, the death rate ranged between 30 and 50 percent. Napoleon's troops encountered plague when they invaded Egypt and the Middle East in 1801.

Beginning early in the eighteenth century, Europe was protected from the spread of plague from Ottoman areas by a barrier erected by Austria (the Habsburg-Ottoman frontier), primarily running through Hungary. Over 100,000 men manned it, with quarantine and checkpoint stations. This "Sanitary Cordon" limited human traffic and trade, and thus the spread of infectious diseases such as plague. The term cordon sanitaire has been used since for any attempt to wall off and prevent disease (or unwanted political influences).

Plague was endemic in England from fourteenth through the seventeenth centuries, with numerous outbreaks in the seventeenth century, some of them shutting down Shakespeare's theater. Severe epidemics occurred in London from 1604 to 1610, and 1640 to 1649, with at least four milder epidemics between those two larger ones. Outbreaks of plague in London ended with great fire of 1666.

The gradual ascendance of brown rats over black rats has been suggested as a factor in the subsidence of plague epidemics. Black rats tend to live in inhabited areas of houses, whereas brown rats prefer dark cellars and sewers, in less close contact with people. Because the rat flea can jump only 90 mm (3.5 inches), proximity to people may be important. However, the theory weakens, when we consider that brown rats had replaced black rats in Moscow before a particularly severe epidemic of plague struck during the 1770s, and brown rats did not reach England until 1727, over 60 years after the last "bout of the plague." Plague is not very particular about which species it affects. Rabbits, ferrets, dogs, and cats were also involved in other outbreaks, with the pattern of disease similar regardless of the original source.

Plague reappeared in England in 1902–1903, and again in 1906–1918, when twenty-four cases were described in a rural area of Suffolk. Six cases recovered (four bubonic and two pneumonic). Only four cases were confirmed bacterio-logically; the rest were considered likely to be bubonic plague. Investigators found infected rats and rat fleas-*Ceratphyllus fasciatus,* not the usual tropical rat flea-and a couple of infected rabbits, but no black rats were found in Suffolk dur-ing the period of that outbreak. To control the outbreak, rat catchers were used, and all 15,332 of the rats caught were dissected. Infected rats were found in twenty-seven areas. A key town in this outbreak was a port on River Orwell, where ocean-going traffic tied up. Investigators concluded that the most likely source of the disease was infected rats coming ashore. In subsequent years, investigators found infected ferrets, rabbits, and rats in rural areas.

Another theory about the history of plague is that a new, less pathogenic form of the causative organism, *Yersinia pestis,* may have evolved, or that resistance appeared in rats and man, decreasing the amount of plague in rats. The appear-ance and spread of a closely related organism, *Y. pseudotuberculosis,* may have been a factor—human infections with that organism are mild and give rise to cross resistance to *Y. pestis.* This observation is compatible with the theory of a famous parasitologist, Theobald Smith, who postulated that parasites evolve to less virulent forms that become able to co-exist with their hosts. Genetic stud-ies have shown that two genes play an important role in the pathogenic differ-ences between *Y. psuedotuberculosis* and *Y. pestis.* A mutation in one or both of these genes may account for the emergence of less virulent organisms, and these organisms may have replaced *Y. pestis* in rat populations, thus accounting for the subsidence of the disease.

The Plague of the 1890s. During the 1890s, a major epidemic of plague devel-oped in Hong Kong and mainland China. It was spread by maritime commerce, as plague usually is, and appeared in major port cities around the world. Ports in Thailand, Indo-China, and Java were affected, as were Manila, Sydney, Capetown, Buenos Aires, Oporto, Honolulu, Glasgow, Mauritius, and Auckland. It returned to China, where a severe epidemic occurred in Yunan. Plague also appeared in Manchuria and Japan. Some cases of plague occurred in Australia and on the Essex-Suffolk border near the coast of England. The progress of this epidemic illustrates the role of human maritime commerce in spreading plague.

FINDING THE CAUSE OF PLAGUE. In 1894, the causal agent of plague was iden-tified simultaneously by two physicians who had participated in the epochal early studies of the germ theory of disease in Europe: Dr. Alexandre Yersin, who had worked with Louis Pasteur in Paris, and Dr. Shibasaburo Kitasato, who had worked in the other main site of discovery of disease-producing agents, the laboratory of Dr. Robert Koch in Berlin. (By that time, after millennia of speculation about disease-producing miasmas, causative agents of the major infectious diseases of the era were being identified at the rate of one a year.) When the plague broke out, Dr. Yersin had left France to go to Hanoi, capital of French Indo-China, and Dr. Kitasato had returned to his native Japan. During the 1890s, public health authorities in various countries became concerned, even alarmed, by reports of outbreaks of plague in the Far East, knowing how it spread by sea to commercial ports worldwide. The French government set up a commission to study the disease and asked Yersin to head it. Concerned for their own safety, the Japanese took a similar step, sending Kitasato to China. The plague bacilli turned out to be relatively easy to observe, stain, and culture. Almost simultaneously, both investigators identified the organism that became known as *Pasteurella pestis*. Kitasato apparently was the first to make the observation but published his findings in Japanese and English. Yersin found the same organism and recognized its role, but he published in French in a leading scientific journal of the time that quickly published short reports. Thus, his results appeared first. Yersin's priority of publication prevailed, and in 1970, the bacillus was renamed *Yersinia pestis*.

Although the role of the rat flea was not yet known, insect vectors were suspected. In 1894, Yersin found that the flies in his Hong Kong plague laboratory died in great numbers, their bodies "crowded with the specific bacillus." He injected tissues from the dead flies into guinea pigs, which developed plague and died of it. Later in 1894, Simond identified the tropical rat flea, *Xenopsylla cheopis*, as the vector in an article in the journal of the Pasteur Institute. This theory had been put forward previously by Ogata, a Japanese investigator, but disregarded. Since then, a wide variety of small mammals, including marmots and rabbits and their fleas, have been shown to be capable of carrying plague bacillus.

Twentieth Century Epidemics of Bubonic Plague in the U.S.   A series of plague epidemics occurred in California between 1900 and 1924. In 1899, two cases of plague were known to have occurred on a ship from Hong Kong bound for San Francisco. Although the victims had recovered by the time it arrived, the ship was quarantined on Angel Island and searched. Eleven stowaways were discovered The next day two of them were missing; later, their bodies were found in the Bay. The plague bacillus, identified during the outbreak in the Far East a few years earlier, was relatively easy to culture, and it was recovered from the two bodies. Although officials were worried that the disease would spread in California, no further cases appeared at that time. However, nine months later, on March 6, 1900, plague bacilli were found in an autopsy of a Chinese man, and California officials felt that some action was needed to prevent an epidemic of the disease.

At that time, despite earlier observations establishing the relationship of the disease to rats and their fleas, the most likely means of spread was thought to be contaminated food or water, or direct acquisition of the organism through defects in the skin. During the previous decade, such mechanisms of infection were shown to occur in other major diseases, including typhoid fever, dysentery, cholera, diphtheria, and wound infections. Disinfection campaigns were instituted, including pouring carbolic acid into sewers, which actually hastened the spread of the disease by flushing out infected rats and their fleas. Strong anti-Chinese sentiment led to efforts to quarantine Chinatown. The Chinese objected, as did the business community, believing it was bad for business for people to think there was plague in the city. The quarantine of Chinatown was lifted, but health officials conducted house-to-house inspections of the area. Despite resistance to the inspectors, two more plague victims were discovered.

When the Board of Health finally admitted that plague was present in the city, the governor refused to believe it and rejected suggestions that he do something about it. However, the denials of the existence of plague by some officials were not convincing, and more and more states began to avoid trading with California. The Surgeon General of the U.S. Public Health Service finally got permission from President McKinley to enforce standard anti–plague regulations. Commissions and boards were formed, disbanded, and reformed, continually fighting with the governor, who persisted in denying the existence of the disease, still fearing what he felt would be needless alarm. A prominent epidemiologist from the Rockefeller Institute in New York, Simon Flexner (1863–1946) headed one commission responsible for a massive cleanup campaign of the houses and shops in Chinatown. In 1903, a new governor took office and vowed to help the boards of health in every way. Despite little having been done, new cases stopped appearing, and the last victim of this outbreak died on February 29, 1904. The known cases totaled about 120, of whom all but eight died; the high mortality rate probably meant that most nonfatal cases were not discovered.

In 1906, plague reappeared in San Francisco after the devastating earthquake and fire. Rats, as well as people, were made homeless by the destruction and both took up residence in refugee camps. This time, officials launched a new kind of campaign that was based on the scientific knowledge that had been accumulated about the plague: They offered a bounty on rats. A similar rat-catching campaign had been used successfully a few years earlier to fight an outbreak of plague in New Orleans, and it helped in San Francisco. Although this second epidemic was larger than the first, it was brought to halt in 1909 and was the last urban outbreak of plague in the United States. Scattered cases continued to occur in rural areas, however, with marmots apparently the main reservoir of the disease.

RATS AND PLAGUE. Despite the success of rat-catching campaigns, it is worth noting that decreasing the rat population could have increased the spread of plague, at least temporarily. Eliminating rats minimizes the reservoir of infection, but leaves hungry fleas looking for a new source for their blood meals. Humans are a satisfactory alternate source of nutrition. Therefore, the infected fleas are more likely to bite and infect humans as a result of the depletion of the rat population, at least until the population of infected fleas dies off. In many medieval epidemics, the records show that the finding of large numbers of dead rats in a community was shortly followed by outbreak of human cases of plague. (The New Mexican couple who recently became ill with plague in New York City had found a dead rat on their property just before leaving for New York, but they were not aware that they had been bitten by its fleas.)

The fact that rats were associated with the disease was noted long before the role of their fleas was elucidated. In Manson's *Tropical Diseases* (1898), he pointed out, "Many observers have remarked the great mortality among rats and other animals which sometimes precedes and accompanies outbreaks of plague in man." He quotes a report that, in a Himalayan town where plague was epidemic in 1864, "the rats quitted the various villages in anticipation of the advent of the disease; the people, taught by experience, on seeing this exodus recognized it as a warning." During an epidemic in Canton in the 1890s, "from districts of the city where the plague had been raging for some time the rats entirely disappeared, whilst they kept on dying in other quarters to which the disease afterward spread."

Recent studies have elucidated the complexities of the relationship between rats and people and help us to understand the history of this disease. When fleas feed on an infected rat, the fleas become infected. When the infected rat dies, its fleas leave and search for a new host. The fleas usually find other rats, infect them, and spread plague through the rodent community. The spread in rats is slow: When the density of rats is low, as it is when rats die in large numbers, fleas are forced to find alternative hosts such as humans, and a human epidemic begins. Rarely, person-to-person spread of pneumonic plague occurs, usually after a human epidemic has already begun. Studies of the disease in recent years suggest that if the infection rate in a given rat population is low (e.g., 25–50 percent), human infection is rare or unlikely. If over 80 percent of a given rat population is infected, human infection occurs. Thus a rat epizootic can smolder for long periods without the appearance of human cases.

Once the disease appears in humans, control of the rat population can actually be deleterious. If the rat population is kept at a permanently low level, then the risk of a large rodent outbreak is low, and therefore the risk of human cases is reduced. However, if a cull is brought into effect after the first human cases have been reported, it can create a far larger pool of infection for humans, since a cull releases many infected fleas that seek human hosts. Any area with a rat population density of about 3,000 per sq km exceeds the threshold and is at risk for appearance of the disease. Areas with rodent reservoirs of plague include the United States, southern Africa, southern Asia (including Vietnam, where American servicemen encountered the disease), and South America.

Cases of bubonic plague continue to be reported from many parts of the world, sometimes with long intervals between outbreaks in a given area. In the 1990s, bubonic plague was observed in Madagascar, Mozambique, and Surat. These modern outbreaks suggest that the disease can exist in animals as an epizootic that later starts to infect people, or that it can be reintroduced from other areas, probably by commercial trade.

VACCINATION TO PREVENT PLAGUE. Infection can be prevented in individuals through vaccination, but vaccination cannot eliminate plague. Because of its rodent reservoir, the infection can reappear whenever unvaccinated people appear in a given vaccinated area. One hundred percent of a population must be vaccinated to prevent any cases of the disease. The vaccination of American troops in Vietnam prevented the infection in the troops, but it did occur in the native population.

SUMMARY. With its tragically high mortality and seemingly inexorable spread, bubonic plague remains the prototype of severe outbreaks of disease. Although the plague is a primarily a zoonosis—a disease of rats and other small animals, especially rodents and their fleas, its effects on humans are legendary. It has been spread by humans through the inadvertent transport of rats and their fleas. It has been purposely induced as a form of biowarfare since the first appearance of the Black Death in the Crimea, through World War II, and it may be used again in the future.

Although thought of as an ancient disease, severe human outbreaks still occur in areas where animal reservoirs exist, and people traveling into those areas can be infected. A vaccine exists, but because it is not possible to immunize the entire population in affected areas, the disease will undoubtedly continue to appear in humans because of its persisting animal reservoirs.

ADDITIONAL READING

Bosier PM, Rasolomaharo M, et al. Urban epidemic of bubonic plague in Majunga, Madagascar: epidemiological aspects. *Trop Med Int Health* 1997;2:422.

Bray RS. *Armies of Pestilence, The Impact of Disease on History.* New York: Barnes and Noble, 2000.

Cartwright FF. *Disease and History.* New York: Crowell, 1972.

Chernin E. Richard Pearson Strong and the Manchurian Plague Epidemic of Pneumonic Plague. *Bull Hist Med Allied Sci* 1989;44:296.

Cleri DJ, Vernaleo JR, et al. Plague pneumonia disease caused by *Yersinia pestis. Sem Respir Infect* 1997;12:12.

Communicable Disease Center. International notes update: Human plague—India, 1994. *MMWR Morb Mortal Wkly Rep* 1994;43:761.

Communicable Disease Center. Plague vaccine *MMWR Morb Mortal Wkly Rep* 1982;31:301.

Crook LD, Tempest B. Plague. A clinical review of 27 cases. *Arch Intern Med* 1992;152:1253.

Dubois, RJ, ed. *Bacterial and Mycotic Infections of Man.* Philadelphia: JB Lippincott Co, 1848.

Eidson MJ, Thilsted P, Rollag OJ. Clinical, epidemiologic and pathologic features of plague in cats: 119 cases (1977–1988). *J Am Vet Med Assoc* 1991;199:1191.

Gottfried RS. *The Black Death, Natural and Human Disasters in Medieval Europe.* New York: Fress Press, 1983.

Heath DG, Anderson GW Jr, et al. Protection against experimental bubonic and pneumonic plague by a recombinant capsular F1-V antigen fusion protein vaccine. *Vaccines* 1998;16:1131.

Inglesby TV, Dennis DT, et al. Plague as a biological weapon, Medical and Public Health Management. *JAMA* 2000;283:2281.

Keeling MJ, Gilligan CA. Metapopulation dynamics of bubonic plague. *Nature* 2000;407:903.

Madon MB, Hitchcock JC, et al. An overview of plague in the United States and a report of investigations of two human cases in Kern County, California, 1995. *J Vector Ecology* 1997;22:77.

Marks G, Beatty WK. *Epidemics.* New York: Scribner, 1976.

McEverdy C. Bubonic plague. *Sci Am* 1988;258:118.

Pollitzer R, Li CC. Some observations on the decline of the pneumonic plague epidemic. *J Infect Dis* 1943;72:160.

Poos LR. Plague mortality and demographic depression in later medieval England. *Yale J Biol Med* 1981;54:227.

Prinzing F. *Epidemics Resulting from Wars*. Oxford: Clarendon Press, 1916.

Scott S, Duncan CJ, Duncan SR. The plague in Penrith, Cumbria, 1597/8: its causes, biology and consequences *Ann Hum Biol* 1996;23:1.

Shrewsbury JFD. *A History of Bubonic Plague in the British Isles*. London: Cambridge UP, 1970.

Shrewsbury JFD, *The Plague of the Philistines, and Other Medical-Historical Essays*. London: V. Gollancz, 1964.

Skurnik M, Peippo A, Ervela E. Characterization of the O-antigen gene cluster of *Yersinia pseudotuberculosis* and the cryptic O-antigen gene cluster of *Yersinia pestis* shows that the plague bacillus is most closely related to and has evolved from *Y. pseudotuberculosis* serotype 0:1b. *Molr Microbiol* 2000;37:316.

Sloan AW. The Black Death in England. *S Afr Med J* 1981;59:646.

Smith MD, Vinh DX, et al. In vitro antimicrobial susceptibilities of strains of *Yersinia pestis*. *Antimicrob Agents Chemother* 1995;39:2153.

Solomon T. Alexandre Yersin and the plague bacillus. *J Tropical Med Hygiene* 1995;98:209.

Suntsov VV, Huong LT, et al. Plague foci in Viet Nam: zoological and parasitological aspects. *Bull World Health Organ* 1997;75:117.

Thornton DJ, Tustin RC, et al. Cat bite transmission of *Yersinia pestis* infection to man. *J S Afr Vet Assoc* 1975;46:165.

Titball RW, Williams ED. Vaccination against bubonic and pneumonic plague. *Vaccines* 2001;19:4175.

Viseltear AJ. The pneumonic plague epidemic of 1924 in Los Angeles. *Yale J Biol Med* 1974;1:40.

Von Reyn CF, Barnes AM, et al. Bubonic plague from exposure to a rabbit: a documented case, and a review of rabbit-associated plague cases in the United States. *Am J Epidemiol* 1976;104:81.

Williams JE, Moussa MA, Cavanaugh DC. Experimental plague in the California ground squirrel. *J Infect Dis* 1979;140:618.

Ziegler P. *The Black Death*. Phoenix Mill, UK: Alan Sutton Pub, New York: John Day & Co, 1969.

Zinsser H. *Rats, Lice and History*. New York: Bantam Books, 1934.

Zwanenberg D. The last epidemic of plague in England? Suffolk 1906–18. *Nature* 1970;14:63.

CHAPTER 2

THE "LITTLE FLIES" THAT BROUGHT DEATH, PART 1

MALARIA OR THE BURNING AGUE

M ALARIA AND YELLOW FEVER, TWO DEVASTATING DISEASES spread by the bite of specific species of mosquitoes, are prime examples of how human activities may cause epidemics. Although effective treatment and prevention has been available since 1633, malaria is still prevalent worldwide and is a major cause of death, especially in children.

For ages, malaria was thought to have been caused by toxic emanations from decaying organic material, or *miasmas*. The observation that the worst such emanations arose from swampy areas was based on the occurrence of the disease near wetlands. Because another name for such airborne poisons was *mal-aria* or *bad air*, the term malaria originally referred to all diseases thought to be caused by miasmas.

M ALARIA IN HISTORY.   Until late in the nineteenth century, the sporadic and recurring fever and chills of malaria were considered the disease, rather than symptoms, and so it was called intermittent fever. In the famous song, Molly Malone was selling her "Cockles and Mussels" until she "died of a fever." References to intermittent fevers, or the "ague," a popular abbreviation for the chills and fever of malaria, can be identified in numerous Biblical passages and in the writings of Hippocrates, and physical evidence of the disease is detectable in Egyptian mummies from long before Hippocrates' time.

The malaria parasite is close to one that affects Old World apes. The disease is thought to have spread from the rain forest of tropical Africa, moving gradually into the Nile Valley and the Fertile Crescent, and then to the northern shore of the Mediterranean. Although evidence for the presence of malaria in Greece after 500 BCE is convincing, it is uncertain when it first appeared in that area.

Evidence for malaria in ancient Egypt is much less abundant, but one very interesting possible example is the mummy of a weaver named Nacht, also known as ROM-I, who was a servant of the Pharaoh Setnakht, first ruler of the twentieth dynasty.[E1] After having resided in the Royal Ontario Museum for some years, Nacht was autopsied in 1974. Nakht is an unusual mummy, since he was a commoner rather than a member of the royal family. He apparently was a teenage priest who died at about age sixteen of a ruptured spleen that may have been due to malaria; intracellular inclusions were found in his red cells, but it has not been conclusively shown that these are malarial parasites. Immunofluorescent studies, although positive for two of five malarial antigens, are difficult to interpret because of nonspecific fluorescence. Mummies of that era also show evidence of schistosomiasis, a parasitic disease caused by blood flukes, which affects the liver and can cause enlargement and rupture of the spleen, another possible explanation of Nacht's fatal illness.

In the Old Testament, Leviticus 26:16 states, "I will even appoint over you terror, consumption, and the burning ague, that shall consume the eyes, and cause sorrow of heart...." The Hebrew word *quaddachath*, used in Leviticus, is translated in the King James version of the Bible as "burning ague;" ague was a common name used for malaria in King James' time. The "terror," in Hebrew "*behalah*," or "trouble," presumably was the severe shaking chill of a potentially fatal malarial attack. During the third century BCE, when the Bible was translated into Greek by a group of Alexandrian scholars, the term was translated as "intermittent fever." Such a reference offers clear evidence that these Hebrew scholars were familiar with malaria and the term intermittent fever used by Hippocrates whose works were written two centuries earlier and were gathered and written in present form in Alexandria at virtually the same time as the Biblical translation was being prepared. The Hippocratic works carefully describe the periodicity of the chills and febrile episodes, using the terms such as *quotidian*, *tertian*, and *quartan*, and even mentioning rare forms such as *quintans*, *septans*, and *nonans* (Epidemics I. xxiv), which were descriptions of the interval between the chills.

The periodicity of the attacks is based on the time it takes for the causative *Plasmodium* organisms to mature and multiply in the red blood cells. Once mature, they cause the red cells to rupture, releasing innumerable tiny organisms into the blood stream, causing chills and fever, and allowing the organisms to enter new red cells and start the cycle over. The most common organism, *Plasmodium vivax,* takes about 48 hours to complete the cycle, and thus the chills and fever occur every other day. This cycle was called "tertian" by the Ancient Greeks, because they counted the day of the chill as the last day of a cycle and the first day of the next cycle. Thus, the next chill occurred on day three of the new cycle. This confusing terminology probably resulted from the lack of a zero in the mathematics of ancient Greece and Rome.

Evidence suggests that Greek settlers brought malaria with them to "Magna Grecia," including Sicily and southern Italy, where it became common long before the time of Christ. Malaria was known throughout the era of the Roman Empire, and some historians have suggested that malaria, rather than decadent luxury, weakened the Roman legions and was responsible for the slackness of spirit that characterized the declining empire. An explosive epidemic that began in 79 CE was most severe in the Campagna, the "garden" of the city of Rome. As a result, cultivation in that area disintegrated, and the area remained marshy—a good breeding ground for mosquitoes, and thus for the spread of malaria, until late in the nineteenth century. The area around Rome remained malarious long after the decline of the Roman Imperial period, through the Dark and Middle Ages, and into the Renaissance. Malaria in Italy was thus the result of failure of a commercial enterprise—farming—that left marshy, wet, untended areas, ideal for breeding mosquitoes.

Changes have occurred in the distribution of the *Anopheles* genus, which includes the dominant malaria-carrying mosquito species. In ancient times, malaria may have been less severe and less often fatal because the most deadly form of the disease—the cerebral form caused by *Plasmodium falciparum,* was not well supported by the common *A. atroparvus* mosquito of ancient Greece and Rome. By late classical times, species of *Anopheles,* that preferred humans as the source of their blood meal (anthrophilic species) had been introduced from North Africa and Asia and spread along the coasts of Southern Europe. In northern Europe, malaria was not a problem until the seventeenth and eighteenth centuries, when periodic outbreaks were recorded in the Netherlands, Germany, Scandinavia, and Poland.

Malaria has always been a serious problem in Venice and its surrounding towns, which were built around a lagoon for protection from barbarian invaders. Recurrent outbreaks have occurred because a great deal of the land in the lagoon is marshy, and thus favorable for mosquito breeding.

Malaria has been blamed for the deaths of many famous people, including Alexander the Great, the famous Roman artist Caravaggio, popes, and cardinals.

"The ague" was a common disease in early seventeenth–century England. Sir Walter Raleigh reportedly was concerned that a recurrence of malarial chills while he mounted the scaffold to be beheaded might be misinterpreted as trembling. The death of Queen Elizabeth's successor, James I, has been attributed to malaria, occurring only shortly before effective treatment for the disease was discovered in Peru.

THE JESUITS' POWDER: QUININE. In 1633, Father Calancha, an Augustinian monk residing in Peru, announced that extracts and powders made from bark of a local tree was an effective treatment for "the fever." According to historians of this subject, the indigenous people of Peru were not aware of the therapeutic properties of the bark. Rather, its value was discovered accidentally, by Europeans, in the seventeenth century. The Peruvian bark was sent back to Europe, and the Society of Jesus became the main dispenser of it; thus it was known as "the Jesuit's powder." In 1658, Oliver Cromwell, Lord Protector of England, was seriously ill with the ague. When told that effective treatment was available, he refused to use it because of its association with the Jesuits, convinced that the powder was really part of a Jesuit plot to poison non-Catholics, and so he died of the disease. (Malaria was endemic in Britain at this time, and settlers to Jamestown brought it with them to the New World.)

In the eighteenth century, Linnaeus named the bark "cinchona," in honor of the Count and Countess of Chinchon. From 1629 to 1640, Don Luis Geronimo Fernandez de Cabrera de Bobadilla Cerda y Mendoza, fourth Count of Chinchon, was the Viceroy of Philip IV in Peru. Legend has it that Dona Francisca, his countess, brought the bark back to Spain and treated feverish peasants with it, but this story is probably not true, since Dona Francisca died at Cartegena, Colombia, on January 14, 1641, just after beginning her homeward voyage from Peru. Whether the Chinchons introduced it or not, the Spanish imported the Jesuits' powder, and it was widely used in Europe—worth more per pound than the Inca's gold.

The famous English physician Thomas Sydenham was slow to accept this treatment for fever, but it was used very successfully by another British physician, Robert Talbor. After the Restoration, Talbor became personal physician to Charles II. When the heir of Louis XIV was suffering from malaria, Charles, who had been harbored by the Sun King while in exile, sent Talbor to treat him. Impressed with the effectiveness of Talbor's therapy, Louis in turn dispatched him to treat the Queen of Spain.

The bark was introduced into Italy by Francesco Torti in 1711. Torti deserves to be remembered for inventing the term mal-aria to describe the supposed origin of the disease in the "bad air" that arose from the swamps and marshlands. Fevers were not divided into different etiologic categories during that period. According to Sydenham and other leading medical theoreticians of the time, fever was the disease (rather than a symptom) and resulted from an imbalance of "humours." Not until the nineteenth century were different forms of fever delineated. Therefore, the Peruvian bark was used in earlier centuries to treat all fevers, because it acts as a mild antipyretic, like aspirin. Its real antipyretic effect was seen when the fever actually was caused by malaria, and it was this response to quinine that helped to define malaria as separate from other "fevers."

Because of its great commercial value, authorities in Peru and neighboring South American countries where cinchona trees grew attempted to protect their treasure. During the eighteenth century, several French, English, and Dutch attempts were made to steal seed or transplantable seedlings, but none succeeded. Finally, in 1859, a British expedition was successful, and cinchona plants were grown in India and Ceylon in 1860. These plantations thrived and supplied the London market for six years, until they were destroyed by an invasion of insects and replaced by plantings of tea. Fortunately, however, in 1865, a Dutch expedition succeeded in obtaining about a pound of cinchona seed, which was successfully grown in Java. Because the British venture in India was thriving at that time, the Dutch attempt seemed of little commercial value at first, but after the British sources failed and South American supplies were exhausted, the Dutch East Indies became the prime source of cinchona.[E2]

Early in the nineteenth century two chemists, Pierre-Joseph Pelletier and Joseph-Bienaimé Caventou, had been isolating active principles from natural products, such as emetine from the ipecac plant and strychnine from the strychnos plant. Earlier, because of the alkaline nature of these substances, the German chemist Meissner had named them alkaloids. In about 1820, a student assigned the task of finding an active principle in cinchona bark found that its extract was alkaline. Thinking that the student had discovered another possible alkaloid, Pelletier and Cavandou began to study the problem themselves. They found that a gummy product isolated from yellow cinchona bark was effective against malarial fever and, because an old Peruvian name for the bark was *quinaquina*, they decided to call their substance *quinine*.

In 1853, Louis Pasteur, a French chemist known for his early investigations of stereoisomerism, identified an optical isomer of quinine, which he named *quinidine*. Quinidine was the most potent drug available to treat cardiac arrhythmias for over a century.

MALARIA IN THE WESTERN HEMISPHERE. Malaria was introduced into the Western Hemisphere from Africa at end of the fifteenth century; studies of primate infections support this conclusion. It is clear that the initial introduction was coastal and was spread from port areas by the *Anopheles* mosquitoes, which had probably arrived in the New World in ships' water supplies. The disease became a major health problem in the Western hemisphere shortly after it appeared on the island of Cuba early in the sixteenth century, its arrival attributed to Spanish colonists who imported slaves from Africa. From Cuba, the disease is thought to have spread all through the Western Hemisphere.

As with so many other epidemic diseases, commercial travel spread the disease to new areas, and reintroduced it when it died out. In colder areas, where mosquitoes are killed off by winter frosts, malaria had to be reintroduced every summer. It occurred episodically in such areas, appearing during some summers, when ships brought the vector mosquitoes and people infected with the parasite, and remained absent other summers. In tropical areas, on the other hand, malaria was a constant threat, with rare disease-free intervals.

Malaria was widespread in the United States during the nineteenth century, particularly in warmer areas of the country. Our early presidents from Virginia almost all had several bouts of the illness early in life, but only George Washington had any major attacks after reaching national prominence. Attacks occurred repeatedly throughout his lifetime and, in 1786, after his election to the presidency, he had a severe episode of "ague and fever." His physician, Dr. James Craik, a Scottish graduate of the prestigious medical school of the University of Edinburgh and a close personal friend, accompanied him on the Braddock expedition in the French and Indian War and throughout the War of Independence. Craik used "the bark" to treat his patient for the first time during his 1786 attack. Washington responded well to it.

Many subsequent presidents from the South suffered from recurrent malaria; Jefferson had only a few, relatively mild episodes, but Madison suffered frequent attacks. There is no evidence that either Adams, father or son, had the disease, but William Henry Harrison had numerous attacks while serving in the army, as did Zachary Taylor during the campaign in Mexico. Franklin Pierce had several bouts with the disease, and Lincoln had malaria as a youth in Illinois.

It is uncertain whether malaria contributed to the deaths of Lincoln's sons, Tad and Willie, who were treated with quinine, since at this time the drug was still used in the treatment of all fevers, and the clinical manifestations of their illnesses were not clearly recorded. Willie's death, in February 1862, which was attributed to "bilious fever," was probably typhoid fever.

Malaria figured in at least one life-and-death decision made by one president. Andrew Johnson, whose problems with alcohol before becoming president are well known, also suffered from "chronic dysentery" and renal calculi, and he had endured several episodes of malaria early in his career, in Tennessee. As president, he was bedridden due to a recurrent malarial attack when presented with the writ for the execution of Mrs. Mary Suratt, who had been convicted of participating in the conspiracy to assassinate Lincoln. Although the plot had been planned in the boarding house that she owned, the evidence upon which she was convicted was considered circumstantial and unconvincing to many people. Nevertheless, petitioners on her behalf with requests for clemency were denied access to the sick president. Many speculate that her execution was judicial murder, vengeance for the death of Lincoln, and that a healthy Johnson might have commuted it.

MALARIA DURING THE CIVIL WAR.   Experiences with malaria during the Civil War were typical of that of all armies fighting in tropical or semitropical areas before the mid-twentieth century. The detailed records kept during that war are particularly revealing but rarely noted. Still officially called the "intermittent fevers," malaria was the second most common disease that affected troops on both sides of the conflict. Only acute diarrhea, which was ubiquitous, was more common. The Union forces had almost a million recorded cases of intermittent fevers, accounting for almost 16 percent of the 6.5 million episodes of illnesses recorded among Union soldiers. A total of about 4,700 deaths were attributed to malaria, a fatality rate of 0.5 percent. "Congestive intermittent fever," probably *falciparum* malaria, the rarest and most malignant form of the disease, was diagnosed in 2.1 percent of the cases in black troops and 1.2 percent in white troops. This deadly variety caused the bulk of the fatalities from the illness (86 percent of the deaths among blacks, 79 percent among white). Even with modern antimalarial drugs, it remains the most difficult to treat and the most malignant.

The incidence of malaria in Civil War troops depended on the region and season in which the military action occurred. In addition, once a soldier acquired malaria, recurrences could occur without further exposure. Not surprisingly, as more and more soldiers acquired the disease and became susceptible to recurrences, the overall incidence increased as the war went on. Modern studies have shown that the *vivax* and *ovale* forms of the parasite, those that produce the most common forms of the infection (tertian and quartan malaria), can persist in the liver and re-emerge at intervals to invade red blood cells and produce new attacks. Attacks may continue to recur for one to five years after the initial infection; during this period, the gametocytes of the parasite are infectious to mosquitoes, and thus the disease can be transmitted to mosquitoes and induce new secondary cases. Modern treatment prevents these recurrences.

The highest incidence of malaria in any of the Union forces occurred during General Ulysses S. Grant's campaign to take Vicksburg, where the army was engaged in the swampy areas along the banks of the Mississippi River. The incidence peaked just before and after the fall of Vicksburg, during the months of June, July, and August 1863, when the incidence varied between 116 and 136 cases per thousand troops *per month*.

The overall incidence of malaria during the four years of the fighting averaged 1.8 diagnosed attacks per soldier annually (actually, 1,794 cases per thousand per year). Although figures are calculated on an annual basis, most cases occurred during the four warmest summer months. Chills and fever from malaria were so common that one soldier wrote, in a letter home, he thought if the Union soldiers could synchronize their chills, they could shake the rebels into submission.[1]

Civil War physicians used quinine effectively to control malaria, and also used it prophylactically. It was difficult to get the soldiers to take the quinine when they were well, especially in view of its bitter taste, but in many outfits the medical staff solved this problem by mixing quinine in whiskey. The Confederate medical department was chronically short of quinine, and it was one of the most valued substances imported by blockade runners.

MALARIA AND TEDDY ROOSEVELT. The career of Theodore Roosevelt was greatly influenced by malaria, although he escaped infection himself. Roosevelt first achieved national prominence during the Spanish American War, when the press was enamored with this New Yorker who resigned his post as Assistant Secretary of the Navy to organize a cavalry unit containing volunteers from all over the country. He was the real life John Wayne of his day and his unit, the First United States Volunteer Cavalry, became known as "Roosevelt's Rough Riders." But Roosevelt was sufficiently wise to have a more experienced military man, Col. Leonard Wood, serve as commander.

Wood was an army doctor serving as White House physician under McKinley who had met Roosevelt while he was still Assistant Secretary of the Navy, and the two had become close friends. Wood had served in the field, in the West, at the beginning of his army career. During the campaign to capture Geronimo, he was surgeon for the expedition as well as its second in command, and later in his career was awarded a Medal of Honor for his exploits. Wood failed to receive a field command in 1898, but when Roosevelt was offered one by Territorial

Governor Myron McCord of Arizona, he accepted it on the basis that Wood would be the colonel, commander of the regiment, and he would be second in command, with the rank of lieutenant colonel. Following their first clash with the Spanish at Las Guasimas, Wood's enormous abilities led to his battlefield promotion to Brigadier General on June 24, 1898. At that point, Roosevelt became the commander of the "Rough Riders" himself and led the famous charge up Kettle Hill at San Juan, a battle generally known as "San Juan Hill." The Rough Riders' horses had not made the trip to Cuba (the men, knowing the press referred to them as Roosevelt's Rough Riders, called themselves Wood's Weary Walkers) and, during that famous battle, Roosevelt was the only one on a horse. Despite being such an obvious and tempting target, he was not wounded.

The Rough Riders and other troops in Cuba were weakened by typhoid fever, malaria, and after the war, by a severe outbreak of yellow fever. Casualties from disease far outnumbered the few battle casualties sustained during fighting against the Spanish, but war Department officials in Washington would not permit the removal of the army from the most malarious areas. Aware of the difficulties the local commander, General Shaffer, was facing, Roosevelt pressured the war department by going directly to the press, who idolized him. Having no military career to risk, his effective use of such publicity got the army bases moved and saved many lives in the expeditionary force. His actions gained Roosevelt a great deal of personal credit and, added to his battlefield exploits, played a major role in furthering his subsequent political career. President McKinley commented that no one had benefited from the war as much as Roosevelt.

Roosevelt was recommended for a Congressional Medal of Honor by three Army generals above him in the chain of command, including two who had already won the Medal of Honor themselves. However, Secretary of war Russell Alger refused to act because Roosevelt had criticized the McKinley administration's failure to bring the troops home from Cuba promptly to protect them from disease. Not until October 21, 1998, during the war's centennial year, was a Congressional Medal of Honor finally awarded to Roosevelt posthumously by a unanimous vote of Congress.

Wartime publicity led to Roosevelt's nomination and election as Governor of New York, where his zeal and effectiveness as a reformer made him very unpopular with state Republican Party leaders. To get rid of him, they prevailed on McKinley to accept him as his vice-presidential running mate when he ran for re-election in 1900, his first vice president Garret A. Hobart having recently died. When McKinley was assassinated by an anarchist in September 1901, Roosevelt became president.

THE PANAMA CANAL.   Malaria figured in Roosevelt's career again during the construction of the Panama Canal. Disease, especially yellow fever and malaria, had killed so many workmen that the French effort to build a canal in Panama (under the direction of Ferdinand De Lesseps, who supervised the construction of the Suez Canal) was given up in 1889, after eight years. When the United States began construction of a canal in 1904, yellow fever and malaria spread again through the construction force.

In May 1905, an outbreak of yellow fever reminded locals of the epidemics of 1885 and 1886 that had demoralized the French workmen. Hundreds of recently arrived American workers hurriedly departed from Panama, including the chief engineer, John Wallace, who decided that an offer of a position in private industry was much more attractive. The epidemic, which lasted about five months, resulted in numerous deaths from yellow fever and malaria. Additional deaths from pneumonia, typhoid fever, and dysentery, as well as the large number of nonfatal cases of all these diseases, contributed to the panic, crippling efforts to construct the canal.

Colonel William C. Gorga was the chief sanitation officer for the Canal Zone. He attempted to apply the lessons learned during the successful effort to control mosquito-borne diseases in Cuba, where he had been assigned by the Reed Commission to implement the conclusions of the research done in Havana. Because he required a great deal of money and manpower for his mosquito control program, strong opposition arose, particularly from those who felt despite convincing research, that the mosquito theory was ridiculous and that malaria was in fact caused by "bad air," as its name implied. They complained that the anti-mosquito campaign diverted funds and men from the real task at hand, and thus delayed the building of the canal.

An effort was made to have Gorgas removed, and a successor was recommended to Roosevelt. The President consulted with several people, including William Welch, Professor of Pathology at the Johns Hopkins Medical School, who responded that, "The best man is already on the job." Roosevelt supported Gorgas, and success was achieved after 18 months of effort. His program had eradicated yellow fever and malaria in Havana after only eight months, and Gorgas' efforts finally brought the same dramatic success in Panama.

Roosevelt had learned his lessons about malaria and yellow fever in Cuba, and his use of the press to publicize the problem and promote a solution to it was far more than a political gesture. Thus, whereas presidents have been victims of disease, they have also played critical roles in their conquest.

MALARIA TODAY. Malaria is still the most common parasitic disease affecting humans. Factors not related to human activities can spread the disease, especially wet weather, which increases breeding areas for the mosquito. Global warming may be a factor in increasing the range of insect vectors and increasing the areas in which the vector can persist through the cold season.

Malaria is known to be present in ninety countries, with more than 300 million cases occurring each year. It is blamed for more than a million deaths, probably mostly in young children. It is mostly present in tropical areas such as Central America and Northern South America, sub-Saharan Africa, coastal Arabia and Yemen, India, Afghanistan, southern Iran, all of Southeast Asia, the Philippines, all of Indonesia but not the mountainous areas of New Guinea. That the areas affected are increasing may possibly be a result of climatic warming.

In the Western Hemisphere, malaria is no longer present in the Unites States except for those cases introduced from travel to other areas; some soldiers returning from Vietnam had attacks of malaria, but secondary outbreaks did not occur. The disease is greatly reduced in Argentina, much of Costa Rica, and Panama, but is still a problem in thirteen South American countries, which reported a little more than half the cases in 1984. The most affected are Hispaniola (Haiti and the Dominican Republic), most of Central America and Mexico, and several Andean countries, including Bolivia, Colombia, Ecuador, Peru, and Venezuela. The Caribbean Islands are free of the disease (except for Hispaniola). Africa remains hyperendemic. Malaria is also found in some areas of Turkey.

Malaria can be transmitted by means other than by the bite of a mosquito. Blood transfusions have long been recognized as a means of transmission; if a blood donor had malaria many years before, he may still harbor the parasites in a quiescent state, but in numbers sufficient to multiply and produce the disease in a recipient. Similarly, contaminated needles shared by drug users can contain enough infected blood to transmit the infection. Malaria can also be transmitted from a mother to her fetus, and newborn babies can have this congenital form of the disease.

Some groups of people are resistant to malaria, including people with some blood groups, individuals with an enzyme deficiency (glucose-6-phosphate dehydrogenase deficiency), and those with the sickle cell trait, the heterozygotic form of sickle cell disease, AS. The high incidence of the AS trait in some African populations is thought to be the result of its protection against malaria.

About sixty-seven of more than 400 species of *Anopheles* mosquitoes can transmit the malarial parasites, and thirty are considered important vectors.

Transmission of malaria is affected by the density of the mosquito population, as well as the flight ranges, feeding habits, and blood meal preferences of various species. Resistance to insecticides is a factor affecting the distribution of these agents and of the disease.

Older children and adults gradually acquire resistance; newborns have transplacental antibodies, but young children are most susceptible and most malarial deaths occur during the first years of life. Repeated attacks of malaria impair resistance to other diseases, and improved malarial control decreases morbidity and mortality from all causes. Resistance is spreading to the most valuable antimalarial drugs, chloroquin and sulfadoxine-pyramethamine; for example, 90 percent of the parasites are resistant to chloroquin in some areas. New antimalarial drugs are being developed, such as Artemisinin, which is from the wormwood plant *Artemisia annua,* although it is difficult to establish the safety of new drugs in infants and young children.

Attempts are also being made to develop a vaccine against malaria. However vaccines are of limited value, because immunity is specific to species and even stages of the life cycle of the parasite. New techniques of vaccine production involving DNA and irradiated parasites are being tried, but antibodies are less effective than cells of the immune system. New techniques being developed to induce cell-mediated immunity offer the best hope for an effective vaccine in the future.

Human factors that increase the incidence of malaria are those that increase breeding sites for mosquitoes and travel by infected people into an area with the appropriate mosquitoes and susceptible people. Rain is the primary meteorologic factor that can increase the availability of breeding sites, especially in areas where standing water can accumulate. Mosquitoes like abundant rainfall and relatively clean, gently flowing water; their optimum survival temperature is 20° to 30° C. Below 16° C, mosquito development ceases. Adults need relatively high humidity, greater than 60 percent. Containers that collect rain water, from flower pots to old tires, are important factors in the reproduction of mosquitoes, and human activities often provide standing water to form breeding sites, such as drainage ditches, construction trenches, and building techniques that leave shallow pits in the earth. Social factors of importance are the proximity of human dwellings to mosquito breeding sites and housing construction that allows easy entry for mosquitoes. Work and social patterns that encourage people to be outside at night are very important.

ADDITIONAL READING

Bray RS. *Armies of Pestilence, The Impact of Disease on History.* New York: Barnes and Noble, 2000.

Cartwright FF. *Disease and History, The Influence of Disease in Shaping History.* New York: Crowell, 1972.

Cockburn A. *The Evolution and Eradication of Infectious Disease.* Westport, CT: Greenwood Press, 1963.

Dubois RJ, ed. *Bacterial and Mycotic Infections of Man.* Philadelphia: JB Lippincott Co, 1948.

Duffy J. *Epidemics in Colonial America.* Baton Rouge, LA: Louisiana State Univ Press, 1966.

Harrison G. *Mosquitoes, Malaria, and Man: a History of the Hostilities Since 1880.* New York: Dutton, 1978.

Jones WHS. *Malaria and Greek History.* Manchester: Univ of Manchester Press, 1909.

Kelly HA. *Walter Reed and Yellow Fever.* New York: McClure, Phillips, 1906.

McNeill WH, *Plagues and Peoples.* Garden City, NY: Anchor Press, 1976

Poser CM, Bruyn GW. *An Illustrated History of Malaria.* New York: Parthenon Pub. Group, 1999.

Ritchie CIA. *Insects, The Creeping Conquerors, and Human History.* New York: Elsevier/Nelson Books, 1979.

Taylor N. *Cinchona in Java. The Story of Quinine.* New York: Greenberg Press, 1945.

Wills C. *Yellow Fever, Black Goddess, The Coevolution of People and Plague.* Reading MA: Addison Wesley, 1996.

[E1]Setnakht's reign, which ended about 1182 B.C.E., occurred after the exodus of the Hebrews from Egypt and at the time of invasions by the so-called the Sea Peoples, who may have been refugees from the fallen city of Troy or Greeks driven from the mainland by major weather changes. These same Sea Peoples are also thought to be the Philistines of the near East. Setnakht's greatest claim to fame is that he was father of the great warrior Pharaoh, Ramses III, who claimed to have fought off the Sea Peoples.

[E2]By the time of World War II, this was the only significant source of quinine in the world, and the occupation of the East Indies by the Japanese led to a crash program to successfully develop new anti-malarials to protect Allied troops in the South Pacific. This effort led to the discovery of Atabrine.

[1]Wiley BI: *The Life of Billy Yank. The Common Soldier of the Union.* Baton Rouge, LA: Louisiana State Univ. Press, 1952, p. 142.

CHAPTER 3

THE "LITTLE FLIES"
THAT BROUGHT DEATH,
PART 2
YELLOW FEVER

ALTHOUGH YELLOW FEVER HAS PROBABLY ALWAYS existed in tropical areas of the Old World, it did not appear in the New World until the middle of the seventeenth century, probably brought across the Atlantic from Africa by the slave trade. For centuries, it remained endemic in tropical areas of the Western Hemisphere and, outside of those areas, it caused frequent, devastating summertime epidemics spread primarily by commercial travel. The mortality rates for yellow fever were 30 to 50 percent, similar to the outbreaks of other deadly diseases such as smallpox, cholera, and even bubonic plague.

The appearance of yellow fever in the Western Hemisphere, the devastating outbreaks that influenced the course of major historical events, and the convincing demonstration of its mode of spread of by the unlikely means of a mosquito (*little fly* in Latin) provide some of the most interesting chapters in the history of medical research.

Yellow fever is a widespread infection, a form of viral hepatitis that causes massive necrosis of the liver and results in severe jaundice, hence the name. Nicknames for the disease, such as "yellow jack" and "bronze john" also emphasize the typical discoloration of the skin. The patients suffer severe headaches, kidney abnormalities, and gastrointestinal hemorrhage that leads to vomiting of black material.

The disease is transmitted by a mosquito that can survive year round in tropical areas. It first appeared in the Western Hemisphere in the Caribbean, and those islands became a prime site for the disease. Port cities in the continental United States that had close commercial relationships with Caribbean islands had the worst outbreaks of the disease, especially during and after the slave revolt in modern Haiti and Santo Domingo. The severity of the epidemics, and the panic they produced, inspired the Domingé idea that this disease would be a form of divine biological warfare. During the American Civil War, after Union forces captured New Orleans, Southerners prayed for the appearance of the disease to drive away the invaders. No yellow fever epidemics occurred in New Orleans during the war, but the disease returned when military quarantine measures were lifted; the most severe outbreaks of yellow fever in American history occurred long after the war ended.

Later in the nineteenth century, yellow fever severely hindered the building of the Panama Canal. However, after the Spanish-American war, the discovery was made in Havana that mosquitoes transmitted the disease, the same mosquito control measures that eradicated the disease there were employed, and construction of the canal was ultimately completed. This is discussed in greater detail towards the end of this chapter.

Before the disease was controlled, knowledge of its spread by maritime commerce led to quarantine measures that successfully prevented outbreaks, especially during the American Civil War. The symbolic significance of quarantine is well-illustrated by the legend of the *Flying Dutchman*, a ship condemned to roam the seas because it carried yellow fever.

YELLOW FEVER APPEARS IN THE WESTERN HEMISPHERE. Because yellow fever was not known in the West Indies until after the importation of black slaves, it was presumably introduced from Africa, although no records confirm its prior existence there. The first unquestionable epidemic of yellow fever in the Western Hemisphere occurred in 1647. A large number of refugees from the English Civil War (1642-1651) migrated to Barbados; these immigrants had never been exposed to yellow fever. When the agriculture of Barbados changed from cereal crops to the more profitable sugar cane, Africans were imported to run the plantations. Most authorities believe that yellow fever came to the island when *Aedes* mosquito larvae were carried in the water casks of slave ships, along with people sick with the disease. Between one-third and one-half of the white population of Barbados died in that epidemic, a mortality rate typical of subsequent epidemics.

The record of Captain Thomas Sherman, commander of *HMS Tiger*, stationed at Barbados during the 1680s, provides a picture of the deadliness of such epidemics. During a two-year period, 600 of his crew members died of yellow fever. (He repeatedly replenished his standing crew of 200 by impressing merchant seamen who had arrived in the port aboard other vessels.)

As the importation of slave labor displaced white English immigrants from agricultural jobs in Barbados and other British Caribbean colonies, many turned to buccaneering. This form of "commerce" helped spread yellow fever among the islands: In 1648, initial outbreaks of yellow fever occurred in St. Kitts, Guadeloupe, and Cuba.

Yellow fever affected numerous American port cities. In 1668, epidemic jaundice in New York was described as "autumnal bilious fever in its infectious form;" it caused so many fatalities that the governor ordered a fast day, a traditional means of combating epidemics. (There is some doubt whether this truly was yellow fever; no mention was made of the characteristic black vomitus, and the fatality rate was not as high as is typical of yellow fever. The outbreak could have been leptospirosis, a form of hepatitis caused by spirochetal bacteria.) The first definite outbreak of yellow fever in the Continental American Colonies occurred in Boston, in 1693, after the British fleet arrived there from Barbados. Cotton Mather (1663-1728) described "a most pestilential Feaver ... which in less than a week's time usually carried off my Neighbors, with very direful Symptoms, of turning Yellow, vomiting and bleeding every way and so Dying." In the Colonies, the disease was often called Barbados Fever.

In 1699, epidemics of yellow fever occurred in Charleston and Philadelphia; in both cities mortality was high and normal activities were disrupted. In 1702, an epidemic occurred in New York, with 570 deaths recorded before it ended. (The total population of New York at the time is uncertain; it reached 8,000 in 1730.) During the first half of the eighteenth century, many epidemics occurred in Charleston, and several in Virginia, Philadelphia, and New York.

No yellow fever occurred in British North America from 1763-1792, but around the first of August 1793, an epidemic began in Philadelphia, then the capital of the United States, after a ship from Tobago arrived on July 22. The British Caribbean islands had been infected by a group of English colonists who had first landed on Portuguese Bolama Island, in the Bissagos Island chain, off the coast of Portuguese Guinea. On February 17, 1793, the settlers arrived in Grenada on the *Hankey*, bringing yellow fever with them, and it quickly spread to other British islands. When the epidemic affected Philadelphia, between August 1 and November 9, 1793, at least 4,031 people died of "fever of Bolama" and were buried inside the city. The total death toll was undoubtedly greater than 5,000 out of a total population of 60,000. Philadelphia was largely deserted by the time the epidemic subsided. President Washington left the city on September 10; Secretary of State Thomas Jefferson, Members of Congress, and other members of the federal government all fled the capital city. Secretary of the Treasury Hamilton and his wife were among those who became ill, and when they left Philadelphia, they had difficulty finding lodging because innkeepers feared contagion.

Benjamin Rush, a physician who signed the Declaration of Independence, is famous for his efforts during that outbreak of yellow fever. Probably the first doctor to recognize the beginning of the outbreak, he described public reactions to the disease, based on their concept that "miasmas" or "bad airs" were the etiologic factor. He wrote: "People shifted their course at the sight of a hearse... Many... went into the middle of the streets, to avoid being infected in passing houses wherein people had died.... The old custom of shaking hands fell into such general disuse that many were affronted at even the offer of a hand."[E1]

THE FRENCH CONNECTION TO YELLOW FEVER IN AMERICA. Yellow fever played a major role in the history of the island of Hispaniola. Part of the island, known as Saint-Domingé, was ceded in 1697 to the French by the Spanish government under the Treaty of Ryswick. A warm relationship still existed between France and the United States when, on October 23, 1790, slaves in Saint-Domingé, inspired by the revolutionary ideas in the *Doctrine of the Rights of Man*, revolted. Fighting erupted repeatedly on the island over the next 15 years. During the revolt, several slave armies initially fought each other, as well as the various French and Spanish armies, but eventually they coalesced under the brilliant generalship of Pierre Dominique Toussaint L'Overture.

By 1792, the French were at war with many European countries, including Spain. In February 1793, the French Republic declared war on Britain. This development cut off Saint-Domingé from support, because the British navy controlled the Caribbean. The British in Jamaica began preparing to invade Saint-Domingé. That same month, King Louis XVI was guillotined, and royalist and conservative white planters and petit blancs on the island decided it was time to leave.

A British force from Jamaica tried to take that part of the island, landing a force of 7,500 men. They had considerable military success initially, but when summer came, the troops were immobilized by the heat. This exposed them to the *Aedes* mosquitoes, which prefer to inhabit human dwellings, and yellow fever broke out. Reinforcements were brought from Jamaica. The death toll reached 7,530; the British withdrew their troops from the island.

In 1802, Napoleon dispatched a force of 23,000 men under his brother-in-law General Le Clerc to regain control of the island. Le Clerc's army landed on February 1. After much barbarity on both sides, the French campaign to subdue the rebellious slaves was victorious. Toussaint L'Overture was captured after being falsely induced to attend truce talks that offered amnesty, but he was imprisoned and sent to France where he died, still in prison. However, yellow fever reappeared when the summer heat began. Despite reinforcements of 10,000 men in the autumn, the weakened French forces remained bottled up. When hostilities with Britain again erupted and the British fleet cut the French off from supplies, the situation became hopeless. Le Clerc died of yellow fever in November 1802, and his successor, Rochambeau, capitulated. The French troops were allowed to leave the island, picked up by a British squadron. At that time, out of a total of 33,000 French soldiers sent to the island between February 1 and November 28, 1802, 24,000 were dead and 7,000 were dying.

The population of the colony had been about 520,000 in 1789, the most populous and richest in the French West Indies. In 1804, after the new Haitian leader Jean Jacques Dessalines (who called himself Emperor Alexandre I) instituted a general massacre of all remaining whites, not a single white person was left, and the total population was reduced to 10,000 mulattos and 230,000 blacks.

Many French colonists joined their exiled countrymen in New Orleans, which was the major source of supplies and reinforcements for the French on the island, since transatlantic voyages were too susceptible to British capture. The interchange between New Orleans and Saint-Dominisé probably was the source of repeated epidemics yellow fever into New Orleans in the years between 1790 and 1805. After Saint-Domingé, renamed Haiti, became totally independent and free of white Europeans, contact with that island became negligible and yellow fever epidemics in New Orleans became much less frequent.

YELLOW FEVER AND THE LOUISIANA PURCHASE. Once Napoleon lost Saint-Domingé, he had no further need for New Orleans and its loss of strategic importance played a major role in his decision to sell Louisiana to the United States. (Some historians, including a near contemporary, Henry Adams, think that Napoleon had intended to use Saint-Domingé and New Orleans as the base for an invasion of the southern United States, but that yellow fever thwarted this plan.)

In 1804, with the French gone from Saint-Domingé, Napoleon sold the United States his supply base in New Orleans and with it all the land in the area-ever afterwards known as the Louisiana Purchase. Once American contact with Saint-Domingé ceased in 1805, the series of almost annual major yellow fever epidemics of the eighteenth and early nineteenth centuries came to an end. That same year, 1805, outbreaks occurred in both New York and Philadelphia, but yellow fever did not recur as a serious epidemic again until 1819. It flared up for the last time in New York City in 1822. After that, although cases were fre-quently found on ships introduced into the quarantine grounds, the ships were not allowed into the city until all signs of the disease had disappeared, and yel-low fever never again gained a foothold in the coastal cities of the northeast.

YELLOW FEVER DURING THE CIVIL WAR.   New Orleans was severely affected by yellow fever in the decades prior to the Civil War. Outbreaks occurred in late summer almost every year, increasing steadily in intensity and virulence throughout the nineteenth century. The decade of the 1850s was the peak period for the disease in the city. Between 8,000 and 9,000 people died of it in 1853, and severe epidemics also occurred in 1854 and 1855. In 1858, another 5,000 people died from "the yellow jack."

However, to the surprise of New Orleans' citizens, no outbreaks of yellow fever occurred in their city during the Civil War. In 1861, Union ships blockaded the entrance to the Mississippi River, an effective form of quarantine. In April 1862, Union forces under Adm. David Glasgow Farragut forced their way past the forts guarding New Orleans, and the Union army occupied the city. After the "Crescent City" fell, a Union physician wrote: "the Southern press at once endeavored to soothe the feelings of the people by assuring them that they had an ally in Yellow fever, which would soon drive the Union army from the soil of Louisiana."

Residents of cities familiar with yellow fever knew that visitors were more sus-ceptible to the disease than natives, probably because a high proportion of the local population were survivors of previous epidemics and thus were immune. General Benjamin Butler, Union Military Governor of Louisiana, recorded that "the rebels are relying largely on yellow fever to clear out northern troops . . . whom they had learned from experience were usually the first victims of the scourge." Butler added that he had also heard "that in the churches prayers were put up that the pestilence might come as a divine interposition on behalf of the brethren."

The native population could not use yellow fever for purposeful biological warfare, but they could use it for psychological warfare, and they did their best to keep Yankee soldiers in fear of the disease. Within hearing of Union officers, their conversations would turn to the devastation of previous epidemics. Children playing in the street would chant,

"Yellow jack will grab them up
    And take them all away."

Some adults went around measuring the height of soldiers, explaining that they had a contract to provide 10,000 coffins. As a result, General Butler was deluged with requests for transfers and leaves from his officers.

Medical officers stationed in the city were worried that yellow fever would return to New Orleans and decimate the Union forces. Chief surgeon of Admiral Farragut's fleet, Dr. Jonathan M. Foltz, sent a letter to General Butler, urging "a strict quarantine and positive nonintercourse with ports where yellow fever existed." General Butler had appointed a port physician as his own quarantine officer, and Foltz recorded that the general gave the physician the following instructions: "In this matter your orders shall be absolute. Order off all you may think proper, and so long as you keep yellow fever away from New Orleans your salary shall be [paid]. When yellow fever appears in this city your pay shall cease." His order for strict enforcement of quarantine included firing on any ships that tried to evade it. All vessels entering the river were required to stop below the quarantine station for inspection. If there was suspicion that yellow fever was on board, the vessel was held for forty days (the classic time peroid from which the name "quarantine" was derived, dating from the era of the bubonic plague epidemics in fourteenth-century Europe). All vessels that had touched ports afflicted by yellow fever were kept in quarantine for the full forty days, regardless of the inspection findings.

Butler instituted other measures intended to keep out the "seeds" of contagion. He ordered the streets cleaned of debris and decaying animal matter, the source of the "miasmas" thought to cause disease. The waterfront French market was particularly filthy: Decades of spoiled produce and animal wastes had composted into the dirt. Butler ordered the market scrubbed until free of odors, city drains and ditches cleaned, streets flushed by the water works, and a refuse collection system set up. The sanitary regulations were strictly enforced and violators threatened with imprisonment. Although mosquitoes were not suspected as vectors of the disease, the sanitary measures had the unplanned effect of decreasing areas where mosquitoes could breed.

Butler's combined quarantine and sanitary measures were kept in force throughout the Union occupation and no yellow fever appeared during the war. In 1864, Union physician George M. Sternberg wrote that Southerners believed the Union occupation of New Orleans would be temporary because of the disease but "two summers have now passed, and their hopes have been disappointed." Sternberg later became an early investigator in the field of bacteriology in the United States and, as surgeon general, appointed the army commission headed by Dr. Walter Reed that firmly established the mosquito's role in the etiology of yellow fever after the Spanish-American War.

The first recorded post-Civil War epidemic in New Orleans occurred in 1867. Severe epidemics again became frequent until 1905, after which knowledge of the mosquito's role in transmission led to effective preventive measures.

Butler's policies and harsh reactions to insults directed at Union troops led the citizens of the city to call him "Beast Butler." He was proud of his success in keeping yellow fever out of New Orleans, but the locals refused to give him any credit. They attributed freedom from the disease to divine intervention, saying that, "God was merciful and would not send them both General Butler and yellow fever at the same time."

Elsewhere, although yellow fever was kept from most southern ports by the Union blockade throughout the war, the disease appeared in some Union-occupied port cities, including Galveston, Pensacola, Key West, and New Bern. A small outbreak occurred in Hilton Head, South Carolina, and its surrounding areas, after troops from the 7th New Hampshire arrived from Key West, where the disease had been introduced by a ship from Havana. An epidemic occurred in Union-occupied New Bern, North Carolina, in September, October, and November of 1864. A total of 571 Union soldiers were affected, with 278 deaths, a typical case-fatality rate for the disease (48.7 percent).

THE EPIDEMIC OF 1878.   Epidemics of yellow fever returned later in the nineteenth century and often spread up the Mississippi River. Previously, the epidemics were not as severe upriver as they were in New Orleans, but their severity increased gradually. In 1873, epidemic yellow fever caused 6,000 deaths in Memphis, and the great Memphis epidemic of 1878, one of the last major outbreaks of yellow fever in the continental United States, was typical of the sequence of events that occurred when the disease appeared.

Sanitary conditions in that city were abysmal, especially along the river, where garbage, dead animals, and outflow from privies accumulated. On June 3, 1878, news of a yellow fever outbreak in the West Indies led the president of the Board of Health to propose quarantining the city and cleaning it to remove the sources of miasmas, but merchants protested the quarantine as a deterrent to summer business. They persuaded thirty-two doctors to sign a statement indicating that there was no danger from yellow fever, and no need for quarantine. The City Council turned down the proposal from the Board of Health.

When thirty-six cases of yellow fever were reported in New Orleans on July 26, the Memphis City Council finally acted, arranging to wash the streets with carbolic acid and to spread lime and other chemicals as "germ killers." The Board of Health set up a quarantine station on an island to hold arrivals coming upriver until it was certain they were not carrying the infection. Similar quarantine stations were set up along the river in Baton Rouge, Natchez, and Vicksburg; Jackson, Mississippi, being inland, set up shotgun roadblocks along all the roads leading to it.

On August 9, yellow fever broke out in Granada, Mississippi, 100 miles from Memphis; during the course of the epidemic 1,040 cases were reported and over 350 deaths occurred in a total population of about 2,000. On August 13, a Memphis newspaper assured the city that all was well, and that it was "not likely" that yellow fever would appear in their city. It advised the populace to "Avoid patent medicines and bad whiskey! ... be cheerful and laugh as much as possible." But on that day Mrs. Kate Bioda, whose husband ran a snack shop in the waterfront district, died of yellow fever. By August 16, thirty-four cases were recognized in Pinchgut, a slum section of the city.

On August 22, twelve deaths from yellow fever occurred in Memphis; the next day, seventeen. The Board of Health officially declared an epidemic, but by then half the population had fled the city. The roads out of Memphis were clogged with wagons piled with bedding, furniture, women, and children. Within the city, looting of abandoned houses was widespread. Refugees were turned away from many communities, but Holly Springs, Mississippi, 36 miles away, had no cases and permitted them to enter, believing that the germ of yellow fever could not live in their higher, drier climate. A few weeks later, half of that town's original population of 4,000 were dead.

Within Memphis, 1,500 cases were reported during the first bad "fever week," with 10 deaths a day; the next week 3,000 cases were recorded, with 50 deaths a day; by mid-September there were about 200 deaths a day. One undertaker buried 2,000 bodies between August 15 and October 1, using converted furniture transporters as "dead wagons."

The populace tried to avoid the disease by carrying rags soaked in turpentine, putting garlic and mustard powder in their shoes, and wearing other foul-smelling items to defeat the miasmas. Tar was kept burning and cannons booming. Benjamin Rush's measures of a century before were still standard: Medical treatment consisted mainly of purging and inducing blisters, especially on the head and over the kidneys. The recommended treatment published in the *Memphis Appeal* consisted of an emetic of mustard salt and warm water, hot foot baths to induce sweating, and administration of a variety of teas.

One "doctor," just graduated from a New Orleans school of hydropathy, packed his patients in ice and sprinkled them continuously with ice water from huge watering cans. When he contracted the fever himself, he insisted on the same treatment, which was administered in an operating amphitheater, thus enabling him to explain his theories to an audience of medical personnel as he died.

The entire country became aware of the disaster occurring in Memphis, and President Rutherford B. Hayes, speaking in Minneapolis, raised $100 when he auctioned off a Bible given him by an ex-Union soldier seeking to aid "some suffering Confederate soldier caught by the pestilence." The Howard Association, named after an English philanthropist, sent volunteers to care for patients, as they had in all towns subject to epidemics of yellow fever since their founding in 1867. The medical hero of the Memphis epidemic was Dr. R. W. Mitchell, who had resigned as president of the Board of Health and had become medical director of the "Howard Medical Corps." The association raised a half million dollars and sent nurses and other medical personnel, food, and supplies to the city. During the epidemic, twenty-three of the Howard Association volunteers developed yellow fever and ten died.

Ten policemen, twenty-four firemen, and fifty newspapermen died during the epidemic. One newspaperman was widely considered a hero; Robert Catron, a correspondent for the Associated Press, sent out telegraphic dispatches twice a day, which drew the attention and sympathy of the nation and generated a flood of aid in the form of food, supplies, money, and volunteers. He filled in for sick friends on all three daily newspapers until he developed yellow fever himself and died on September 24.

Another hero was the madam of the Mansion House, the most opulent bordello in Memphis. She dismissed her prostitutes and used her rooms to nurse victims of the epidemic, doing much of the nursing herself until she, too, died of the disease. An editorial in the *Memphis Appeal* paid tribute to "this sinner with a golden heart."

Overall, about 16,000 people died of yellow fever along the Mississippi valley area during the epidemic of 1878, with Memphis the hardest hit. Many refugees never returned, and the city was so bankrupt that it surrendered its corporate charter in January, 1879, to become a mere "taxing district" by act of the Tennessee legislature. But despite the virtual destruction of the city by yellow fever, Memphis was heard from again.

YELLOW FEVER DURING THE SPANISH-AMERICAN WAR. At the time of the 1878 Memphis epidemic, the germ theory of disease was becoming accepted and the science of bacteriology established. However, the possibility of insect transmission of an infectious agent had not yet been demonstrated, and the concept was ridiculed. The control of yellow fever (and malaria) required proof of the mosquito's role in the spread of disease, and the studies that established this role— some of the most dramatic and important episodes in the history of preventive medicine—were a direct consequence of the Spanish-American War.

The war lasted only 118 days in 1898, but American troops occupied Cuba until May 20, 1902. Although there were relatively few battlefield casualties, there were constant casualties from disease during the entire period of warfare and occupation.

Typhoid fever was the main cause of illness and death among the American forces, until yellow fever appeared after the fighting, in the summer of 1900. During the build-up and training of the troops, no large camp avoided an outbreak, and typhoid fever caused more than five times as many deaths as occurred as a result of military action. Because of the severity of the problem, a Typhoid Board was created, which included Drs. Walter Reed, E. O. Shakespeare, and Victor Vaughan. They demonstrated that filth, feces, and flies were responsible for spreading typhoid and that it could break out in camps that had previously been disease-free. Because all camps included soldiers from cities or towns where typhoid fever had been rampant, it became clear that apparently healthy people could carry typhoid bacilli in their intestinal tract, excrete them in the feces, and cause an outbreak of the disease. These observations contributed to understanding of the concept of a *carrier state*.

When the yellow fever epidemic became widespread in Cuba, the prevalent theory of its etiology was that it, too, was caused by filth, particularly the decay and dirt found around docks. The association with docks was correct, since most major outbreaks of the disease occurred in port cities and began in the harbor area, spreading from ships carrying infected passengers. This theory led to the institution of rigorous clean-up measures similar to those of General Butler in New Orleans during the Civil War, beginning in Santiago, where Dr. Leonard Wood, the original commander of the Rough Riders, had become a brigadier-general and post-war military governor. Later, when he became military governor of all Cuba, he instituted the same measures in Havana. He insisted on strict sewage disposal and set forces to work scrubbing the city streets. His thoroughness in cleaning up Santiago reportedly led one of his sergeants to comment "When Wood gets through, the flies will starve to death in Santiago!" According to the "contagionist theory" these measures would wipe out both typhoid fever and yellow fever; however, while typhoid was virtually eliminated, malaria and yellow fever persisted. Because quinine was available, treatment for malaria was fairly satisfactory. Thus, yellow fever caused the most concern, particularly in view of the panic it had caused in many cities during previous epidemics.

Once it became clear that improved sanitation had no effect on the spread of yellow fever, Army Surgeon General George Sternberg appointed a special Army Board to study the problem. Major Walter Reed was its chairman and Drs. Aristides Agramonte, James Carroll, and Jesse Lazear were members. On June

25, 1900, the Reed Commission set up a field station for experimental studies at the Columbia Barracks, near Quemados, Cuba .

ESTABLISHING THE ROLE OF THE MOSQUITO.[E2]   In 1879, when an American Yellow Fever study team, including Dr. George Miller Sternberg, was sent to Cuba, no fruitful results came of their inquiry. Sternberg, who became Surgeon General of the Army by the time of the Spanish-American War, was a distinguished bacteriologist and an authority on yellow fever. In the studies he conducted as part of the 1879 team, he had tried, unsuccessfully, to transmit the disease through mosquitoes. However, he had not allowed for the "extrinsic incubation period" in the mosquito, a phenomenon unknown at that time. This probably accounted for his failure, as a result of which, he opposed the mosquito theory and requested that the Reed commission begin its studies by looking for the "icterus bacillus," an etiologic agent apparently found by an Italian bacteriologist named Sanarelli.

When Sanarelli studied yellow fever in Brazil, simultaneous outbreaks of leptospirosis (Weil's disease) and yellow fever occurred. Weil's disease is caused by the bacterial organism, *L. icterohemorrhagica*, and it was often confused with yellow fever. Sanarelli probably saw both types of disease, but believed them to be exclusively yellow fever.

Implications for the role of insects in the transmission of diseases had been made earlier in the nineteenth century. In 1807, a Dr. Crawford, in Baltimore, suggested the insect transmission theory for yellow fever. In 1848, Dr. Josiah Clark Nott, a Connecticut native practicing in Mobile, Alabama, lost four of his own children during an epidemic, even though he had moved them outside of the stricken city to the country. His observation on the spread of the epidemic led him to postulate an insect vector. In 1854, Dr. L.D. Beauperthuy, working in Angostura, Venezuela (later Ciudad Bolivar), advanced a similar hypothesis. In 1880, the great tropical disease investigator, Dr. Patrick Manson, identified the role of the mosquito in the transmission of filariasis, the same year that Dr. Charles Laveran, a French military surgeon working in Algiers, identified the parasite of malaria. Finally, in December of 1897, Dr. Ronald Ross, a British physician, published a paper demonstrating that the Anopheles mosquito transmits malaria only after a period of incubation in the insect's abdomen (the extrinsic incubation period). This report, which caused quite a stir, stimulated Dr. Jesse Lazear at Johns Hopkins University to attempt to confirm his findings. Ross' observations had a major impact on the willingness of the Reed Commission to consider the theory that the mosquito was involved in the spread of yellow fever.

The observations of Dr. Carlos Finlay of Cuba also had a great influence on the Reed Commission. Finlay, a native of Havana, had graduated from Jefferson Medical College in Philadelphia in 1855, then returned to Havana to practice. He was much loved and respected as a person and a physician, and despite his busy practice he found time to study the problem of yellow fever and its transmission. He knew of the suggested vector role of mosquitoes, and undertook an in-depth study of the mosquitoes of Havana. Among 700 species, he correctly identified the *Culex fasciatus* (also called *Stegomyia fasciatus* and later renamed *Aedes aegypti*) as the agent, and recognized that only the female sucks blood from mammals. He showed that this occurred after fertilization by the male, and that the warmth of the blood stimulated the female to ovulate. He postulated that the mosquito would prefer a patient with fever, since the warmer the blood, the sooner ovulation occurred. Thus, mosquitoes would be most attracted to patients with yellow fever, thus enhancing spread of the disease.

Finlay observed the *Culex* mosquito thoroughly, noting that while it does not fly great distances, it could be transported by humans in their clothing or in a ship's cargo. He tested his theory of the role of the mosquito in the transmission of yellow fever by subjecting twenty people, including himself, to the bite of mosquitoes that had bitten patients suffering from yellow fever. He stated that the results were "favorable to my theory," but inconclusive. He wanted to have his theories tested further, but was concerned over the ethics of such experimentation; in conducting his own studies, he had subjected the test subjects, including himself, to mosquitoes that had very recently been exposed to yellow fever patients, in the hope that only mild disease would result. On August 14, 1881, his comprehensive report on the biology of the *Culex* mosquito and the clinical and pathological aspects of yellow fever was presented to the Royal Academy of Medical, Physical, and Natural Sciences of Havana. Although this paper is now considered a classic, Finlay had a stammer, and his hesitating, hour-long presentation was received with silence. According to a contemporary, "the presiding officer of the Academy tabled the paper to obviate discussion and embarrassment to everyone."

While yellow fever was raging in Memphis, and in the towns of Orwood and Taylor, Mississippi, Dr. Henry Rose Carter made a critical observation, that was important to the Reed Commission. Carter noted that the time interval between the arrival of an infected case in isolated farmhouses and the occurrence of secondary cases in the vicinity of these houses was generally from two to three weeks. However, susceptible people who subsequently visited the houses for a few hours would fall sick with the usual incubation period of one to seven days. Carter named the initial interval "the extrinsic incubation period."

This "extrinsic incubation period" resembled the period Ross had observed for the incubation of malaria in the mosquito before it was able to transmit the disease. On June 26, 1900, Carter sent a note to Lazear suggesting that Findlay's "theory has much in its favor." Carter was a fellow alumnus of Reed's at the University of Virginia, and he was in Cuba to discuss these findings when Reed arrived there. Reed later wrote Carter that, "your own work in Mississippi did more to impress me with the importance of the intermediate host than everything else put together."

Jefferson Randolph Kean, another University of Virginia alumnus, was acting sanitary officer for Havana and an early convert to the mosquito theory, perhaps because of his friendship with Reed. He insisted on putting kerosene atop cisterns and eliminating every conceivable site that might contain standing water. Kean made inspectors responsible for any case of yellow fever that occurred in their territory.

On October 22, 1900, Reed described the course of the work of his "board of medical officers" in a presentation to the American Public Health Association in Indianapolis and in the Commission's first publication, which appeared in the *Philadelphia Medical Journal*, late in 1900. The report noted that, after failing to find Sanarelli's "icteroid bacillus," the Commission was faced with a choice of seeking the etiologic agent (presumably bacterial) by studying the intestinal flora of patients with yellow fever, or "to give attention to the theory of the propagation by means of the mosquito—a theory first advanced and ingeniously discussed by Dr. Carlos J. Finlay of Havana (*Anales de la Real Academia*, 18:1881, 147-169)." In this original publication, the Reed Commission pointed out that Ross' observation on malaria and Carter's work in Mississippi influenced them to look into the mosquito theory.[E3]

Because of his earlier experience with studies of mosquitoes confirming Ross' observation on the malarial parasite, Lazear was put in charge of the mosquito phase of the study. After hatching *Culex* mosquitoes from eggs supplied to him by Dr. Carlos Finlay, Lazear allowed them to feed on yellow fever patients and, after various periods of incubation, to bite volunteers. Nine of the volunteers, including Lazear himself, stayed healthy, but two developed yellow fever. These cases engendered considerable excitement and were the main subject of the initial report. One case, Dr. James Carroll, a member of the Reed Commission, had been bitten by a mosquito that had bitten a severe case of yellow fever on the second day of the disease, 12 days before biting Carroll. The other case, a soldier designated only as "X.Y." was bitten by the same mosquito, four days after it bit Dr. Carroll and two days after it had bitten another yellow fever patient.

After giving a detailed report of its attempts to find Sanarelli's bacillus, the commission drew the conclusions that the icteroid bacillus was not part of the etiology of yellow fever, and that "The mosquito serves as the intermediate host for the parasite of yellow fever, and it is highly probable that the disease is only propagated through the bite of this insect."

However, because of the way that the studies were performed, Dr. Carroll could have contracted yellow fever from other types of exposure during the course of his work. In their first report, the Commission members carefully documented all the possible additional ways in which Dr. Carroll and "X.Y." could have acquired the infection other than by the experimental bite of the mosquito. They believed that these other possibilities were unlikely, but noted the obvious need for a carefully controlled environment, in which other means of infection were rigorously excluded.

In this initial report in the *Philadelphia Medical Journal*, Reed detailed how Dr. Jesse Lazear, as part of the study, was bitten on August 16, 1900 by a *Culex fasciatus* mosquito that had bitten a very mild case of yellow fever in the fifth day of the patient's illness. Lazear did not develop an illness as a result of this experimental exposure to the mosquito. However, on September 13, while collecting blood from yellow fever patients on one of the hospital wards, Lazear was accidentally bitten by another mosquito, which he recognized as a *Culex*, although he could not determined the species. The report added, "As Dr. Lazear had been previously bitten by a contaminated mosquito without after effects, he deliberately allowed this particular mosquito, which had settled on the back of his hand, to remain until it satisfied its hunger." Five days later, Lazear felt ill and developed a chill, the next day he had a temperature of 103.8°, and on the third day he became jaundiced. The disease became inexorably progressive and Lazear died on September 25.

Because Dr. Lazear had been bitten by a mosquito while on the wards of a yellow-fever hospital, and the insect was most likely contaminated by biting a yellow fever patient, the experience added to their conviction that the disease was transmitted in that fashion.

After Lazear's death, all attention focused on the mosquito theory. Major Walter Reed, who had been in Washington to present the report of the Typhoid Board, returned to Havana and checked all the records left by Lazear. Because the possibility existed that Carroll, and perhaps even "X.Y." had other types of exposure to yellow fever, a carefully controlled experiment was designed in which all volunteers would be kept isolated from exposure to mosquitoes or other possible vectors. One group would be bitten by mosquitoes that had been allowed to feed on yellow fever patients at carefully selected intervals in the course of the disease and with known incubation periods after feeding on the patients. A second group would be exposed to various forms of "contagion" known to spread other infectious diseases, such as typhoid fever.

Obtaining funds to set up the new study became a problem. Surgeon General Sternberg was still unconvinced by the mosquito theory, probably because of his own failure to show their role, and Reed knew that he could not get the money he needed from Washington. Reed received a great deal of help from General Leonard Wood, now military governor of Cuba. Appalled by the extent of yellow fever there, Wood played a major role in persuading Sternberg to appoint the commission to study the cause of the disease and its mode of transmission, in the hope of preventing future cases. Later, after Lazear's death, when Reed needed funds to conduct the second phase of the studies, Jefferson Kean, acting sanitary officer and a friend of both Reed and Wood, suggested that Reed seek General Wood's assistance. Both Reed and Wood knew that the Surgeon General was stubbornly skeptical about the mosquito theory, and that if Wood passed Reed's request for funds through regular channels it would result in a permanent end to the experiments.

Wood also remembered his lack of success in preventing yellow fever through cleaning up Santiago and the similar failure of such measures in Havana. He felt that the "contagionists" must be wrong—that yellow fever was transmitted directly from person-to-person—and he was impressed with the studies Reed's team was conducting. In Wood's office, they discussed the definitive studies Reed was planning, and Wood decided to find the necessary funds himself. That morning he signed a bill providing $10,000 to strengthen the police force in Havana. Wood told Reed that "This work is of more importance to Cuba than the capture of a few thieves. I will give you the ten thousand dollars, and if that proves insufficient I will give you ten thousand more."

Wood cautioned Reed to get in writing "informed consent" from his volunteers, and then protected Reed from interference with his work; twice Wood intervened to save the project when the Surgeon General ordered it discontinued because he needed the doctors for service elsewhere. Reed later called Wood's support invaluable.

On October 9, 1900, at a dinner in honor of his fortieth birthday, Wood told his staff, "I have a most important thing to tell you. We have got at the cause of yellow fever. That achievement is going to be of more importance to Cuba and to the rest of the world than anything else we could possibly do here...." Later, Wood played a role in convincing Major Gorgas, who had become the sanitation officer, to undertake mosquito control.

The new facility that Reed constructed with Wood's funds was called Camp Lazear. It consisted of two temporary buildings 80 yards apart, but totally screened to keep out all mosquitoes. One was intentionally designed to have bad ventilation, and was provided with bedding and garments soiled with urine, feces, and vomit from yellow fever patients. The other was clean and well ventilated, and screened in the middle. Volunteers allowed themselves to be placed in each facility, and some in the clean house were purposely subjected to the bites of mosquitoes known to have bitten yellow fever patients.

The volunteers in the humid, ill-ventilated dirty house remained healthy. The first volunteer to be bitten by an infected mosquito, Private J. R. Kissinger, developed yellow fever. One of the volunteers who initially stayed on the other side of the screen in the clean house, Private J. J. Moran, insisted that he be bitten, too; he also developed yellow fever, as did three Spanish volunteers.

Altogether, twenty volunteers during this phase of the study contracted yellow fever, with no fatalities. The volunteers were paid $100 in gold, plus an extra $100 if they actually developed yellow fever. The volunteers probably reasoned that since everyone was going to catch the disease in any case, they might as well be paid for it. Since few people believed the mosquito theory, the most heroic volunteers were probably those who slept in the filth, bedclothes, and blankets of patients who had the disease, not only from an aesthetic standpoint but because such material was known to spread other diseases, especially typhoid fever.

In addition to Lazear one other death occurred among the volunteers who participated in the Cuban studies. Clara Maas, a civilian serving as a "contract nurse" with the Army, volunteered during a later series of experiments that were designed and carried out by the Cuban physician Juan Guiteras and Major William Gorgas. These experiments were designed to demonstrate that a mosquito that bit a patient with mild yellow fever would transmit only mild disease, analogous to the concept underlying the use of inoculation in smallpox. Walter Reed, no longer in Cuba, advised against these experiments when shown the protocol. They were carried out despite his cautions, and Clara Mass, bitten by a laboratory mosquito that had previously bitten a patient with mild yellow fever, died of the disease on August 24, 1901. Miss Mass, who trained as a nurse in the Belleville, New Jersey, hospital that now bears her name, was honored on a U.S. postage stamp in 1976.

On April 30, 1901, Walter Reed presented a preliminary report of his commission's observations to the Association of American Physicians; in his report he gave public credit to Finlay and concluded that, "the mosquito serves as intermediary host for the parasite of yellow fever." His data showed that the mosquito is capable of transmitting the disease between 9 and 16 days after biting an infected person. Further studies by Reed Commission members showed that blood taken from a patient early in the disease was also capable of transmitting the disease directly, without the intervention of a mosquito. About a year later, at the suggestion of Dr. William Welch of the Johns Hopkins Medical School, they designed experiments similar to those that had shown that hoof-

and-mouth disease, an illness of animals, could be transmitted by a filtrate that contained no cells or bacteria. A similar filtrate of the blood of yellow fever patients was shown to transmit the disease, thus satisfying the concept that underlies the definition of a filterable virus. This observation was a critical step enabling the later development of an effective vaccine.

Major William C. Gorgas implemented the standard sanitation measures after he succeeded Kean as public health officer in Havana, but epidemic yellow fever continued to rage. Gorgas met Dr. Finlay and discussed his mosquito theory with him, but remained unconvinced. After the initial findings of the Reed Commission, Major Gorgas did agree that mosquitoes could transmit yellow fever, but he did not think they were the only, or the most important, mode of transmission. However, in March 1901, under pressure from General Wood, Gorgas began the campaign to eradicate mosquitoes.

Initially, Gorgas decided that the only way to obtain convincing evidence for the role of the mosquito was to eliminate it and measure the incidence of yellow fever. The *Aedes aegypti* mosquito prefers to live near human habitation and it has a very limited flight range. The female lays up to 120 eggs, which develop into larvae and then grow into adult mosquitoes in under 10 days. Adults live only three or four weeks. The mosquito population of Havana was quickly reduced by fumigating houses, especially those in and near where cases of yellow fever had occurred, and removing standing water—barrels, cisterns, even tin cans and broken dishes that could serve as breeding sites. The number of mosquitoes around Havana dropped precipitously and, concurrently, so did cases of yellow fever. Havana was free from yellow fever for the first time in 200 years. With the success of that campaign, Gorgas was converted to the mosquito theory and went on to the more difficult task of eliminating the Anopheles mosquitoes that transmitted malaria.[3]

Walter Reed was greatly honored for his classic definitive epidemiological studies. (The main referral hospital of the U.S. Army in Washington, D.C. is named in his honor.) Unfortunately, he died of appendicitis two years after his discovery. Dr. Carlos Finlay continued to practice medicine in Cuba until six years before his death in 1915, at the age of 82.

YELLOW FEVER AND THE PANAMA CANAL.   Faulty engineering, poor knowledge of local conditions, and the inroads of yellow fever, malaria, and typhoid combined to defeat the French effort to build a canal across the isthmus of Panama. The construction effort, led by Ferdinand de Lesseps, was maintained for nine years, and during each summer yellow fever broke out, with mortality rates that varied between 10 to 12 and 50 percent. The French carefully avoided keeping detailed records of the deaths, but American sources subsequently estimated that between 20,000 and 22,000 workers died of disease. Senior officials, including successive chief engineers sent from France to run the effort, brought coffins with them, so that their bodies could be shipped back to France.

After Theodore Roosevelt negotiated the independence of Panama from Colombia, American civil engineers took over construction of the canal. An outbreak of yellow fever in May 1905 reminded locals of the epidemics of 1885 and 1886 that had demoralized the French workmen. Hundreds of recently arrived American workers hurriedly departed Panama, including chief engineer John Wallace, who decided that an offer of a position in private industry was much more attractive. (Wallace scoffed at the idea that mosquitoes could spread the disease and refused to divert funds to mosquito eradication projects.) The May 1905 epidemic, which lasted about five months, resulted in numerous deaths from yellow fever and malaria. Additional deaths from pneumonia, typhoid fever, and dysentery, and a large number of nonfatal cases of all these diseases, contributed to the panic that crippled efforts to construct the canal.

The army assigned William C. Gorgas, fresh from his success in Havana, as public health officer and President Roosevelt was advised to back his efforts. Once given the resources he needed, Gorgas undertook a thorough effort to clean up the city of Panama and concentrated on removing all possible mosquito breeding sites.[E4]

The 1905 epidemic ended in September, 1906, at which time seven cases of yellow fever occurred, resulting in four deaths. One afternoon during this period, as Gorgas and several of his staff were performing an autopsy at the Ancon Hospital, he is reported to have told them, "take a good look at this man," expecting him to be the last case of yellow fever they would see.

The effectiveness of the campaign is illustrated by the admissions book of the Ancon Hospital (now the Gorgas Hospital), which gives the name, age, date of admission, diagnosis, and outcome for each case admitted for treatment. Page after page lists yellow fever and malaria, with occasional isolated entries for typhoid fever, pneumonia, or injury, until the month when Gorgas' efforts were instituted. In the middle of a page, the listings for yellow fever and malaria cease; the rest of that and subsequent pages list pneumonia, typhoid, etc. but no further cases of mosquito-borne diseases. Gorgas' program limited deaths during the American endeavor to about one-tenth those that affected the French effort. The twenty-year effort to build a canal across the Isthmus of Panama culminated with the opening of the canal on August 15, 1914.

YELLOW FEVER, BOARDS OF HEALTH, AND BIOTERRORISM. The yellow fever epidemics provided a sharp impetus to developments in public health. The first board of health was set up in Philadelphia, and others soon followed throughout the nineteenth century. In 1855, the Louisiana State Board of Health was created, the first of its kind in United States. In 1879, a national board of health (intended to function as a national quarantine system) was created by Congress. It was opposed by municipal and state health boards, however, so it merged with the United States Maritime Hospital Service. Then, in 1888, in response to a yellow fever epidemic, the Florida State Board of Health was created. Thus, by the epidemic of 1905, government health organizations were fully prepared to eradicate yellow fever.

Yellow fever still exists, finding its hosts mostly in jungle primates, but affecting humans entering jungle areas where its mosquito vector cannot be eliminated. However, an effective vaccine exists, and travel in such areas can be safe. Yellow fever is not a disease likely to be spread purposely, because the essential vector of the *Aedes aegypti* mosquito would have to be introduced as well. Nonetheless, in areas where appropriate mosquitoes exist, yellow fever could be a potent form of bioterrorism.

ADDITIONAL READING

Adams HH. *History of the United States During the Administrations of Jefferson and Madison.* Chicago: Univ of Chicago Press, 1967 (orig. pub 1921).

Bean WB. *Walter Reed: A Biography.* Charlottesville: Univ Press of Virginia, 1982.

Blake JB. Yellow fever in eighteenth century America. *Bull NY Acad Med* 1968;44:673.

Bray RS. *Armies of Pestilence, The Impact of Disease on History.* New York: Barnes and Noble, 2000.

Cartwright FF. *Disease and History, The Influence of Disease in Shaping History.* New York: Crowell, 1972.

Crosby AW. *Ecological Imperialism, The Biological Expansion of Europe.* Cambridge, UK: Cambridge Univ Press, 1986.

Dubois RJ, ed. *Bacterial and Mycotic Infections of Man.* Philadelphia: JB Lippincott Co, 1948.

Duffy J. *Epidemics in Colonial America.* Baton Rouge: Louisiana State Univ Press, 1953.

Duffy J. Yellow fever in the continental United States during the nineteenth century. *Bull NY Acad Med* 1968;44:687.

Hagedorn H. *Leonard Wood, A Biography* New York: Harper & Brothers, 1931.

Hobbs WH. *Leonard Wood, Administrator, Soldier, and Citizen.* New York: G.P. Putnam's Sons, 1920.

Keating JM. A History of the Yellow Fever. The Yellow Fever Epidemic of 1878, in Memphis, Tenn., Embracing a Complete List of the Dead, The Names of the Doctors and Nurses Employed, Names of All Who Contributed Money or Means, and the Names and History of the Howards, Together with Other Data, and Lists of the Dead Elsewhere. Memphis, TN: Printed for the Howard Association, 1879.

Kelly HA. Walter Reed and Yellow Fever. New York: McClure, Phillips, 1906.

Manchester K. The Archeology of Disease. Bradford, West Yorkshire, England: Univ of Bradford Press, 1983.

Marks G, Beatty WK. Epidemics. New York: Scribner, 1976

McCullough, D. The Path Between the Seas, The Creation of the Panama Canal, 1870-1914. New York: Simon and Shuster, 1977.

McNeill, WH. Plagues and peoples. Garden City, NY: Anchor Press, 1976

Powell JH, Bring Out Your Dead; The Great Plague of Yellow Fever in Philadelphia in 1793. Philadelphia: Univ of Pennsylvania Press, 1949.

Ritchie CIA. Insects, The Creeping Conquerors, and Human History. New York: Elsevier/Nelson Books, 1979.

Spink WW. Infectious Diseases, Prevention and Treatment during the Nineteenth Century . Minneapolis: Univ of Minnesota Press, 1978.

Strode GK, ed. Yellow Fever. New York: McGraw-Hill, 1951.

Taylor N. Cinchona in Java; The Story of Quinine with an Introduction by Pieter Honig. New York: Greenberg, 1945.

Wills C. Yellow Fever, Black Goddess, The Coevolution of People and Plagues. Reading, MA: Addison Wesley, 1996.

[E1]During the great Philadelphia epidemic, an article in American Daily Advertiser of August 29, 1793, presages Dr. Walter Reed's classic observations by 107 years: "As the late rains will produce a great increase of mosquitoes in the city ... I imagine it will be agreeable to the citizens to know that the increase of these poisonous insects may be much diminished by a very simple and cheap mode, which accident discovered. Whoever takes the trouble to examine their rain-water tubs, will find millions of the mosquitoes...in a state not quite prepared to emerge and fly off .... Into a wine glass ... pour half a teaspoon full, or less, of any common oil, which will quickly diffuse over the surface, by excluding the air, will destroy the whole brood. Some will survive two or three days, but most of them sink to the bottom, or adhere to the oil on the surface within twenty-four hours. A gill of oil poured into a common rain-water cask will be sufficient: large cisterns may require more; and where water is drawn out by a pump or cock, the oil will remain undisturbed...."

[E2]In retrospect, we know that the duration of infectivity in individual cases is so brief that yellow fever could have spread only rarely from ill people aboard ships. They would either have died or recovered and no longer have been infectious by the time the ship reached port. Thus, ships could have passed through quarantine regulations, since these regulations usually were based on finding sick passengers. Therefore, mosquitoes infected with the virus, which they most likely caught from feeding on infected passengers early in the voyage, must have been carried aboard ships in the water supply and brought the epidemic to the port city.

[E3]Nevertheless, the role of the mosquito was still doubted by most people. Newspaper editorials belittled the mosquito theory: On November 2, 1900, the Washington Post commented: "Of all the silly and nonsensical rigmarole about yellow fever that has yet found its way into print ... the silliest beyond compare is to be found in the mosquito hypothesis."

[E4]The thoroughness of the mosquito control effort was amazing. One of the plagues of life in Panama was enormous ants that would crawl up the legs of workers' cots to bite them at night. To deter the ants, cot legs were placed in small pans of water, which formed an effective barrier. Gorgas ordered that a skim of oil be placed in those pans. He even went so far as to remove flower pots from staff offices and insist that the Panama City Cathedral change the holy water daily.

CHAPTER 4

SYPHILIS

THE GREAT POX

THE SIEGE OF NAPLES DURING THE FIFTEENTH CENTURY IS
often blamed for the first great outbreak of syphilis in Europe. Troops from
many nations were involved in the siege: when Charles VIII of France set out to
claim his rights to the kingdom of Naples, which he had inherited as an
Angevin, his troops were mercenaries of French, Spanish, German, Swiss,
Hungarian, and Polish origin. According to some authorities, Spanish mercenaries also fought in defense of Naples, and some of the Spanish troops on both
sides had been with Columbus on his first trip to the New World.

When the French were finally able to occupy Naples on February 21, 1495,
after a long siege, they were already afflicted with a new disease. Whether the
disease first appeared among the invading, besieging troops or appeared inside
the walls of the city is debatable. One observer who was inside Naples at the
time, the father of the great anatomist Fallopius (1523-1562), wrote that the
defenders "finally with violence drove their harlots and women out of the
citadel, and especially the most beautiful ones, on the pretext that the food had
come to an end. And the French, gripped by compassion and bewitched by their
beauty took them in...." Exchange of women between opposing forces was usual
during campaigns of the time, so the act itself was not surprising. However, it
points to a clear knowledge of the mode of transmission of the new disease,
probably because of the location of the initial lesions on the genitalia, and constitutes an early form of biological warfare.

In 1514, Giovanni de Vigo, in describing the new disease, stated, "it is above
all a contagious disease. The contagion is derived above all by coitus, that is to
say by sexual commerce of a healthy man with a sick woman or inversely of a
sick man with a healthy woman." Thus, syphilis was known to be a venereal

disease, from its first appearance in Europe, although that term was not used at the time. The word "venery," derived from the name of the Roman goddess Venus, was first used in 1497 to describe the pursuit of sexual pleasure. Although the term "venereal," which describes the mechanism of disease transmission, did not come into use until 1658, sexually transmitted urethritis, either gonorrhea or a similar infection, was known and well described in the early books of the Bible. Passages in Leviticus mandated that men with "an issue, flow of the seed of copulation" be isolated to prevent contagion; the same passage prescribes the isolation of menstruating women, suggesting that the "issue" of menstrual flow was confused with the "issue" of infectious urethritis. The term gonorrhea, introduced by Aristotle, was derived from the Greek terms *goneh*, seed, and *reos*, a flow, interpreting the urethral discharge as flow of "the seed of copulation." Thus Aristotle's term gonorrhea had the same meaning as the Hebrew term used to describe infectious, sexually transmitted urethritis in Leviticus. Venereal urethritis, then, was known at least two millennia before syphilis appeared in the Old World, and the transmission of disease by sexual contact was not a new concept to the combatants at Naples.

The Neopolitans called syphilis "the French disease," blaming it on their attackers. Charles' troops were devastated by it; the high initial mortality rate depleted their numbers and physically wrecked and disfigured the survivors. Although they eventually took Naples, the gathering of opposing forces elsewhere in Italy required them to head home shortly after they captured the city. Their march through hostile territory all the way up the Italian peninsula was originally unopposed, but soon became a rout. Faced with disease from within and attack from without, the French army disintegrated. Charles blamed his problems on "the Neopolitan disease."

As his troops staggered to their homes across Europe, they brought the disease with them. It appeared, and was recognized as a new disease, in England in 1496, Poland in 1499, and in Russia and Scandinavia in 1500. Because it was thought that Charles' mercenaries were the original sufferers, and that they were spreading it as they staggered toward their homes, the disease was usually called "the French disease."

Syphilis appeared in India in 1498, where its arrival coincided with the famous visit of the Portuguese Explorer Vasco da Gama, who rounded the Cape of Good Hope and landed at Calicut on the Malibar coast on May 20 of that year. It is reasonable to assume that Da Gama's sailors behaved as sailors usually do, and when the new disease appeared it became known as "The Portuguese Sore." A sixteenth-century medical work by Bhava Misra, from the Goa area of Portuguese occupation, blames the Portuguese for the introduction of syphilis into India and refers to it as *firangi roga*, which translates as the "European illness."

Despite the French suggestion that syphilis be called "*La Grosse Verole*," (the Great Pox) the name usually used in that country was "the Spanish disease." The Spanish, in turn, looked to see who they could blame, and noted that when Columbus landed at San Salvador in the Bahamas, the native Arawak Indian population was friendly and peaceful, nudity in both sexes was common, and it was their custom to share their women freely. Anxious to please the godlike strangers, a great deal of sexual contact occurred between Arawak women and members of Columbus' crew.[E1]

On March 15, 1493, Columbus returned to Palos, Spain, from his first trip to the islands later known as the Bahamas, Cuba, and Hispaniola. His crew of 44 disbanded, some apparently joining Gonzalo de Cordoba, whose forces joined those of Charles VIII for the march on Naples. In a book published in Venice in 1518, the theory that the new disease was imported from the West Indies by Columbus' crew was already expounded. This theory was supported and popularized in a 1525 book by Gonzalo Fernandez do Oviedo. Oviedo had been present in Barcelona when Columbus reported details of his journey to Queen Isabella, presenting to her six natives from the New World. They were displayed naked before the court; Oviedo commented on their color and handsome appearance, but made no mention of any evidence of the new disease. Oviedo later made several trips to the West Indies himself and reported evidence of the disease among the natives. He did not consider the possibility that it could have been introduced into the New World by Europeans, who had been arriving in considerable numbers for many years before he made his trip.

In 1539, Rodrigo Diaz de Isla published a good description of syphilis, calling it "The West Indian Disease." He claimed to have treated at least one of Columbus' crewmen for it, and his report was generally accepted as evidence for the New World origin of syphilis. Thus, the Spanish blamed syphilis on someone else.

WAS SYPHILIS TRANSMITTED FROM THE NEW WORLD TO THE OLD? The American origin of syphilis has been controversial, but recent studies have found supporting evidence for its presence in pre-Colombian Native Americans. Diseases such as yaws and pinta, which are caused by treponeme organisms similar to those that cause syphilis, were widely distributed in ancient societies, including the pre-Columbian Amerindians. Hence, there is good reason to believe that nonvenereal or endemic syphilis (also called treponarid) was similarly prevalent, spreading by skin contact and affecting people in early childhood or infancy. Recent careful studies of the effects of these "benign" treponemal illnesses have shown that patients develop sequelae resembling those of venereal syphilis, including congenital abnormalities, central nervous system lesions, and visceral pathologic changes. Bone disease also occurs, but it is distinguishable from the bone lesions of venereal syphilis.

The organisms that cause treponemal diseases are antigenically similar to those that produce venereal syphilis, and positive serologic tests for syphilis are found in natives of various parts of the world where yaws, endemic syphilis, and other treponemal diseases are found. Recent studies of the DNA of these organisms have shown no identifiable differences to the organism of venereal syphilis.

The prevailing theory that different treponemes exist in different parts of the globe and that venereal syphilis does not coexist with endemic syphilis has been disproved in recent years. Opponents of the theory of the New World origin of syphilis have suggested that syphilis was present, but rare, in Europe before Columbus, but that it was not correctly diagnosed, perhaps being confused with leprosy. According to this theory, an outbreak of the disease and a change in its character occurred around the time of Charles VIII's siege of Naples. A careful paleontologic search for bone lesions suggestive of true, venereal syphilis in pre-Columbian European skeletons has not supported this concept. On the other hand, an extensive study of pre-Columbian New World skeletal specimens has revealed a small number of specimens with bone lesions characteristic of venereal syphilis. The conclusion of these studies supports the concept that syphilis developed in the New World, probably as a mutation of the organism that causes yaws.

When syphilis first appeared in Europe it was debilitating, with severe disfiguring skin lesions and a high early mortality. Then, a rapid decline in the severity of syphilitic lesions occurred during the first half of the sixteenth century, and we can trace changes in the descriptions of the disease by various authors at that time, including Ulrich van Hutten, Diaz de Isla, and Girolamo Fracastorius. This change suggests a gradual adaptation between the organism and its hosts. Some decrease in the frequency of syphilis may have occurred during this period. In 1529, Sir Thomas More wrote that its incidence had declined significantly, and that one sufferer from the "French Pox" now attended hospital for every five in 1499. However, in 1579, William Clowes stated that fifteen of every twenty patients admitted to St. Bartholomew's Hospital suffered from syphilis.

In 1530, a classic description of the disease by Girolamo Fracastorius, in which the name syphilis was first used, presents a vivid picture of what the disease was like shortly after it appeared:

"Let us now study the symptoms of this disease," he wrote. "The disease does not affect dumb inhabitants of the wave, nor the wild beasts of the forest, nor the birds of the sky, nor horses or cattle. It only has to do with man. Man alone is prey....

"One of the most surprising facts is that, after having contracted the germ of contagion, the victim attacked by the scourge does not often present any lesion that is well marked before the moon has four times accomplished its travels. The disease, in fact, does not show itself at once by accusing symptoms directly that it has penetrated the organism. For a certain time it broods in silence, as if it were gathering its forces for a more terrible explosion. During this period, at all events, a strange languor seizes the patient and depresses his whole being; his mind seems heavy, his limbs are soft and weakening, fail to work; the eye loses its flash and the face is depressed in its expressions and has become pale.

"It is in the organs of generation that the virus is first transported, to irradiate from there to the neighboring parts and on the regions of the groin.

"Soon after, more well-defined symptoms show themselves ... Atrocious pains suddenly bursts forth in the limbs charged with vitiated humors and tortured articulations, the arms, the shoulders, the calves...

"The most subtle of these humors, those which are most easily evacuated, take refuge either in the skin or in the extremities of the limbs. They then produce hideous eruptions on those points, and these exanthems soon spread over the whole body and over the face with a repulsive mask.

"Unknown to our days, these eruptions consist of pustules and conical pimples, which, gorged with corrupted liquids, are not slow in opening to allow the escape of a mucous and virulent sanious fluid. Even, sometimes, the pimples that are similar or develop in the depths of organs and noiselessly corrode the tissues. It is thus that horrible ulcers are seen covering the limbs, denuding the bones, eating the lips and penetrating the throat, from which there issues only a weak and plaintive voice. At other times, again, there exhales from the skin thick humors which dry into fearsome crust on the surface of the integument.

"Ah! How many patients, sorrowful victims of this plague have contemplated with horror their faces and their bodies covered with hideous taints, deploring their youth in its boom, and have cursed the gods and threatened the sky. Unfortunate!"

Fracastorius went on to describe treatment with an ointment of mercury mixed with bear grease or horse fat, applied over the entire body surface except the head and over the heart. He even describes mouth ulcers, a result of heavy metal poisoning from absorption of the mercury. In his section on prevention, he makes the key point about the mode of spread. "At all event," he wrote, "do not succumb to the attractions of love; nothing could be more harmful, and your kisses would taint the tender daughters of Venus with a detestable contagion."

Famous Cases of Syphilis.   Many famous people have been reported victims of syphilis, beginning appropriately enough with Charles VIII of France, who died in 1498, at the age of 28, supposedly of syphilis. He was succeeded by the Duc d'Orleans, who became Louis the XII (1498-1515). Louis, in turn, was succeeded by Francis I (1515-1547), and the saga of syphilis in the French monarchy resumed. Francis took as his mistress the model for Leonardo da Vinci's famous *La Belle Ferromiere*. Her husband was not pleased with the royal honor accorded his wife and apparently decided on an unusual form of revenge. He deliberately acquired syphilis at a bordello and infected his wife, who in turn passed it on to Francis. If this legend is true, then syphilis has figured in social as well as military biowarfare. However, descriptions of Francis I's illnesses in his later years and his terminal symptoms are more typical of tuberculosis rather than complications of syphilis.[E2]

The long list of prominent historical figures reported to have had syphilis includes three Popes, Alexander VI, Julius II, and Leo X; two czars, Peter I (The Great) and Ivan IV (The Terrible); one czarina, Catherine the Great; two kings, Henry VIII of England and Louis XIV of France; three authors, John Keats, Oscar Wilde, and Guy de Maupassant; and one physician, John Hunter, who acquired the disease inadvertently while inoculating himself with pus from a patient with gonorrhea during studies on the transmission of that disease.

Romantic fashions change, and the spread of syphilis in the sixteenth century was not regarded in the same fashion as it was, for example, in Victorian times. It was long considered by aristocrats as a "gallant disease." Erasmus, who was homosexual and is thought to have had syphilis and possibly Reiter's disease, mentions that a nobleman who had not yet had syphilis was regarded as "ignobilis et rusticanis." In Paris, about one-third of the inhabitants were said to be infected with syphilis, so perhaps the name of "The French Disease" was appropriate after all.[E3]

ADDITIONAL READING

Ackernecht E. Paleopathology. In: Landy D, *Culture, Disease, And Healing: Studies In Medical Anthropology.* New York: Macmillan, 1977.

Brothwell D, Sanderson AT. *Diseases in Antiquity.* Springfield, IL: C.C. Thomas, 1967.

Cartwright FF. *Disease and History.* New York: Crowell, 1972.

Chamberlain NR, Radolf JD, et al. Genetic and physicochemical characterization of the recombinant DNA-derived 47-kilodalton surface immunogen of *Treponema pallidum subsp. pallidum. Infect Immunol* 1988;56:71.

Cockburn A, Cockburn E, eds. *Mummies, Disease, and Ancient Cultures.* Cambridge, New York: Cambridge Univ Press, 1980.

Crosby AW, Jr. *The Columbian Exchange, Biological and Cultural Consequences of 1492.* Westport, CT: Greenwood Press, 1972.

Crosby AW, Jr. The early history of syphilis. In: Landy D. *Culture, Disease, and Healing: Studies In Medical Anthropology.* New York: Macmillan, 1977.

Díaz del Castillo B. *The Discovery and Conquest of Mexico, 1517-1521.* [Edited from the only exact copy of the original ms (and published in Mexico by Genaro Garcia.) Translated with an introduction and notes by A. P. Maudslay.] London: G. Routledge & sons, Ltd, 1928.

Dubois RJ, ed. *Bacterial and Mycotic Infections of Man.* Philadelphia: JB Lippincott Co, 1948.

Fracastorius H. Concerning contagious diseases and their treatment. In: Major RH. *Classic Descriptions of Disease, With Biographical Sketches of the Authors.* Springfield IL: C. C. Thomas, 1945.

Hart GD, ed. *Disease in Ancient Man.* Toronto: Clarke Irwin, 1983.

Henschen F. *The History and Geography of Diseases* [transl. Joan Tate]. New York: DelaCorte Press, 1966.

Kilduff RA. The next great plague to go. *The Military Surgeon* 1942;90:374.

Marks G, Beatty WK. *Epidemics.* New York: Scribner, 1976.

Miao R, Fieldsteel AH. Genetics of Treponema: relationship between *Treponema pallidum* and five cultivable treponemes. *J Bacteriol* 1978;13:101.

Noordbhoek GT, Engelkens HJ, et al. Yaws in West Sumatra, Indonesia: clinical manifestations, serological findings and characterisation of new Treponema isolates by DNA probes. *Eur J Clin Microbiol Infect Dis* 1991;10:12.

Rothschild BM, Heathcote GM. Characterization of the skeletal manifestations of the treponemal disease yaws as a population phenomenon. *Clin Infect Dis* 1993;17:198.

Rothschild BM, Rothschild C. Treponemal disease revisited: skeletal discrimination for yaws, bejel, and venereal syphilis. *Clin Infect Dis* 1995;20:1402.

Rothschild BM, Calderone FL, et al. First European exposure to syphilis: the Dominican Republic at the time of the Columbian contact. *Clin Infect Dis* 2000;31:936.

Wells C. *Bones, Bodies, and Disease; Evidence of Disease and Abnormality In Early Man.* London: Thames and Hudson, 1964

Wills C. *Yellow Fever, Black Goddess, The Coevolution of People and Plagues.* Reading MA: Addison Wesley, 1996.

E1Columbus omitted these details in his report to Queen Isabella. However, the huge bronze Columbus Doors at the entrance to the rotunda of the U.S. Capitol building have bas relief sculptures depicting Columbus' arrival. The work of Randolph Rogers, these doors contain a series of historical episodes based on Washington Irving's *Life and Voyages of Christopher Columbus* (1835). In one scene, one of Columbus' men is carrying off a local woman, memorializing an episode that may depict the first transmission of the causal agents of syphilis from the New World to the Old.

E2Voltaire memorialized Francis I's syphilis in a poem in which he referred to his *"corona veneris,"* the rash on his forehead, presumably secondary syphilis. Part of that poem was dedicated to Belle Duchos, a famous actress of the time, also known to have had the disease.

E3In addition to changes in the fashionability of venereal infections, the diseases themselves have changed. Syphilis and gonorrhea are minor problems, thanks mostly to penicillin, whereas *Chlamydia* has become the most common venereal infection, *Herpes simplex* the most troublesome, and acquired immune deficiency syndrome (AIDS) the most fearsome. In AIDS, the fear of a major, uncontrollable, and untreatable sexually transmitted disease fast became reality. However, amazing progress in understanding the etiology, mechanism of transmission, and biology of AIDS and the viral agent that causes it has led to the development of agents that inhibit its multiplication and greatly improve the prognosis. The huge numbers of infected people and high death rate in certain areas, particularly sub-Saharan Africa, coupled with the cost of the treatment and failure of some populations to adopt the precautions necessary to control it, leave open the possibility that AIDS will be a repetition of the story of great past plagues.

CHAPTER 5

THE SMALL POX

W ITH THE DISCOVERY OF THE NEW WORLD IN THE
fifteenth century, two Old World diseases—smallpox and measles—
were introduced to Native American populations, both with devastating results.
Because these two diseases were not clearly separated before the seventeenth
century, it is not certain whether either or both were responsible for the enormous mortality rates among the native population following their introduction.

These two diseases form the most extreme example of how human actions
can induce epidemic disease; the fatality rate for smallpox and measles is among
the highest on record at any time, anywhere, surpassing even the medieval Black
Death epidemic. In the New World, the introduction of these diseases was the
result of greed, both personal and political. Imperialistic attempts to establish
colonies and extract wealth from newly discovered lands virtually wiped out the
indigenous population of many areas and led to their replacement by imported
slaves. These episodes are among the bleakest in the history of the world, and
were typical of the thinking and actions of the early modern era. Although in
some cases new diseases were accidentally introduced by well-intentioned missionaries, evidence suggests that smallpox and measles may have been intentionally introduced in some areas to deplete the native population and make it
easier to overcome resistance.

The history of smallpox is one of wholesale human suffering and the devastation of populations, as well as of the death or disfigurement of historically
important people. Smallpox also had a critical impact on the outcome of many
battles and military campaigns.

Recently both diseases have been brought under good control or eliminated
by the development of vaccines, the last known spontaneous case of smallpox
having occurred in Somalia in 1978. On the other hand, while naturally occurring human smallpox has been completely eliminated, laboratory infection of

humans has occurred subsequently, and fears of laboratory samples getting into the hands of bioterrorists has revived concern about the disease. Nevertheless, unless smallpox is purposely reintroduced, it is possible to write the obituary of a disease that was among the most devastating and disastrous plagues to have affected mankind, a disease whose epidemiology holds important lessons relevant to medicine today.

THE GLOBAL SPREAD OF SMALLPOX. Smallpox was clearly absent from many regions of the world until relatively recent times. Although its origin is unknown, good evidence suggests the presence of the disease in China as far back as 1122 BCE. The use of inoculation to prevent severe disease was described in Chinese medical texts as early as 590 BCE. Smallpox was also present in India for several thousand years, and inoculation or variolation was described in Sanskrit medical texts.

Smallpox probably did not occur in the Western world until agricultural development and the creation of cities crowded susceptible individuals together in populations large enough to sustain active infection by the virus. In smaller population groups, many diseases die out once all susceptible individuals have become infected and either died or developed immunity to it. The disease reappears only when a new population of susceptibles appears through birth or immigration.

No evidence of smallpox occurs in Egyptian medical papyri, and no depiction of people with the disfiguring skin lesions typical of the disease exists. However, Ruffer, a nineteenth-century Egyptologist, believed that the skin changes present in a single mummy, that of Ramses V, were the result of smallpox. If so, he is the only recorded case from that era, and recent electron microscopic examination of skin cells shed from the mummy failed to show evidence for viral inclusions. However, Egyptian authorities refused a biopsy, which would have provided a more definitive specimen.

Although numerous other epidemic diseases or "plagues" occurred in Egypt, Greece, Rome, and other countries of the ancient world, none resembling smallpox is identifiable in early medical works, including those attributed to Hippocrates, Aristotle, and Galen, and none of the afflictions described in the Old and New Testaments resembles smallpox.

The first accurate description of smallpox in the Western world, written in 930 CE, is attributed to Rhazes, physician to the hospital of Baghdad. However, evidence suggests that the disease appeared earlier, in Syria, perhaps as early as in 302 CE. Smallpox reached Mecca between 569 and 571, where it affected a party of Abyssinians, led by Prince Abraha, who were besieging the city aided by one elephant, an episode referred to as "the elephant war." Abraha died of the disease and retreating Abyssinians were "continually falling by the wayside, dying miserably by every waterhole."

Smallpox became permanently established in the Arabian peninsula among the followers of Mohammed; the caliph Yezid, who died in 683, was said to have been pitted from it and, in 753, the Caliph Abdul-abas Alaffah died of it. Along with Islam, smallpox spread across North Africa, into Spain, and across the Pyrenees. Epidemics of smallpox raged in Europe for the next thousand years, reintroduced periodically from the Middle East by returning Crusaders.

Remarkable changes in disease ecology resulted when Europeans discovered the New World. Several diseases can be identified in pre-Columbian artifacts of Aztec and Peruvian origin, including images on pottery jars that show spinal deformities characteristic of tuberculosis of the spine (Pott's disease) and distorted grimaces characteristic of facial nerve paralysis (Bell's palsy). All ancient populations suffered deaths from crop failures and famine, warfare, accidents, and exposure. Childbirth was always an important cause of death; burials have been found with the fetal bones still in place in a woman's pelvis. Skeletons and the mummified human remains of pre-Columbian Indians demonstrate the existence of osteoarthritis, spinal arthritis (ankylosing spondylitis), bone infections (osteomyelitis), iron deficiency, bone lesions of tuberculosis, and treponemal diseases such as yaws.

Evidence for trauma is abundant, but there is little to show that epidemic disease existed in the Americas before the time of Columbus.[E1] Many early explorers of the New World and the Pacific islands mention the freedom from disease in native populations not previously exposed to the benefits of European civilization, as well as the general good health and impressive physiques of many native peoples. The usual age of death was clearly quite young by our standards, but all evidence points to trauma, exposure, famine, and childbirth as the main causes of early demise, not epidemic disease.

Smallpox first appeared in the New World among the natives of Hispaniola in 1517 or 1518, probably when African slaves were brought to work the sugarcane plantations, newly established after the Spanish gave up on finding gold on the island. The local Arawak Indians had refused to go into bondage and many were killed outright; by 1530, disease and the atrocities of the Spanish forces had eliminated the original Indian population of that island, estimated to have been about two million when Columbus landed.

Smallpox was introduced into Mexico in May 1520, when Panfelo de Narvaez arrived from Cuba on an expedition intended to compete with that of Hernando Cortez, then in Mexico City. His party included one slave who was reported to be suffering from a mild attack of smallpox when he landed.

The disease spread among the native population of Mexico with an unbelievable mortality.

Smallpox defeated the Aztecs in Tenochtitlan, now Mexico City, when Cortez could not. When, after a long siege, the Spaniard's small force reconquered the city in August 1521, he found nearly half the inhabitants dead of disease. The canals of Mexico City, on Lake Texcoco, were choked with the bodies of smallpox victims. According to William Hickling Prescott's *History of the Conquest of Mexico*, "The floors of the dwellings were covered with the prostrate forms of the miserable inmates, some in the agonies of death, others festering in their corruption.... Death was everywhere." He quotes Cortez as saying, "A man could not set his foot down unless on the corpse of an Indian." In Mexico, it is estimated, based on existing taxation records, that the combined ravages of smallpox and measles killed more than 18 million of the original population of 25 million.

In South America, Francisco Pizarro and his men purposely tried to spread smallpox among the native Incas by distributing blankets used by people with the skin lesions of the disease, believing that the "miasma" that caused it stuck to the blankets. Although wrong about the true cause of smallpox, they were right about the contagiousness of the blankets: Smallpox virus has been isolated from patients' bedclothes. The same strategy was used in an attempt to spread smallpox among Native Americans during the French and Indian War. The British and their American colonists purposely gave gifts of contagion-laden blankets to Indians allied with the French.

Early Spanish explorers of the Amazon River had no problem with disease; an expedition in 1543 lost three men to Indian attack, seven to starvation, but only one to "fever." No disease was noted among people in the Amazon basin until sometime after 1650, when malaria appeared. This fact stands in striking contrast to reports that early European explorers of central African rivers virtually all died of disease. Naval vessels and trading ships learned to anchor well off the African shore to avoid massive outbreaks among their crews.

French records indicate that a great pestilence appeared among the Indians of the Massachusetts Bay area in 1616-1617, causing a marked decrease in the population of the area into which the Pilgrims settled three years later. In 1633, an outbreak of smallpox among the Indians further diminished the capacity for effective resistance to the original European settlers of New England.

Evidence of the appearance of disease in the New World is reviewed by Col. P. M. Ashburn in his book *The Ranks of Death: A Medical History of the Conquest of America*. He quotes Jesuit missionaries in Canada, who were distressed because, "Disease, war, and famine are the three scourges which God has been pleased to smite our Neophytes since they have commenced to adore him and submit to his laws. Hardly have they heard of the Doctrine that we preach to them, and commence to receive his divine seed, when a contagious disease [probably smallpox] spread through these nations, carrying off the healthiest of them.... Hardly had they left Tadousac, where they had listened with love to the Christian truths and presented their children for baptism, when death fell upon these little innocents, and disease upon a great part of their parents...."

A Spaniard, Antonio de Herrera, described events in the Mexican region of Tabasco: "There used to be a great number of Indians, but by reason of many diseases and pestilences, they diminished greatly, because being sick with measles, smallpox, catarrhs, bloody flux, and great fevers, they bathe in the rivers, without waiting for the diseases to subside, and so they die."

When smallpox was introduced among more isolated populations, such as those on remote islands, the mortality rate during the resulting epidemics was extremely high; for example, in 1707, in Iceland, 18,000 out of a total population of 50,000 died of smallpox. In 1853, smallpox was introduced into the Hawaiian Islands, in an epidemic that lasted eight months and killed over 80 percent of the population, despite efforts to control the disease by vaccination. Over 15,000 deaths occurred on Oahu, 10,000 recorded in Honolulu alone.

During the 1860s, Peruvian slavers raided the Polynesian population of Easter Island. One thousand men were taken; they were exposed to smallpox when they arrived in Peru, and nine hundred of them died. The Peruvians sent the remainder back to the island, and smallpox developed aboard ship on the way back, killing all but fifteen of the Polynesians. The returnees then spread the disease on the island. When the islands were originally "discovered" and named by the Dutch admiral Roggeven, on Easter Day in 1722, he estimated the population to be 4,000. There are no good estimates of the population in the interim, but after the Peruvian epidemic of smallpox, the population numbered 111; by 1954, it had increased to 764.

SMALLPOX IN EUROPE. Smallpox likely became much more virulent in Europe after the Spanish and their African slaves brought the disease to the New World and then reintroduced it back into Europe. In the early seventeenth century, a period of severe outbreaks began that lasted well into the eighteenth century. Outbreaks became particularly frequent and virulent in Great Britain and Western Europe during this period, making smallpox the most feared disease of the era. The usual mortality in these epidemics ranged between 20 and 40 percent, and it is estimated that, during this period, 80 percent of the entire population of Europe was struck by the disease. According to one report, one-sixth of the population of Ireland died of smallpox in a single year.

The attention of the British public was focused repeatedly on smallpox epidemics that affected members of the royal family. The 29-year-old Queen Elizabeth I nearly died of the disease in October 1562, and a law of succession was hurriedly drawn up during her illness to cover such a contingency. When she recovered, a special medal of thanksgiving was struck. In 1660, when Charles II returned to England to assume the throne at the time of the Restoration, smallpox accompanied the royal party on its trip from The Hague, causing the death of Charles' brother, the Duke of Gloucester, as well as of Princess Mary of Orange. Pepys' diary of 1661 records smallpox outbreaks in London, and the famous Doctor Sydenham described the epidemic of 1667-1668.

Smallpox altered the succession to the British throne. When William and Mary came to power in 1688, the succession was based on Queen Mary's claim to the throne as the daughter of the Roman Catholic King James II, deposed by the "Glorious Revolution." But Mary died of smallpox on September 28, 1694, without progeny. William was allowed to reign as William III to the end of his life, although technically he was not entitled to the British throne. (He was the son of Mary Stuart, daughter of Charles I and William, Prince of Orange.) When William III died in 1702, he was succeeded by Mary's younger sister, Queen Anne, but orderly succession to the British throne was fatally disrupted when Anne's son, now the Duke of Gloucester, died of smallpox acquired during a trip abroad. This precipitated a constitutional crisis that resulted in passage of a law forbidding travel of royalty abroad without the permission of Parliament; it also provided for the succession of the German-speaking Hanoverian, George I, on Anne's death. The Hanoverians eventually anglicized their name and became the Windsors, the present royal family of Britain.

In addition to its effect on the succession to the British throne, smallpox affected royal families in other countries as well. An Austrian emperor, a King of Spain, and a Queen of Sweden all died of the disease, as did King Louis XV of France and Tsar Peter II of Russia. The "Sun King," Louis XIV, had a nonfatal attack. In 1661, the disease affected the succession to the throne of China, when the emperor died of smallpox. K'ang Hsi was chosen to succeed his father over his two older brothers because he already had survived smallpox; he reigned for 61 years.

Smallpox also affected the course of the American Revolution. Inoculation (discussed in the next section) was introduced in England in the early 1700s to minimize outbreaks of the disease by inducing a mild form of it and hence life-long immunity. The practice became widespread in eighteenth-century Britain and routine in the British Army before the time of the American Revolution. In 1776, when Montgomery led the American attack on Quebec along with

Benedict Arnold, his second-in-command and hero of the ill-fated attack, an outbreak of smallpox developed. The defending British garrison had been inoculated, but the besieging Americans were badly affected; the disease and the hurried inoculation of the troops cut the effectiveness of Montgomery's force. Fewer than 5,000 out of a total attacking force of 8,000 men remained in fighting condition at the crucial point in the battle. Although military accounts rarely mention the disease, in 1951, a British authority who analyzed that battle concluded, "It can hardly be an exaggeration to say that smallpox was the main cause of the preservation of Canada for the British Empire."

INOCULATION AND VACCINATION. Attempts to avoid death or disfigurement from smallpox are among the earliest recorded forms of preventive medicine.[E2] It was obvious that epidemics varied in severity, and that infection acquired during mild outbreaks resulted in mild disease, but still protected against future attacks even of severe disease. As early as 590 BCE, in China, smallpox was intentionally induced by a process that came to be called inoculation, or variolation. ("Inoculation" referred to introducing a "seed" with the disease, the seed being analogous to the eye of a potato, hence the derivation from the word for eye. "Variola" was the technical name for smallpox, thus purposely introducing it was "variolation.") The procedure consisted of transferring infectious material from mild cases into susceptible individuals in the hope of causing a mild but protective form of the disease. Because freshly inoculated people, usually children, were infectious and could spread the disease while sick, they were usually kept in a primitive form of isolation hospital, away from other people until all lesions had healed. A mortality rate of one to two percent followed inoculation.

Chinese inoculators removed dried scales from the lesions of mild cases, ground them into a fine powder, and blew this into the nose of the recipient. The process was known as "pock-sowing." The custom may have been introduced into China from India, where it is recorded in a Sanskrit text, the *Sacteya*. This text is attributed to Dhanwantari, roughly comparable to Aesculapius of classical Greece, whose traditional writings were compiled in the second and third centuries CE. In Brahmin mythology, a special god, Kakurani, was associated with smallpox; in China there was a goddess of smallpox.

Inoculation was practiced by Greek and Turkish physicians before it appeared in Western Europe. By the early eighteenth century, physicians Giacomo Pylarini of Smyrna and Emanuel Timoni of Constantinople used inoculation; Timoni wrote to Dr. John Woodward of London about Pylarini's methods and, in 1714, Woodward reported these observations in the *Philosophical Transactions of the Royal Society*.

A notable British intellectual, Lady Mary Wortley Montague, is credited with playing a major role in fostering the adoption of inoculation in England in the early decades of the eighteenth century, although the anatomist Thomas Bartholin of Copenhagen is said to have practiced inoculation as early as 1675. Lady Montague was the wife of Edward Wortley Montague, Ambassador to "the Porte" of Turkey; they arrived in Constantinople in May 1717 and resided there just over a year. Lady Mary learned a little Turkish and, after being told of the practice of inoculation, she wrote letters home accurately detailing the procedure. In 1714, she had been disfigured by an attack of smallpox, which caused her to lose her "very fine eyelashes," and she had written, "My beauty is no more." Wanting to avoid similar disfigurement of her children, she had her three-year-old son inoculated while still in Turkey, and "took much pains to introduce the practice upon her return to England." In April 1721, her five-year-old daughter was inoculated in London when an epidemic of smallpox broke out.

Lady Mary was an influential member of British society, much admired by the poet Alexander Pope, and her efforts led to an interest in the concept of inoculation by the royal family. The cautious King George I ordered trials of inoculation on six condemned prisoners at Newgate, who volunteered on promise of reprieve if they survived. They were inoculated on August 9, 1721, and all had mild cases. On April 17, 1722, Claude Amyand, the king's surgeon, inoculated Princess Amelia, age 11, and Princess Caroline, age 9, and also inoculated his own children and various other members and servants of noble families. One of Aymand's footmen died of smallpox, but whether he acquired it by inoculation or naturally was not clear, since the epidemic was raging all over London at the time.

Inoculation became a routine procedure in many European countries; it began in 1749 in Holland, 1750 in Germany, and 1755 in France. Nevertheless, controversy arose because of concern over its safety. Because some severe cases of smallpox and deaths followed instances of inoculation, fear minimized its use in America, and there was strong ecclesiastic opposition to such interference with the "will of God."

During 1721, the epidemic of smallpox reached Boston; the famous minister Cotton Mather had read of Timoni's experiments with inoculation in Turkey and suggested a trial to Boston physicians. Dr. Zabdiel Boylston (1679-1766) introduced the practice and was almost lynched. He inoculated his own son and two slaves on June 26 and, despite the threats to his safety, inoculated 244 people before the epidemic subsided. Of nearly 12,000 people in the city at the time, one-half developed smallpox and 844 (seven percent) died. Of those inoculated by Boylston, only two per cent died. Boylston was invited to London by one of its leading physicians, Dr. Hans Sloane, to report on his experience.

The mortality during a severe epidemic in Charleston in 1738 was apparently decreased by mass inoculation, and Benjamin Franklin and George Washington, who set up Army hospitals for the purpose, supported the procedure. In France, Voltaire was an ardent supporter of inoculation, and he convinced Catherine the Great of Russia, who was inoculated along with her sons and members of her court.

The first edition of the *Encyclopedia Britannica*, published by a "Society of Gentlemen" in Edinburgh in 1771, included a long passage on smallpox that accurately described the disease in great detail, ending with the following paragraph: "The method of abating the rigour of this disease, and preventing the great mortality with which it is attended, by inoculation, is now so well known and so generally practiced, that a particular detail of it in this place is unnecessary."

It was into this milieu that Edward Jenner added his observations on the relationship between cowpox infection and smallpox immunity 25 years later. Cowpox, a local infection of cow udder, was a distinct entity communicable to the hands of farmers or their aides who milked the cows. It was common folk knowledge that a farmer or milkmaid who had contracted cowpox did not catch smallpox.

The beauty of milkmaids was legendary in England, probably because they did not become scarred by smallpox as most people did. However, protection by prior cowpox was disputed, because inoculation was practiced so commonly that it was uncertain which factor was responsible for the protection. The facts were never systematically collected for analysis. In 1765, a Mr. Fewster presented a paper to the Medical Society in London, stating that an individual who had cowpox was protected from smallpox. In 1769, another paper coming to the same conclusion was presented in Germany. In 1774, a farmer named Jetsy, in Dorset County, purposely inoculated his wife and sons with cowpox to protect them during an outbreak of smallpox. He and his servant girls had previously had cowpox, and he felt that they were immune. None developed smallpox, but Jetsy's efforts were not brought to light until 1802 or 1803, after Jenner's procedure was widely adopted and his fame established.

However, the credit for being the first to purposely induce cowpox to prevent smallpox is given to Edward Jenner. At the age of eight, Jenner was inoculated with smallpox; the procedure resulted in a severe, nearly fatal attack of the disease. In 1770, he became a friend and protégé of the great John Hunter and subsequently won a Fellowship in the Royal Society for his study of the "Natural History of the Cuckoo." He received backing from Hunter, although in commenting on Jenner's research, Hunter advised him "to speculate less and experiment more." After becoming a physician and developing a practice in Berkeley, Gloucestershire, Jenner continued to conduct studies in biology and became interested in diseases of animals. For the remainder of his life, he maintained that certain animal diseases are a source of human disease, and he experimented with swinepox, similar diseases of horses, and cowpox.

In 1778, Jenner observed a relationship between cowpox and smallpox: He noted that people who previously had cowpox did not develop smallpox when he tried to inoculate them. In 1796, Jenner decided to test this hypothesis; he took material from a sore on the hand of a milkmaid named Sarah Nelmes "who had been infected by her master's cow." On May 14, he inserted this matter into the arm of an eight-year-old farm boy, James Phipps, who had never been inoculated or had spontaneous smallpox. The boy developed a local sore and was "perceptibly indisposed" for only one day. Jenner later wrote, "In order to ascertain whether the boy, after feeling so slight an affection of the system from the Cow-pox virus, was secure from the contagion of smallpox, he was inoculated on the 1st of July following with variolous matter taken from a pustule..., but no disease followed.... Several months afterwards, he was again inoculated with variolous matter, but no sensible effect was produced on the constitution."

Jenner submitted a report of his experiments to the Royal Society, which rejected the paper. He then repeated his experiment, collecting a total of eighteen cases, and published his observations in his book, *An Inquiry into the Cause and Effects of Variola Vaccinae, A Disease, Discovered in Some of the Western Counties of England, Particularly Gloucestershire, and Known by the Name of Cowpox*.

Jenner invented the term *vaccination* from the bovine origin of the infective material (*vaccus* means cow in Latin), but it has since been adopted to describe all types of purposeful immunization. The practice of vaccination was only slowly adopted in place of inoculation, partly because of public relations setbacks that occurred when the procedure was done in smallpox hospitals; some vaccination recipients were exposed to real smallpox while awaiting vaccination and subsequently developed severe disease.

In 1802, the House of Commons voted Jenner 10,000 pounds as a reward for his research. He moved to London to supervise vaccination at the Royal Jennerian Society, founded with the consent of King George IV, and having the Queen as patron. However, Jenner remained a controversial figure, in part because of his practice of inventing involved theoretical explanations for instances of apparent failures of vaccination, and the gradual realization that, contrary to his claims, vaccination did not give lifelong protection against smallpox.

Vaccination was introduced into the United States by Dr. Benjamin Waterhouse, Professor of the Theory and Practice of Physic at Harvard, when he received some of the "lymph" used for the purpose from England. He began by vaccinating seven of his own thirteen children. The support of vaccination by President Jefferson assisted in its adoption; Jefferson had his entire household, including slaves, vaccinated, and predicted that vaccination for smallpox "would finally extirpate the disease from the earth."

In 1805, Napoleon had his entire army vaccinated. In 1807, government-ordered, compulsory vaccination of all children commenced in Bavaria and gradually spread to other countries during the nineteenth century. However, major epidemics continued to occur during the nineteenth century: The Prussian army vaccinated its troops, but the French did not. As a result, during the Franco-Prussian war of 1870-1871, a smallpox epidemic caused about 200,000 cases and 24,000 deaths among the French forces. During the siege of the city of Paris, 18,000 people died of smallpox. The disease caused no problems among the attacking Prussian forces and, on January 28, 1871, after a four-month siege, Paris capitulated.

Opponents of vaccination fought the spread of the procedure in many countries, with varying motives. Some objected on scientific grounds; other opposition was religious objection to the concept that a disease of beasts could affect man. Confusion persisted over the issue of whether immunity was lifelong until it became clearly established that periodic revaccination was necessary.

The "lymph" material used for vaccination was usually taken from the sore that developed on a previously unvaccinated person, without sterile technique (antiseptic and aseptic techniques were adopted in the 1870s and 1880s). Consequently, the occurrence of secondary infections at the site of injection was nearly universal, and when virulent *Streptococci* were around, fatal "blood poisoning" could result—one full-time vaccinator working in a public clinic after 1900 was known to the medical students as "Septic Sam." The transmission of syphilis occurred in some cases, especially when soldiers were vaccinated, as during the 1863 smallpox epidemic of the Civil War. Controversies concerning the method of introducing the vaccine, the number of sites to use, and similar details became resolved as convincing statistics were amassed, and gradually the disease became less and less of a menace.

During the Civil War, both armies set up about 400 military hospitals, most with separate facilities for smallpox patients, called "pest hospitals." The isolation of smallpox patients was practiced whenever possible; in November, 1863, President Lincoln developed a mild case when he returned to Washington after his famous speech dedicating the cemetery at Gettysburg, and he was isolated in the White House until his symptoms resolved. Lincoln is quoted as being upset at the quarantine, saying, "I finally have something I can give everybody."

The mild nature of Lincoln's illness is puzzling, since no record shows that he was vaccinated at any time. However, late in the nineteenth century, a variant of smallpox, *variola minor*, was identified; it had a much lower mortality rate (1 to 2 percent) than standard, *variola major* smallpox (20 to 30 percent or higher). It is possible that Lincoln's mild case was *variola minor*, although no evidence proves the existence of the variant at that time.

THE WORLDWIDE CAMPAIGN TO ELIMINATE SMALLPOX. Once it was discovered that no nonhuman reservoir of smallpox existed, a successful effort to eliminate the disease became possible. It was not practical to vaccinate the entire population of the world and, fortunately, this was not necessary thanks to a United Nations-led campaign to eliminate smallpox that began with the identification and reporting of all outbreaks of the disease in the world. The practical and political difficulties in achieving this objective were enormous in themselves, and bounties were offered to ensure the reporting of new cases. Once outbreaks were identified, a medical team was dispatched to vaccinate all susceptibles until smallpox was eliminated from that area.

When the campaign began in 1967, smallpox was still endemic in 33 countries, and an estimated 10 to 15 million cases of the disease occurred each year. The last case in Asia—and the last case of lethal *variola major*—occurred in Bangladesh, in October 1975. The last naturally occurring case of any type of smallpox developed on October 26, 1977, in Somalia, in a man named Ali Maow Maalin.

The program, centered in Geneva under the direction of Dr. Donald Henderson, required several innovations. Freeze-dried vaccine was substituted for liquid vaccine, since the liquid form required refrigeration. The scratch technique was replaced by the use of a jet gun to deliver the vaccine, speeding up the process and decreasing the need for sterile injection equipment. The main innovation was "surveillance containment," the erection of a barrier of vaccinated individuals around an outbreak of the disease until the epidemic burned out for lack of susceptible people. The cost of the program was less than $100 million, 25 percent of which came from the United States, with the Soviet Union supplying the freeze-dried vaccine. International cooperation with the vaccination campaign finally succeeded in eliminating all known traces of this once fearsome plague after a campaign that lasted just 10 years, 9 months, and 26 days.

W ARTIME EXPERIENCE WITH SMALLPOX. The communicability and lethality of smallpox make it a potential biowarfare weapon. With most of the U.S. population never having been vaccinated, and the rest vaccinated too long ago to be fully immune, the susceptibility of the U.S. population may resemble that of the sixteenth-century Mexicans at the time of the Conquistadors.

During the Civil War, both sides were accused of using smallpox as an agent of biowarfare, primarily among prisoners of war.[E3] Neither side was guilty of such a practice, but accusations of the use of "spurious" or poisonous vaccine arose during a smallpox pandemic in 1863 and 1864. All soldiers were supposed to be vaccinated, either before joining the army or immediately after induction. The vaccination technique at that time was neither sterile nor painless; deep scratches were made in the skin, using whatever sharp knife or razor was available, and the vaccination material was inserted—along with any infectious bacteria that were present. Once "lymph" was obtained from vaccinated individuals, soldiers often vaccinated each other. Fear of the painful technique and the possibility of other infections that followed vaccination resulted in whole regiments refusing to be vaccinated. Thus large numbers of soldiers remained susceptible to the disease. When unvaccinated soldiers became prisoners of war, and soldiers incubating the disease were captured and added to the prison camp the disease could spread widely. In many cases of smallpox outbreak, guards vaccinated the entire prison camp (and themselves), but considering the filthy conditions in prison camps and the severe malnutrition of the prisoners, bad infections were frequent. The resulting illnesses and deaths led to accusations that prison authorities were purposely using poisonous ("spurious") vaccines, and these accusations were repeated for decades after the war in various partisan publications. However, it is clear that the same vaccine material was used on the guards as on the prisoners, and that no purposeful introduction of disease occurred.

In her memoirs, Phoebe Pember, a matron at the most prominent Confederate hospital, the Chimborazo Hospital near Richmond, gave an excellent portrayal of the complications that could develop after vaccination: "They [vaccinated soldiers] were dreadfully afflicted objects, many of them with sores so deep and thick upon arms and legs that amputation had to be resorted to save life. As fast as the eruption would be healed in one spot, it would break out in another, for the blood seemed entirely poisoned."[1] Mrs. Pember also noted that the poor nutritional status of some of the Confederate soldiers seemed to be a predisposing factor. Other records reveal that Federal prisoners brought to the Chimborazo hospital were vaccinated with the same material that had been used on the Confederate soldiers. They developed similar complications.

A disparity is noted in the recorded incidence of smallpox in white and black Union troops. During the most severe epidemic period (July 1, 1863, to June 30, 1864, when data for black troops begins), the incidence among white troops was 7.4 cases per 1,000. Among black troops, then in their first year of active service, it was much higher, 61.1 per 1,000. The much higher incidence among the black soldiers indicates that they had not been vaccinated as slaves, and the policy of vaccinating newly enlisted troops was not carried out on them. This conclusion is supported by an 1867 article written by a prominent physician in Mobile, Alabama, who recorded that "A large proportion of them [former slaves] had never been vaccinated, scarcely any vaccinated, and they therefore afforded an unprecedented amount of material for the disease. Fully nine out of ten of the deaths from smallpox have been among the Freedmen."[2]

BIOTERRORISM AND SMALLPOX.   The specter of smallpox as an agent of bioterrorism has reawakened interest in smallpox vaccination. As a weapon, smallpox is effective because it is spread from person to person, and it generates widespread fear. However, the disease spreads slowly and, once an attack is discovered, the rapid vaccination of large numbers of people in affected regions could contain it. Large amounts of vaccine are being prepared to prevent mass casualties, but the psychological effect—the main objective of such attacks—would be great.

Despite the fact that smallpox vaccination is quite safe (especially when compared to the danger of the disease), it can be associated with a number of adverse effects. These include *eczema vaccinatum*, a generalized skin infection and, more serious, encephalopathy, which may cause permanent brain damage or death.

Contraindications to receiving the vaccine include preexisting eczema, dermatitis, and other significant skin conditions; any type of severe immunodeficiency or immunosuppression (including patients receiving radiation, high-dose corticosteroids, such as cortisone or prednisone, or cancer chemotherapy); pregnancy; breastfeeding; age less than one year; allergy to the vaccine's components (which can include a variety of antibiotics); and any moderate or severe acute illness at the time of vaccination. Because the vaccinia virus used in smallpox vaccines can spread to others from the site of vaccination, these contraindications apply not only to vaccine recipients, but also to their household and other close contacts. The vaccination site should be considered infectious to others until complete healing occurs.

Because of the small, but nevertheless possible risks associated with smallpox vaccination, present recommendations state that only "first responders"—health care workers likely to come into contact with any cases induced by terrorist actions be vaccinated. The public reaction that many officials fear should an outbreak be confirmed can be imagined based on public reaction to a 1947 outbreak in New York City. Two cases of smallpox appeared, apparently contracted during a trip to Mexico. Although virtually everyone had been vaccinated in childhood, because the immunity from vaccination wanes after ten years, health authorities felt that everyone who had not been vaccinated in the past ten years should receive revaccination. Clinics were set up across the city, and six million people were vaccinated in a few days. Lines outside the clinics wound for blocks, but moved relatively rapidly. All available medical personnel were put to work giving vaccine; I participated as a medical student. A sense of concern led to mass cooperation with the vaccination program, but no reaction that could be called panic occurred.

ADDITIONAL READING

Ashburn PM. *The Ranks of Death, a Medical History of the Conquest of America.* New York: Coward-McCann, 1947.

Chapin CV. Variation in type of infectious disease as shown by the history of smallpox in the United States 1895-1912. *J Infect Dis* 1913;13:171.

Crosby AW. *Ecological Imperialism, The Biological Expansion of Europe.* Cambridge UK: Cambridge Univ Press 1986.

Díaz del Castillo B. *The Discovery and Conquest of Mexico, 1517-1521.* [Edited from the only exact copy of the original ms (and published in Mexico by Genaro Garcia.) Translated with an introduction and notes by A. P. Maudslay.] London: G. Routledge & Sons, Ltd, 1928.

Dubois RJ, ed. *Bacterial and Mycotic Infections of Man.* Philadelphia: JB Lippincott Co, 1948.

Duffy J. *Epidemics in Colonial America.* Port Washington, NY: Kennikat Press, 1972, 1953.

Editorial. The Soviet smallpox accident *The New York Times,* June 18, 2002.

Fenn EA. *Pox Americana: The Great Smallpox Epidemic of 1775-82.* New York: Hill and Wang, 2001.

Fenner F. Human monkeypox, a newly discovered human virus disease. In: Morse SS. *Emerging Viruses.* New York: Oxford Univ Press, 1993.

Halloran M, Elizabeth IM, et al. Containing bioterrorist smallpox. *Science* 2002;298:1428

Henderson DA. Smallpox as a biological weapon; medical and public health management. *JAMA* 1999;281:2127.

Hopkins DR. *Princes and Peasants: Smallpox in History.* Chicago: Univ of Chicago Press, 1983.

Jenner E. *An Inquiry into the Cause and Effects of Variolae Vaccinae, a Disease Discovered in Some of the Western Counties of England, Particularly Gloucestershire, and Known by the Name of The Cowpox.* London: Samson Low, 1798.

Karlen A. Man and Microbes. New York: G.P. Putnam's Sons, 1995.

Koopman J. Controlling smallpox. Science 2002;298:1342.

Marks G, Beatty WK. Epidemics. New York: Scribner, 1976.

McNeill WH. Plagues and peoples. Garden City, NY: Anchor Press, 1976.

Rathbone J. Lady Mary Wortley Montague's contribution to the eradication of smallpox. Lancet 1996;347:1566.

Stetten D, Jr. Victory over variola. Am Soc Microbiol News 1978;44:639.

[E1]Many bones found with embedded arrowheads and speartips, and skull wounds clearly made by axes, reveal the importance of warfare as a cause of death in ancient times. The role of the medical profession in treating combat wounds is the basis for the term "physician" in several languages. For example, the ancient Chinese pictograph for physician shows a figure removing an arrow from another figure. The Egyptian hieroglyph for physician is a seated figure, an arrow, and a jar of medicine. The ancient Greek word for physician, iatros, originally meant "arrow remover."

[E2]The color red was thought to offer therapeutic benefit to victims of smallpox, a "treatment" that can be dated to tenth-century Japan, where red cloths were hung in smallpox sickrooms. As recently as 1902, in the Boston Smallpox Hospital, patients were given a red-light treatment, issued red pajamas, made to drink red juices, and sometimes isolated in rooms painted red and having red curtains.

[E3]The intention to spread smallpox among enemy soldiers was facetiously suggested on at least one occasion during the Civil War. When soldiers rejoined the famous 20th Maine after a furlough early in May, 1863, they were thought to have been exposed to smallpox. The regimental surgeon feared an outbreak would develop, affect the entire regiment, and spread throughout the Army of the Potomac. He suggested quarantining the regiment until it was certain that no smallpox outbreak would appear. The regiment was moved to the rear, just before the Battle of Chancellorsville. Lt. Col. Joshua Chamberlain, who had just been given command of the regiment, was upset at being taken out of the battle. He is supposed to have told his brigade commander, "At least we can give the rebels smallpox."

[1]Phoebe P: A Southern Woman's Story: Life in Confederate Richmond. New York: G.W. Carleton, 1879.

[2]Nott JC: Smallpox epidemic in Mobile during the winter of 1865-6. Nashville Med Surg J. N.S. 1867;2:372-380.

CHAPTER 6

CHOLERA AND THE
WORLDWIDE PLAGUES OF
THE NINETEENTH CENTURY

C HOLERA IS AN INFECTION OF THE GASTROINTESTINAL
tract that can cause more deaths, more quickly, than any other epidemic
disease. Historically, cholera is thought to have ravaged the Indian subcontinent
and the Far East in ancient times and the Middle Ages, but it did not spread out
of that area to cause pandemics until 1817. It is an exclusively human disease,
and it is spread along lines of travel by caravan, ship, or airplane, primarily
through contaminated water or food supplies.

Some authorities consider cholera the most likely cause of the disastrous
plague said to have affected the Assyrian army of Sennacharib during the siege
of Jerusalem, about 700 BCE. According to the Bible, Sennacharib's forces were
struck overnight with an enormous mortality that forced them to abandon the
siege and return to Nineveh, an episode beautifully described by Lord Byron:

The Assyrian came down like the wolf on the fold,
   And his cohorts were gleaming in purple and gold;
   And the sheen of their spears was like stars on the sea,
   When the blue wave rolls nightly on deep Galilee.
   Like the leaves of the forest when Summer is green,
   That host with their banners at sunset were seen:
   Like the leaves of the forest when Autumn hath blown,
   That host on the morrow lay withered and strown...

The Assyrians did abruptly abandon the siege. But in their own records at
Nineveh they describe how Hezekiah, the King of Judah, bought them off with
gold and other gifts, and a later passage in the Bible describes gifts given by King
Hezekiah to Sennacharib in almost the same terms. Thus it is questionable

whether cholera, or any other epidemic disease, caused a great overnight mortality among the Assyrians and resulted in the lifting of the siege. On the other hand, the theory does seem plausible, because cholera can be as devastating and deadly as that Biblical episode suggests, killing thousands in a few days if not overnight.

Cholera typically spreads when large numbers of people share the same water supply for drinking or cooking, bathing or waste disposal. The Ganges and Brahmaputra Rivers, as well as the Yangtze River, have caused disasterous outbreaks of cholera, especially during religious pilgrimages when great crowds of people use inadequate sanitary facilities. Devastating epidemics of cholera repeatedly affected pilgrims during the Haj at Mecca and have affected similar religious pilgrimages in India.

The causative agent of cholera, the bacterium *Vibrio cholera*, is killed by the acidity of gastric juices. If a large quantity of the organism is ingested, however, a sufficient number can survive the gastric acid to enter the small intestine and multiply, causing devastating enteritis. In tropical areas, where the winter temperatures do not get below 50°F, the disease can persist and cause repeated flareups. Temperatures below 50°F kill the organism, so that cholera is a summertime disease in more temperate areas, where it is eliminated by cold weather during the rest of the year and has to be reintroduced.

In reading about cholera, it is important to note the inconsistent usage of the term. Severe diarrhea or dysentery of any cause has been called *cholera* or, when extremely severe, *cholera morbus*. The term has also been used for nonintestinal diseases. To distinguish it from other causes of dysentery, throughout most of the nineteenth century the term *Asiatic cholera* was used and that disease is the subject of this chapter. True, or Asiatic, cholera characteristically causes extremely severe diarrhea with profuse watery stools that often contain white, rice-like particles (rice water stools). The resulting dehydration causes patients to collapse swiftly from falling blood pressure; the skin becomes shriveled, the pulse weak and thready, and the patient can become comatose within hours of the onset of the intense diarrhea, particularly when it is often accompanied by vomiting that aggravates the fluid loss. Circulatory collapse and kidney failure ensue, and death results.

Fluid replacement can reverse the process and save the patient. Fluids are best given by injection directly into the blood stream, but this is impractical when huge numbers of cases occur in areas without adequate medical facilities. Late in the twentieth century, rapidly absorbable, orally administered fluids were devised, and these cut the cholera mortality rate. Vaccines against cholera are unsatisfactory, as they give inadequate levels of immunity and require multiple injections. Indeed, the fact that cholera can be contracted more than once indicates that protective immunity does not develop and therefore that vaccines would not be successful.

SPREAD OF CHOLERA: THE GREAT PANDEMICS OF THE NINETEENTH CENTURY. Some of the most massive epidemics of cholera have resulted from the fecal contamination of rivers that are used as a water supply or for ritual bathing and drinking such as the Ganges in India. Contaminated urban water supplies, such as wells and reservoirs, have also caused huge outbreaks. Cholera existed in epidemic form in India long before the West knew about the disease, although there is detailed evidence for only one major epidemic in India before 1820. However, in Bengal, there is a long tradition of worshipping a Cholera Goddess, and a temple to her was still present in Calcutta in the late nineteenth century. Other records suggest local epidemics of cholera in different parts of India in the late eighteenth century. While these episodes did not become pandemics in the fashion of those seen in the nineteenth century, an epidemic did reach Burma and probably Malaya in the 1770s. During this period, cholera did not spread widely, probably because transportation was limited and travelers died or recovered before reaching their destination. Healthy carriers of the vibrio that causes cholera can spread the disease, but apparently they did not contaminate water supplies to any great extent.

The first great pandemic of cholera affecting many countries outside of the Indian subcontinent started in Jessore in August 1817. This first cholera pandemic was a new phenomenon, killing in hours, spreading quickly over Bengal within three months, and devastating the Grand Army of Lord General Francis Rawdon-Hastings. The outbreak began a pattern of spread from India by sea, first reaching into nearby Ceylon (Sri Lanka) and Burma, then into the East Indies, where it killed 100,000 people in Java alone. In 1820, the epidemic reached the Philippines and also arrived in Chinese ports, especially the treaty ports, such as Canton, with a great deal of Western commerce. Commerce also carried it up the Yangtze Valley and, by 1822–1824, it was reported inland in both Central and North China, including Beijing.

In 1820, when British soldiers were sent from India to the Persian Gulf to help the Sultan of Oman subdue rebellion, cholera came with them. A second group of soldiers carried cholera from Bombay inland to Shiraz in Persia, and to Basra (now in Iraq). In Basra, in 1821, it killed 15,000 to 18,000 people in three weeks. It proceeded with shipping from Basra up the Tigris-Euphrates valley to Baghdad, where Turks were fighting Persians. The Persian army defeated the Turks, but was itself defeated by cholera. It retreated in terror, carrying cholera into Persia and then north to the Caspian Sea area. The army was soon reduced to 10,000 men, and subsequently 5,000 more died of cholera. Persian traders carried it to ports along the Persian Gulf, from which the slave trade took it to the East African coast.

Cholera spread into Russia, where an attempt to stop it by quarantine was ineffective, because the disease is not spread by individual person-to-person contact as much as by water supplies contaminated by waste disposal. The disease spread along the caravan routes around the eastern Mediterranean and, to the consternation of the Egyptian government, to coastal Egypt, including Cairo, where the Egyptians also attempted quarantine. Finally, the severe winter of 1823–1824 stopped the spread of the disease.

The second great pandemic of cholera occurred in 1826, probably again starting from its primary habitat in Bengal. Once more it reached the Caspian Sea and was spread from there by shipping over much of the world. It is possible that the 1817 epidemic never left the Astrakhan coasts of the Caspian Sea, and that the new pandemic arose from this persisting focus. If so, a continuous pandemic of cholera existed from 1817 to 1837, with only a lull during the middle years of that period. Cholera may also have come back to Western Asia from China overland, via the Silk Route. By 1831, the disease appeared in Northern Europe, affecting the Baltic port of Riga, then spreading inland to Warsaw, where it took a terrible toll among the troops on both sides of the fighting between the Poles and the Russians.

This pandemic also caused a great mortality among the pilgrims on the Haj, whose solitary ritualistic water source became contaminated. It killed about half these pilgrims, including the governors of both Mecca and Medina. From Arabia, it spread to Alexandria and Istanbul, along the entire North African coast and into the Balkans, and reached Hungary. It then spread by ships along the Danube. In the north, cholera spread to Cracow and into Russia proper, as far as Archangel. It also swept into Sweden and Germany and, in 1830, reached France from Britain by ship; seaports were the main cities affected. In Western Europe, cholera primarily affected the poor, whose water supplies were most prone to contamination. In France, the poor suspected that the bourgeoisie and the authorities were trying to poison them. There is evidence to suggest that cholera played a role in the unrest that led to uprisings in France in 1830 and 1832, and to small riots in Berlin, Hamburg, and St. Petersburg.

Cholera was brought to North America in 1831. It traveled across the Atlantic and arrived in Quebec on the ships on which many Irish immigrants had already died and been buried at sea. The ships were quarantined on an island in the St. Lawrence River about 30 miles downstream from Quebec, but quarantine broke down and people escaped from the island. The first case of cholera appeared in Quebec City on 8 June 1832, and then the disease appeared upstream in Montreal.

Cholera reached the City of New York by ship from Canada rather than directly from Europe. It came across the St. Lawrence River into New York State, and commerce on the newly improved Erie Canal system provided an efficient means of transport for both goods and disease, which spread throughout New York despite new quarantine laws. The first known case in New York City occurred in a poor Irish immigrant on June 26, 1832; it appeared in Philadelphia on July 5. By August, it had spread from Maine to Wisconsin by means of the Erie Canal system and the Great Lakes. Chicago was badly affected. From Chicago, it spread down the Mississippi River system, affecting St. Louis and Vicksburg. It struck the town of Cairo, the southernmost point in Illinois at the junction of the Ohio River and the Mississippi, and river traffic took it up the Ohio to Pittsburgh. The advent of winter weather cut the epidemic short, but the disease reappeared in 1833 and 1834.

Quarantine is always a controversial measure. Its opponents usually deny the contagious nature of the disease in question and fight its imposition, because in many cases, the disease is not one that actually spreads directly from person-to-person as was true of the original disease that led to the invention of quarantine, bubonic plague. Since cholera rarely spreads directly from person-to-person this lack of evidence for direct person-to-person spread weakened the case for quarantine, and its important economic and social effects fueled the fight against it.

Pronouncing contagion as the reason a disease spread was seen as an antisocial theory that could wreak havoc on many fundamental functions of society. Opponents of quarantine claimed that its widespread adoption as a way to prevent epidemic disease could cause cities to become deserted and commerce to cease. Such economic and social considerations always competed with public health issues, especially before the etiologic agents of disease were identified and the need for effective public health measures accepted. In some countries, such as France, the need for quarantine was dismissed by authorities who believed their people were too clean to become infected. They were wrong, but quarantine was ineffective in controlling cholera. The cholera organisms can be carried on hands or soiled clothing and introduced into food by flies or nightsoil, although the most important transmitting vehicle is contaminated drinking water. Several other huge pandemics of cholera, or flare-ups during a continuing pandemic, occurred throughout the nineteenth century as a result of contamination of water or food supplies.

The disease was particularly severe during the years 1854–1863. Filippo Pacini (1812–1883), a physician and professor at the University of Florence who was particularly skilled in microscopy, observed the comma-shaped bacillus that causes cholera. He called it a *vibrio*. However, his work was ignored until it was rediscovered by Robert Koch (1843–1910) in 1883.

Many other organisms cause dysentery, and severe epidemics of bacterial dysentery that were not cholera have occurred throughout the centuries. Military forces have been most severely affected by such outbreaks, although most epidemics had a much lower mortality rate that did cholera. True cholera affected military activities most severely during the Crimean War (1854–1856), in which British and French forces, with some contribution of Piedmontese Italian troops, joined those of Turkey in opposing Russia.

The British and French first landed at Varna, in Bulgaria in 1854, with the objective of keeping the Russians away from the Bosporus and the Dardanelles. When the Russians backed off and evacuated Bulgaria, the Allies moved their forces to the Crimea, intending to destroy the Russian naval base at Sevastopol. Cholera appeared soon after the troops landed at Varna. The 1852 epidemic of cholera in India had spread to the Middle East by 1853 and moved into Europe. In 1853, cholera was already in France before the troops left for Turkey and Bulgaria, and they probably brought it with them. In July and August 1854, there were 55,000 French troops in Bulgaria; during the entire month of July, 8,230 cases of cholera appeared among them, and 5,030 men died. The next month, 3,043 cases occurred, with an astounding 3,015 deaths. One night, a French commander marched his men out of their camp in an attempt to avoid the outbreak, but 600 more men died between midnight and morning on July 28, 1854.

It has been suggested that one of the reasons the British and French moved their troops from Bulgaria to the Crimea was an attempt to elude cholera, but they carried the disease with them to the Crimea where it affected the troops of all armies involved in the conflict there. It killed Lord Raglan, the commander of the British armies, and spread to the Russian army, killing thousands of their troops as well.

Fortunately, no cholera was present in the United States during the American Civil War. But in 1865, after the Civil War ended, cholera again swept over Europe and reached New York, by then a city of half a million people. There was neither municipal waste disposal nor a clean water supply, but the Board of Health adopted the measures suggested earlier by John Snow in London as described in the next section. They cleaned and disinfected the houses of cholera victims and fear of the disease generated general public cooperation. Street cleanliness was not part of the program and quarantine was not enforced, but the city was cleaner than it had been, and New York had little cholera during that outbreak. Other cities relied on street cleaning instead of Snow's concentration on the water supply, but no other American city gave similar powers to health authorities; all suffered more from cholera than New York during this outbreak, which lasted until 1869.

The opening of the Suez Canal on November 17, 1869 greatly enhanced the opportunity for cholera to spread by ship from its home base on the Indian sub-continent to the Mediterranean and Europe. Cairo and Alexandria in Egypt were affected much more frequently than before. Cholera was epidemic in that area in 1883, and there was great fear of an outbreak in Germany and elsewhere. Robert Koch was already famous for his discovery of the tubercle bacillus and for promulgating the "four postulates" necessary to establish an organism as the eti-ologic agent of a disease, and the German government asked him to head a group of scientists being sent to Egypt to find the etiologic agent of cholera. In August 1883, the group examined and cultured material from the intestines of fatal cholera cases in Alexandria. Koch found a comma-shaped organism pre-sent in these cases, but was unable to obtain it in pure culture or to reproduce the disease by giving it to experimental animals, key components of his own pos-tulates.

The epidemic subsided in Egypt but persisted in India. Koch obtained per-mission for his team to move to Calcutta where, on January 7, 1884, he announced that he had successfully isolated the bacillus in pure culture. He described many characteristics of the organism, specifying that it was always found in patients with cholera (especially in the characteristic "rice water stools"), but was not found in patients with other types of diarrhea. He could not fulfill his fourth and most important postulate, the reproduction of the disease experimentally in other animals and the subsequent recovery of the organism from them. He concluded correctly that other species are not susceptible to cholera. His theory of the cause of cholera was accepted, and Koch became a national hero in Germany and hailed around the world. However, it was for his discovery of the etiologic organism of tuberculosis that he was awarded the fifth Nobel Prize for Medicine and Physiology, in 1905.

The realization that humans are the only species affected by the cholera vib-rio has important public health implications. No reservoir of infection in animals can cause the disease to return to affect humans—as occurs, for example, with bubonic plague. The spread of cholera occurs entirely by human action, and public health measures instituted largely because of the cholera epidemics of the nineteenth century, especially providing clean, uninfected water and food sup-plies, can contain the disease. However, cholera still exists in some areas of the world, and the organism is readily available to people intent on spreading it pur-posely.

In 1892, after Koch firmly identified the causative organism, a severe out-break of cholera struck the port city of Hamburg in northern Germany. At that time, Hamburg was crowded with nearly 17,000 immigrants from Eastern Europe trying to reach America. The Prussian government sent Robert Koch to the area; he confirmed the presence of the cholera vibrio and organized public health measures including a poster campaign to encourage the boiling of drinking water; a ban on raw fruit from coming into the city; and the closing of public baths, schools, dance halls, and all public gatherings. Business forces, as expected, opposed his measures and avoided the quarantine; they arranged for an ocean liner to be allowed to sail, but they could not avoid cholera. When it appeared on the ship, the malady was called diarrhea and vomiting, and when patients died, the official diagnosis was diabetic coma.

How an Obstetrician Was Midwife to the Birth of Epidemiology. Although Great Britain was not affected by the first pandemics of cholera (1817–1823), the next two (1826–1837 and 1846–1863) reached the British Isles. The first great epidemiological study of disease was a study of the cholera outbreaks in London, conducted by a surgeon who was struck by the large numbers of deaths in Soho, the area of London where he lived. In 1831, during the first attack of the disease, John Snow (1813–1858) published a report suggesting that cholera was being spread by contaminated water. The epidemic returned to London in 1854, after killing over 10,000 people in Newcastle and Gateshead. On the night of August 31, "the most terrible outbreak of cholera that ever occurred in the kingdom" affected the Soho area. In three days, 127 people living around Broad Street died. The residents of the area fled from their homes, leaving shops shuttered, houses locked, and streets deserted. It was like a return of bubonic plague. By September 10,500 residents of the area had died, and in some parts of the parish the death rate was over 12 percent, more than double the rate for the rest of London.

Snow was aware that severe watery diarrhea was an early manifestation of cholera, and he thought that the outbreak must be due to "miasmas" originating in water contaminated by sewage. People in the area were aware of undrained cesspits beneath old houses, and Snow guessed that these pits were draining into wells and contaminating the water in that area. While investigating the cases that had occurred, he noted that the cholera cases were clustered around a single pump on Broad Street, in St. James's Parish. He interviewed families of the victims and found that nearly all the deaths had taken place within a short distance of the pump. He also found that there had only been ten deaths in houses much nearer another pump; of those, five of the victims had always drunk the water from the Broad Street pump, and three were schoolchildren who had probably drunk from the pump on their way to school.

Snow took a sample of water from the pump. Checking it microscopically, he thought he observed the white "rice water" particles seen in the stools of cholera victims. Convinced that he had found the source of the disease, he went to the Board of Guardians of St. James's Parish, who, though reluctant to believe him, did agree to remove the handle from the Broad Street pump as an experiment. Once the handle was removed new cases of cholera stopped appearing.

Snow had to explain some puzzling features of the epidemiology of the cholera outbreak in Soho. Of the 530 inmates in the Poland Street workhouse, located around the corner from the pump, only five of them had developed cholera. Snow found that no one from the workhouse drank the pump water, because the building had its own well. The Broad Street Brewery was near the pump, and none of the seventy workers in it died of cholera. Snow found that the men were given a free allowance of beer every day and thus never drank any water at all. Snow also investigated the deaths from cholera of a widow and her niece who lived in another area of London. Neither of these women had been near Soho for a long time; when Snow interviewed the widow's son, he discovered that she had once lived in Broad Street and liked the taste of the well-water there so much that she had sent a servant to Soho every day to bring back a large bottle of it for her. The last bottle of water—from which her niece had also drunk—had been fetched on August 31, the day the Soho epidemic started.

Many authorities, and particularly the Board of Health, still refused to believe that Snow had identified the cause of the outbreak of cholera in Soho. A clergyman came to his defense. The Reverend Henry Whitehead, vicar of St. Luke's Church, Berwick Street, believed that the disease was caused by divine wrath and, intending to prove his point, he investigated the epidemic himself. However, his findings merely confirmed Snow's, and the Vicar became convinced Snow was right. Whitehead even helped Snow to isolate the case that may have started the epidemic: Just before cholera broke out in Soho, a child living at number 40 Broad Street had been taken ill with cholera symptoms, and its soiled "nappies" had been steeped in water that was subsequently tipped into a leaking cesspool situated only three feet from the Broad Street well.[E1]

Although Snow was more famous at the time as an obstetrician, his contributions to epidemiology were more important. Snow's observations on cholera became the basis of public health efforts to improve the quality of urban water supplies. Fear of cholera and knowledge of its mode of spread resulted in urban Boards of Health being created, beginning in the 1850s and 1860s. These focused on sanitation and the prevention of contamination of water supplies. Where successful, their efforts led to the elimination of cholera.

Attempts at cleanups were hampered by the belief that poisonous miasmas were the cause of contagious diseases. It was believed that these miasmas arose in filth rotting in the streets and houses, and that stirring up old dirt could release the toxic vapors into the air and be more harmful than the actual dirt itself. Nevertheless, the concept of miasmas, and the belief that immorality, sinfulness, and poverty were the underlying causes of disease, gradually shifted, and public health measures replaced moral lectures and sermons as the means of prevention. Concerns about cholera, and the work of John Snow, were prime movers in the development of the public health movement.

CAN CHOLERA BE SPREAD BY BIOTERRORISTS? The purposeful contamination of water supplies is one of the possible means of attack by bioterrorists. Cholera and the epidemics it has produced show how contaminated water supplies can cause severe, widespread disease with high mortality. The measures that have been implemented in most urban areas to prevent contamination by disinfecting and purifying water supplies are probably sufficient to prevent such attacks being successful, unless the contaminants are introduced distal to the water purification plants. Authorities have become vigilant to minimize the likelihood of successful attack of this type.

During what is considered the seventh cholera pandemic (which is still in existence), a new cholera strain, called the El Tor strain, was identified. Severe outbreaks of El Tor occurred in Africa in 1971; air travel may have increased the speed with which the infection spread, and subsequently several hundreds of cases of the El Tor variety of cholera appeared in Europe.

The human actions that have led to the spread of epidemic cholera have been inadvertent, mostly based in commercial travel by caravans, ships, and, more recently, airplanes. Tourism may now be a major factor in the spread. Between 2000 and 2002, over forty outbreaks of cholera occurred around the world, mostly in Africa but also in Afghanistan, Russia, and Peru. Cholera can be prevented, and treatment is also effective, but large numbers of cases can easily overwhelm health authorities. We can hope that cholera will never be purposely spread, and that clean water becomes universal enough to eliminate this scourge in the forseeable future.

ADDITIONAL READING

Blake PA. Epidemiology of cholera in the Americas. *Gastroenterol Clin North Am* 1993;22:639.

Bray RS. *Armies of Pestilence, The Impact of Disease on History.* New York: Barnes and Noble, 2000.

Brody H, Vinten-Johansen P, et al. John Snow revisited: getting a handle on the Broad Street pump. *Pharos Alpha Omega Alpha Honor Med Soc* 1999;62:2.

Delaporte F. *Disease and Civilization: The Cholera in Paris 1832.* [Transl. A. Goldhammer.] Cambridge, MA: MIT Press, 1986.

Dubois RJ, ed. *Bacterial and Mycotic Infections of Man.* Philadelphia: JB Lippincott Co, 1948.

Gangarosa EJ, Barker WH. Cholera. Implications for the United States. *JAMA* 1974;227:170

Lacey SW. Cholera: calamitous past, ominous future. *Clin Infect Dis* 1995;20:1409.

Marks G, Beatty WK. *Epidemics.* New York: Scribner, 1976.

McCarthy SA, Khambaty FM. International dissemination of epidemic Vibrio cholerae by cargo ship ballast and other nonpotable waters. *Applied Environmental Microbiology* 1994;60:2597.

McCullum C. Disease and dirt. The social dimensions of influenza, cholera and syphilis. *The Pharos* 1992;55:22.

Reeves PR, Lan R. Cholera in the 1990s. *Brit Med Bull* 1998;54:611.

Rosenberg CE. *The Cholera Years: The United States in 1832, 1849 and 1866.* Chicago: Univ of Chicago Press, 1962.

Sandler DP. John Snow and modern-day environmental epidemiology. *Am J Epidemiol* 2000;152:1.

Synder JD, Blake PA. Is cholera a problem for U.S. travelers? *JAMA* 1982;247:2268.

Vandenbroucke JP, Eelkman Rooda HM, Beukers H. Who made John Snow a hero? *Am J Epidemiol* 1991;133:967.

Weber JT, Levine WC, et al. Cholera in the United States, 1965–1991. Risks at home and abroad. *Arch Intern Med* 1994;154:551–6.

Wills C. *Yellow Fever, Black Goddess, The Coevolution of People and Plagues.* Reading, MA: Addison Wesley, 1996.

[1]Snow went on to become a famous obstetrician, one of the first to use anesthesia during delivery. In 1847, the year after the initial report of the value of ether as a surgical anesthetic, Snow, only 34 years old and only three years beyond his M.D. degree, published a short article entitled, "On the Inhalation of the Vapor of Ether." He subsequently wrote a series of papers on his experiences with anesthesia, including on the use of chloroform.

Queen Victoria and Prince Albert first showed interest in chloroform to ease her childbirth in 1848, but no anesthetic was administered for her seventh delivery of Prince Arthur in 1850. By the time of her eighth delivery (Prince Leopold), she wanted chloroform and her obstetrician, Charles Locock, a friend of Snow's arranged for Snow to give it. Four years later, the Queen had Princess Beatrice, her ninth and final child, also with John Snow providing chloroform. Following Queen Victoria's lead, the social elite in London wanted anesthesia for their deliveries, and Snow became famous.

CHAPTER 7

THE GREAT INFLUENZA
PANDEMIC OF 1918–1919
PRESIDENT WOODROW WILSON
AND THE BLITZKATARRH

"THE GREAT WAR"—FOUR YEARS OF THE BLOODIEST fighting yet seen by man—resulted in about 10 million military casualties and an additional 10 to 11 million civilian deaths. The war still raged when the great influenza pandemic of 1918 occurred, and the disruption caused by the fighting facilitated the spread of this disease, which caused as many fatalities as the war itself, but in a much shorter period of time. More than 21 million people died of it, most of them during the four months preceding the armistice. These figures make it one of the most devastating epidemics in history.[E1] Curiously, the main waves of the epidemic ended in most places virtually simultaneously with the armistice, which became effective at 11 A.M., November 11, 1918.

Crowding is a major mechanism in the dissemination of influenza virus. The transport of large numbers of men to training bases and on crowded troopships to France contributed to the devastating incidence and mortality among Americans. The need to mount and maintain military pressure on Germany in 1918, in a last-ditch offensive, forced the President of the United States to make agonizing decisions that required continued exposure of American troops to the infection. After the war, Wilson's own health failed rapidly, beginning with an attack of influenza during the peace conference at Versailles.

In the United States, 548,452 deaths from flu or pneumonia (the main complication of flu that usually led to a fatal outcome) were recorded during that period, a fatality rate of 0.5 to 1.2 percent of cases. In the American Army, more than 600,000 hospital admissions for influenza were recorded, with 23,007 deaths attributed directly to influenza and an additional 6,364 listed as due to pneumonia. This equaled one-third of the total of battle deaths that occurred in the American Expeditionary Force during the entire war.

Elsewhere, the flu was equally or even more devastating. The United Kingdom lost about 200,000 people. The island of Samoa, without previous experience of influenza, lost 25 percent of its population, and the disease wiped out whole Eskimo villages. India was perhaps the worst affected country, losing about 12 million people. Suffering in Spain was especially severe, and early reports of the devastation in that country received worldwide publicity, because Spain was not involved in the war and there was no censorship. Because Spain was the first country to have its suffering so widely reported, the disease became generally known as the "Spanish Influenza."

Several known varieties of the influenza virus occur. Type A virus is the form that causes the great pandemics; type B usually causes local epidemics, and type C causes a mild disease generally seen among children. Influenza epidemics usually affect young people especially severely, probably because older people have some degree of immunity from exposure to previous epidemics. However, influenza virus frequently mutates and changes its antigenicity; as a result, exposure to previous infections may not provide immunity during a new outbreak.

Influenza virus can also infect some wild and domestic animals, although not all influenza viruses of animals can spread to man. Influenza viruses infective for man can be found in several domestic animals, including pigs, horses, poultry, and several other species of birds. Thus, the reservoir of viruses that can potentially infect people is ineradicable.

The flu virus primarily attacks the upper respiratory tract, especially the trachea and bronchi, but it can lead to secondary bacterial infections in the lungs, pneumonia, thus increasing the likelihood of a fatal outcome. Ordinary influenza can cause high fever with a great deal of sweating, generalized and severe muscular pains, and prostration with distressing weakness. Sneezing and a dry cough are common. The typical attack lasts about six days. The virus is transmitted by droplets in the air released through sneezing or coughing. The disease usually occurs in the winter, and can cause a severe epidemic if large numbers of nonimmune people have appeared in a community since the last epidemic, or if the virus has changed its antigenicity so that previous immunization is no longer protective.

The term *flu* is often used nonspecifically for a wide variety of respiratory tract infections. (It is said that if one person has such an infection, it is called "a cold," but if many people have it, it is called "the flu.") The severe influenza epidemic of 1918 and 1919 was a true pandemic, spreading around the world and wreaking havoc everywhere it occurred.

SPREAD OF INFLUENZA. Although influenza spreads mainly from person to person through aerosolized respiratory droplets, it also can spread from animals to humans, and the great pandemic of 1918–1920, which spread from swine to humans, was a prime example. The infection can also spread from birds, especially chickens, to humans. Fear that the importation of infected chickens will lead to human outbreaks has led to the destruction of huge flocks of them in several locales. However, the spread of the disease among humans occurs so quickly that is hard to blame any one individual cultural phenomenon as causal. Today, it is easy to blame air travel, but the rapidity of intercontinental spread was astounding even during World War I, when it still took 10 days to cross the Atlantic. The dramatic and sudden increase in mortality occurred on both sides of the Atlantic almost simultaneously.

THE HISTORY OF THE 1918–1919 EPIDEMIC. The term "influenza" was first applied to the disease during an epidemic occurring in Florence, in 1580. The Italian word, meaning *influence,* referred to a supposed deleterious influence of the stars on the welfare of humans. The stars must have been exerting a particularly malignant influence in 1918, when influenza became pandemic. The original locus of the outbreak is disputed. The French blamed the disease on Chinese workers brought in to dig trenches. The Spanish decided it began in Russian Turkestan, but the Russians, along with most of the world, thought it began in Spain.

The earliest recorded outbreak of influenza, however, apparently occurred in the United States. Early one morning in March 1918, at Fort Riley, Kansas, a cook named Albert Gitchell reported to the post hospital with fever, sore throat, and generalized achiness. Two minutes after his arrival, another soldier arrived, reporting the same symptoms; by noon 107 cases were logged, and by the end of a week, 522 soldiers exhibited the same syndrome. The outbreak at Fort Riley, which lasted five weeks, affected 1,127 soldiers and caused 46 deaths. The diagnosis of influenza was made, but the deaths were attributed to secondary bacterial pneumonia. In May, the 89th and 92nd Divisions finished their training at Fort Riley and were shipped to France where, according to some reports, cases of influenza began to appear among the French soon after their arrival. The disease then appeared in Britain and Germany, and subsequently in India, Asia, and the Far East.

J.S. Koen, a veterinarian studying hog cholera for the Bureau of Animal Industry in Iowa, reported a 1918 epidemic among pigs that closely resembled the influenza seen in men. He recorded, "... an outbreak in the family would be followed immediately by an outbreak among the hogs, and vice versa, as to present a most striking coincidence, if not suggesting a close relation between the two conditions. It looked like 'flu,' it presented the identical symptoms of 'flu,' it terminated like 'flu,' and until proved it was not 'flu,' I shall stand by that diagnosis." After the discovery of the influenza virus and its ability to undergo frequent mutations and exist as numerous antigenically distinct strains, studies led to the conclusion that the virus of the 1918–1919 pandemic was indeed caused by swine influenza.

The 1918–1919 influenza pandemic caused some of the highest recorded mortality rates among civilians in various cities of the United States. On October 1, 1918, 202 deaths from influenza occurred in Boston; on October 10, 528 Philadelphians died of the disease. In New York City, on October 23, 851 people died of it, the highest daily death toll ever recorded in that city. During the week of October 23, 1918, there were 21,000 deaths throughout the country from influenza, the highest weekly mortality ever recorded in the United States from any cause at any time.

The descriptions of the near panic that developed in those cities resemble similar descriptions of panic in cities during outbreaks of bubonic plague. Theaters, movies, dance halls, bars, and all places of public assembly were closed, including schools and churches. Liberty Loan drives, parades, and even football games were canceled. Ordinances were passed requiring everyone to wear a gauze face mask in public, and stiff fines were imposed on people who sneezed and coughed in public without covering their mouths with a handkerchief. The general attitude is summed up by a line from Ben Johnson's *The Alchemist*, in which, during an outbreak of the plague, one character tells another, "Breathe less, and farther off!"

Police who were not sick themselves had plenty of free time to enforce the new ordinances; in Chicago, the crime rate for the month of October 1918 fell by 43 percent. Firemen were employed to hose down the streets of Philadelphia, where all places of public assembly were closed. The Catholic Charities of Philadelphia hired six horse-drawn wagons to search streets, alleys, and tenements for the bodies of abandoned victims; the 200 they found caused enormous overcrowding in the morgue, since the embalmers refused to come to work. Several cities ran out of coffins, and their mayors set up new manufacturing facilities. On at least one occasion, a rail shipment of coffins passing through one city bound for another was highjacked by a health official for local use.

In Germany, in an attempt to bolster morale on the home front, reports were published in German newspapers that victims in New York were lying heaped in the streets.

Desperate cures were proposed, such as the inhalation of chloroform and the removal of tonsils and teeth. The supposed medicinal value of Scotch whiskey drove the price up to $20 a quart. Both houses of Congress adopted a resolution appropriating emergency funds to combat the disease. Boston was particularly severely hit; Lt. Gov. Calvin Coolidge, acting for the absent governor of Massachusetts, telegraphed the President and governors of nearby states requesting aid for the state, because the State Department of Health reported an estimated 50,000 cases. Coolidge reported that doctors and nurses had been mobilized into the army and that, with hospitals full, many cases were receiving no attention. His cable stated, "Earnestly solicit your influence to obtain for us the needed assistance in any way you can. 100 physicians and 1000 nurses needed immediately." New Hampshire and Connecticut were not asked to send help because of the prevalence of influenza in those states.

The epidemic affected the American forces already in France, as well as those training for service overseas. During October 1918, 70,000 men in the American Expeditionary Force in France reported sick, and General Pershing pleaded for reinforcements. Overall, one-third of the troops stricken with influenza died, and in some small units the mortality rate reached 80 percent.

Meanwhile, in the United States, a typical outbreak struck Camp Funston, Kansas, where the 10th Division was training. The number of new cases per day rose swiftly, from 50 to 100, to 300, 700, 800, to over 1,000. General Leonard Wood was the commander of Camp Funston. He was a former Army Chief of Staff who had been a physician before becoming a regular army officer, and whose role in the Spanish-American War and the conquest of yellow fever in Cuba is described elsewhere in this volume. Wood wrote to the Governor of Kansas: "There are 1440 minutes in a day. When I tell you there were 1440 admissions in a day, you will realize the strain put on our Nursing and Medical force...."

Because mortality was especially high among young people brought together from various parts of the country into crowded recruit training bases, military leaders considered discontinuing the draft. President Wilson was compelled to make a difficult decision. On September 27, 1918, a public announcement was made that, "Because of the epidemic of Spanish influenza in army camps, Provost Marshal General Crowder tonight canceled calls for entrainment between October 7 and 11 of 142,000 draft registrants." In canceling the call-up of draftees, General Crowder was acting upon instructions from General Peyton March, Army Chief of Staff. Every state and the District of Columbia had quotas assigned, and the men had been scheduled to go to every camp in the country. The report added, "The men will probably not be entrained until after the influenza epidemic has been checked.... During the 24 hours ending at noon today, 6,139 new cases of influenza in the army camps had been reported to the Surgeon General of the Army." Two new camps were added to the list of those affected, leaving only 13 recruit training camps free of disease. The total number of cases of influenza in all camps was put at 35,146, with 3,036 cases of pneumonia. It was not until October 23 that the Surgeon General decided to allow resumption of draft calls.

Because crowding of troops on transport ships magnified outbreaks of influenza, President Wilson had to decide whether to save American lives by discontinuing the assembly of troops on transports. At this point in the course of the war, the Germans were reeling from military defeats and the cumulative effects of four years of struggle. Rapid progress was being made by Allied armies, pushing the Germans eastward toward the German border. A breakthrough seemed close, and it was thought essential to keep up the pressure; a slowing of the flow of fresh American troops into the lines would ease the strain on the demoralized Germans.[E2] Publicity about a decrease in the reinforcements for the Allied forces might stem the rising tide of defeatism in Germany.

Wilson was faced with a difficult decision. Medical authorities advised him to stop the assembly of troops until the epidemic waned. Three hundred thousand troops were being sent to embarkation ports monthly, and death rates often reached 20 percent, especially among the soldiers packed on troopships, where the potent bacteria that caused severe secondary bacterial pneumonias were rapidly spread along with the influenza virus. Continuing the transportation of troops to Europe meant thousands of avoidable deaths, but perhaps also a prolongation of the war, which could cause additional thousands to die.

General March, the Army Chief of Staff, had been pressured to stop troop shipments, but he had declined. March went to the White House to discuss the problem with the President on Sunday, October 8, 1918. He informed Wilson of the extent of the influenza epidemic, but advised the President not to discontinue the embarkation of troops for Europe, pointing out that, "Every soldier who has died [of influenza] has just as surely played his part as his comrade who has died in France." Wilson reportedly gazed out the window of his office, silently observing the fall foliage in Washington for a while, and then turned back to General March and agreed not to suspend transporting troops to France. A little over a month later, the armistice was signed and the war ended.

Military histories of the war mention little or nothing about the effect of the influenza on the effectiveness of the various armies in the field, but it must have been devastating, particularly during the important German offensive early in the summer of 1918. That drive, launched on March 21, was Germany's last desperate bid for victory—or at least an attempt to engender sufficient Allied discouragement to bring about peace on favorable terms. The Germans quietly massed troops on the Western Front for an attack that ended the stalemate of previous years by breaking through Allied lines at several key points. Their drive to Paris was finally stopped at the Marne, 37 miles from the capital, at almost exactly the same spot that marked the high point of their advance into France in August 1914. A general consensus among military historians is that the German commander, General Erich von Ludendorff, came extremely close to a major victory that would have changed the outcome of the war.

The failure of Ludendorff to exploit the early successes of that offensive has puzzled historians. A typical analyst described a portion of the offensive as follows: "A month's pause followed.... He needed an interval for rest and preparation, and the delay was fatal, giving the British and French time to recuperate and the Americans time to gather strength....The tactical success of his own blows had been Ludendorff's undoing; yielding to their influence, he had pressed each too far and too long, so using up his own reserves and causing an undue interval between blows. He had driven in three great wedges, and but none had penetrated far enough to sever a vital artery, and this strategic failure left the Germans with an indented front inviting flank counterstrokes."

Could depletion of his forces by influenza been a factor in Ludendorff's delay? A number of reports at the time documented that influenza was devastating the German army during this portion of the campaign. On July 9, a small dispatch published in the New York Times had a headline stating that "Documents Taken from German Prisoners Indicate They Are Having a Hard Time with the New Influenza." Datelined "From the Associated Press, July 8, 1918, With the British Army in France," it mentioned that, "Captured documents and statements of prisoners indicated that the Germans were having a bad time in numerous zones with the new influenza which is running through Europe. An unposted letter [that] was found in the pocket of a man captured on July 4 throws some light on this subject. It read: 'I felt so ill that I should like to report sick. Fever is rampant among us and already a whole lot of men are in the hospital. Every day more go th[ere]. As I have not yet had leave and am expecting to go any day, I shall not report sick yet anyway.'"

The *Times* article pointed out that the letter, "of course, refers to the prisoner's own sector and not to the whole German front, of which he could know little." It added, "The new fever is said to strike down the men so quickly that they drop in their tracks while on duty. They have high fever for two or three days and are usually laid up for at least six days at the hospital." It did not mention the effect that the influenza epidemic was having on the Allied troops.

In a report on July 13, Philip Gibbs, the most prominent war correspondent of the *New York Times*, stated that the "Flanders grip" was rife among German troops in that area of the front. Another report, on July 11, mentioned that Kaiser Wilhelm "himself has fallen victim to the influenza which has been so prevalent in the German army...." adding that he "had gone home from the French front because of an attack of the Spanish grip."

General Ludendorff fled to Sweden after the war and published his memoirs in 1919. In them, he blamed the failure of the offensive largely on the epidemic affecting his forces, which the German soldiers called the "Blitzkatarrh." Ludendorff wrote, "It was a grievous business having to listen every morning to the Chief of Staffs' recital of the number of influenza cases, and their complaints about the weakness of the troops."

The great Allied offensive of 1918 began as Ludendorff's offensive failed, building up greater and greater momentum. With a complete breakthrough threatening, many in the German high command wanted the civilians to negotiate an armistice, hoping to avoid a humiliating admission of military defeat. Pressure for an end to the war mounted inside Germany. Prince Maximilian of Baden was appointed as prime minister, because he was believed to be someone the Allies would accept as a peacemaker. On October 23, overtures requesting an armistice were sent by Prince Max to President Wilson through the Swiss. Wilson rejected them, demanding unconditional surrender.

When Ludendorff was forced to resign on October 26, the new civilian government was free to proceed with an unconditional military surrender. But Prince Max was ill with influenza for two weeks during this critical period and was comatose for three days, publicly attributed to a "sleeping draught given for influenza." When he returned to his office on November 3, he found that, while he had been comatose, both Turkey and Austria had capitulated to the Allies and revolution had spread inside Germany.

The Bolshevik government of Russia, headed by Lenin, had been recognized by the Kaiser's government as soon as peace was signed between Russia and Germany. This allowed the communists to send an ambassador to Berlin. As soon as he arrived, the ambassador began using the embassy to stir up revolt inside Germany. The communists were most effective among the naval forces. The entire German High Seas Fleet had been summoned to Kiel for one last massive raid into the English Channel, an attempt to stop the flow of men and supplies into France. Even submarines were recalled from attacks on commerce in the Atlantic for this desperate attack, which was to start on October 29. But mutiny broke out at Kiel, with red flags appearing over many ships, and the fleet never sailed. A mutiny of the entire fleet occurred on November 3, and revolution spread to Berlin by November 9.

Prince Max resigned as a result of this turmoil, and the Kaiser, finally realizing that he no longer controlled events, was forced to abdicate on November 9. A Soldier's and Worker's Council, claiming to be the government of Germany, appointed the leader of the Social Democratic Party, Friedrich Ebert, as chancellor on November 10. He signed the armistice on the following day. Ebert became the first president (1919–1925) of the German republic.

The devastation of influenza epidemic subsided almost simultaneously with the signing of the armistice. Did the disease affect the course of the war? Most military authorities do not give great weight to this possibility, emphasizing that the disease affected both sides simultaneously, and commanders knew the effect of the disease on their own troops, but not the enemy's. It seems likely that the German psyche was, at the very least, affected by the sickness among their men at a time when Allied forces were building in strength due to the continuing arrival of American troops. However, it is not possible to separate the effect of the influenza from all the other forces in play at that time.

Additional waves of influenza occurred during 1919 and 1920, and almost halted the peace conference in Versailles. The British and French Prime Ministers, Lloyd George and Clemenceau, both had bouts of the disease, and during April 1919, Wilson had a severe attack of influenza while in Paris for the conference. Historians have commented on Wilson's deteriorating physical and emotional status during the Versailles conference, climaxing when he had an impassioned argument with Clemenceau on March 27. While objecting to the French Premier's demand for annexation of the Saar and occupation of the Rhineland, Wilson actually exploded into a verbal tirade at the conference table, leading to his later asking Clemenceau, "...do you wish me to return home?" The French Premier responded, "I do not wish you to go home, but I intend to do so myself." He then picked up his hat and left the room. Wilson became acutely ill a few days later, on April 3, developing a high fever, headache, muscle pains and aches, chills, sweats, and severe malaise.

His influenza was treated with standard measures, and improved after about a week, but some of his associates thought that he never fully recovered. He continued to have headaches, and a diagnosis of persistent viral encephalitis was considered; an increase in cardiac symptoms, particularly shortness of breath, led to the possible additional diagnosis of myocarditis due to the influenza virus. Subsequent medical commentators on Wilson's physical ailments have attributed his deterioration to hypertensive and arteriosclerotic cerebrovascular disease, syndromes better understood by us than by the physicians in Wilson's time.

Biographers also describe a marked personality change in President Wilson after his bout with influenza; he became suspicious of spies in the embassy, leading him to get up at night, sneak downstairs, and insist on rearranging furniture. His favorite mode of relaxation, riding in his "motor car," became a source of agitation; he would become highly upset whenever another car passed his on the highway, demanding arrest and punishment of the motorist for speeding. After returning to the United States, on one occasion he wrote to the Attorney General to ask if, as President, he had the legal power to arrest a motorist. Although his mental and emotional difficulties clearly increased after the attack of influenza, they were only an exaggeration of a trend apparent earlier. These same symptoms are perhaps one reason for his confrontational attitude toward a Senate reluctant to accept the League of Nations, which he had introduced into the Treaty of Versailles, and thus a factor in his failure to obtain ratification. Herbert Hoover, active in relief efforts in Europe after the war, wrote in a biography of Wilson that he never recovered from the flu, and that "the previously incisive, quick mind became a slow and more resisting mind."

In Wilson's defense, it has been pointed out that he had negotiated and compromised to get wording of the Treaty acceptable both to himself and the other Allied governments. He felt that he could not accept the Senate's demand for changes that would have required renegotiating the Treaty with the other heads of state. When it became clear that he was not going to get his cherished Treaty of Versailles ratified, he decided on a personal campaign to convince the American public to pressure the Senate, disregarding the advice of most of his aides, his wife, and his personal physician. On September 4, 1919, Wilson embarked on a 10,000-mile speaking tour by train. On September 26, near Pueblo Colorado, his speech became slurred, his face twitched uncontrollably, and he was carried from the rear platform into the train. The next day, he was noted to have weakness of the arm and leg on one side. His train immediately returned to Washington, where he seemed to make a remarkable recovery, although the subsequent course of his illness has been the subject of much controversy and literature. His wife kept him sequestered from the press and members of his cabinet and, to the end of his administration, he was never again fully functional. He did not hold a cabinet meeting until April 20, 1920, on which occasion each secretary was announced to him by name. His hesitating manner during the meeting distressed those present. Twenty-eight bills passed by Congress went unsigned during his "recuperation," but he did veto one: the bill to enforce the Volstead Act (Prohibition).

During the Democratic convention in 1920, the Assistant Secretary of the Navy, Franklin Delano Roosevelt, was nominated for the Vice-Presidency. Roosevelt had known Wilson well, and had accompanied him to the Paris Peace

Conference. After the convention, Roosevelt visited Wilson at the White House and recorded that he was aghast at the change in the state of the President's health. He found Wilson unable to utter more than a few, barely coherent words.

Wilson's health failed progressively and, after leaving the presidency, he became totally incapacitated, blind, and unable to speak. He died on February 3, 1924.

THE EPIDEMIC THAT WASN'T: THE 1976 VACCINE EPISODE. During the 1950s, influenza vaccines based on an inactivated virus became available. Because the virus mutates and changes antigenicity each year, it is essential to prepare a new vaccine with the appropriate strain of virus before the year's epidemic begins. This cannot be done until the first cases appear and the antigenic characteristics of the new virus are revealed. In 1957, the strain isolated was sufficiently different from previous strains so that older vaccines were not useful. However, the vaccine and the problems it presented were new. Although large amounts of vaccine were prepared, the decision to proceed was made late in the season and only 7 million people were vaccinated in timely fashion—too few and too late—70,000 people in the United States died of flu during that episode. In 1968, the vaccine did not become available until three weeks after the first epidemic cases appeared; only 10 million doses of vaccine were prepared and 33,000 people died.

Late in 1975, at the army post at Fort Dix, New Jersey, sputum from several cases of upper respiratory infection showed influenza virus Type A/Victoria. However, two specimens were difficult for the local lab to identify, and these were sent to the Centers for Disease Control and Prevention (CDC, then called the Communicable Disease Center) in Atlanta. Meanwhile, the disease spread among recruits at the fort, and one soldier died. The CDC identified the virus as resembling or identical to the same swine influenza responsible for the 1918–1919 pandemic. Serum obtained from people over 50 years of age, old enough to have been infected in 1918 or 1919, contained antibodies to this strain. A decision had to be made as to whether to produce large amounts of vaccine against this strain of virus and inoculate as many people as possible, and the decision had to be made immediately if the vaccination was to be prepared fast enough to prevent another severe epidemic—or a repeat of the 1918–1919 pandemic.

The large-scale production of this vaccine was possible early in 1976, but a policy decision had to be made at the governmental level to arrange for not only the production but, also, the stockpiling of it in readiness for widespread administration if an epidemic began. A second option was for the government to arrange for production of the vaccine and to organize a national vaccination program immediately. The third choice was to sit tight and hope that a pandemic would not develop. Because the normal number of annual deaths from influenza totaled 17,000, at a cost to the economy of an estimated $500 million, the CDC favored direct intervention. It undertook both the production and organization of delivery of the vaccine for the whole country. All this had to be done urgently, if it was to occur before the expected start of the epidemic. (It is interesting to note that the British and the World Health Organization, WHO, believed there was insufficient information for such a decision to be made.)

Vaccination programs were not normally a federal government function, but were usually organized locally, and the decision involved many facets: The government had to purchase and distribute large amounts of vaccine and also obtain enormous numbers of syringe, needles, and vaccine guns. The cost of the program was estimated to be only about a $135 million. President Gerald Ford quickly approved the scheme, and the plan went through the necessary Congressional Committees by the middle of April 1976. Because it was obvious the President would sign this bill in a hurry, the Democrats in the Senate slipped a whole series of other health interventions into the bill that he would never have signed if it were not for the urgency of the situation.

Despite the early decision, errors in production of the vaccine and other problems occurred. It became clear that the target of 146 million vaccine doses by October could not be reached. The question of indemnity in case of accidents and unforeseen complications was not addressed. There was a real possibility that an unusual paralytic disease, Guillian-Barré syndrome, could arise in a significant number of people as a result of vaccination. The U.S. insurance industry was not willing to assume the financial burden and would not insure the drug firms for liability in case of accidents or unforeseen complications. The pharmaceutical industry therefore wanted the government to assume this responsibility. However, Congress felt that the government could not involve itself in insurance matters. The date for the arrival of the epidemic moved ever closer.

As these problems were being addressed, Legionnaire's disease developed in a large number of conventioneers in Philadelphia. In desperation, Congress stopped the pay of CDC employees until they identified the cause of Legionnaire's disease. Although this distraction did not help with the problems surrounding the influenza vaccine, the beginning of the influenza epidemic season spurred Congress to action; a bill ratifying government indemnity for pharmaceutical companies was finally passed.

Although vaccine production lagged behind schedule, the vaccination program was started on the target date of October 1. One million people were vaccinated in the first ten days. On October 11, in a Pittsburgh clinic, three elderly people died immediately after vaccination, making headlines even though the CDC showed that no relationship existed between these deaths and the vaccine. Other deaths occurred and one batch of vaccine came under suspicion. The vaccine program continued, nonetheless, and 2.5 million people were vaccinated by the end of the second week. The acceptance rate of the vaccine by the public declined as the epidemic failed to appear, but by mid-December, more than 45 million vaccine doses were delivered to civilians and another .5 million to the military.

Although this total represented about 24 percent of the population, very few side effects had been reported. The number of vaccine-related deaths was below the number of deaths expected by chance in any 48-hour period in the absence of vaccination. However, during the third week of November, a definite case of Guillian-Barré syndrome appeared in Minnesota after vaccination. In the following week, three more cases of the syndrome appeared in that state, with one death, and three more deaths occurred in Alabama. As more cases appeared, investigation showed that <1 percent of the Guillian-Barré cases were vaccine-related, but no data was available on the expected rate of Guillian-Barré syndrome. By mid-December, five deaths had occurred due to Guillian-Barré, and the association with vaccination became clearer. One case of the disease occurred for each 200,000 people vaccinated, compared to 1 case in 1 million people in the absence of vaccination.

The continuing failure of the epidemic to appear was the final blow to the program. Although small outbreaks of swine influenza did occur in the United States, the vaccine was not used to bring it under control because, by that time, concern of side effects was so great that a total moratorium on its use was put into effect.

The heads of the Department of Health Education and Welfare and the CDC were fired. As one observer put it, "such is the fate of bold decision-makers if the decision turns out to be wrong, while those sitting on the sidelines or a convenient fence continue to sit in comfort and safety." In retrospect, premature decisions were made to do more than was strictly necessary at any one time. Medical authorities were overconfident and insensitive to both the public and the media, and failed to consider the uncertainties and problems likely to arise. Thus, no safety nets were in place to deal with situations as they arose.

Today, new data about the spread of disease, the side effects of vaccines, and the outcome of vaccination have been obtained, and computer models can improve the decision-making process for controlling influenza epidemics.

The question of indemnity for unfortunate developments remains thorny and unresolved. In the United States, following the 1976 episode, 743 claims were filed for personal injury and 67 claims for wrongful deaths; a total of over $600 million was claimed and $9,100,000 paid. (These figures do not include one claimant who filed for but did not receive over a $1 billion.) Although some changes have been made in assigning liability for vaccine-related injury, the threat of lawsuits has driven many vaccine manufacturers out of the business.

SUMMARY. Influenza is a prime example of a disease that is spread readily from person to person, and thus can rapidly encompass the globe. It is also an example of disease that people can acquire from domesticated animals. The ease of its spread makes it extremely difficult to prevent influenza through the usual public health measures, and the best means of prevention remains the development of the necessary vaccine for each outbreak, accompanied by rapid production and administration. The legal problems affecting medical issues are not easily solved, but the public cannot expect private industry to develop and manufacture needed vaccines if liability and lawsuits for untoward developments that are not due to negligence or manufacturing errors can wipe out any chance to recover costs and perhaps take other assets as well.

ADDITIONAL READING

Beveridge WB. *Influenza, The Last Great Plague*. London: Heinemnan Co, 1977.

Bray RS. *Armies of Pestilence, The Impact of Disease on History*. New York: Barnes and Noble, 2000.

Crosby AW. *Epidemic and Peace, 1918*. Westport, CT: Greenwood Press, 1976.

Hoover H. *The Ordeal of Woodrow Wilson*. New York: McGraw-Hill, 1958.

Kilbourne ED ed. *The Influenza Viruses and Influenza*. New York: Academic Press, 1975.

Koen JS. A practical method for field diagnosis of swine diseases. *J Vet Med* 1919;14:468.

Liddell-Hart BH. *A History of the World War, 1914–1918*. London: Faber & Faber, 1934.

Ludendorff E. *Ludendorff's Own Story, August 1914–November 1918; the Great War from the Siege of Liège to the Signing of the Armistice as Viewed from the Grand Headquarters of the German Army*. New York: Harper, 1919.

March FA. *History of the World War*. Philadelphia: United Publishers of the United States and Canada, 1919.

Marks G, Beatty WK. *Epidemics*. New York: Scribner, 1976.

McCullum C. Disease and Dirt. The social dimensions of influenza, cholera and syphilis. *The Pharos* 1992;55:22.

Perisco JE. Swine flu in 1918, History of an epidemic. *Am Heritage* 1976;24:28.

Pershing JJ. *My Experiences in the World War*. New York: Frederick A. Stokes Co, 1931.

Rogers N. *Dirt and Disease: Polio before FDR*. New Brunswick, NJ: Rutgers Univ Press, 1992.

Spink WW. *Infectious Diseases, Prevention and Treatment during the Nineteenth and Twentieth Centuries.* Minneapolis: Univ of Minnesota Press, 1978.

Tumulty JP. *Woodrow Wilson As I Know Him.* Garden City, NY: Doubleday, Page & Co, 1921.

Von Ludendorff E. *Ludendorff's Own Story, vol. 2.* New York: Harper Bros, 1919.

Webster RG. Influenza. In: Morse SS, ed. *Emerging Viruses.* New York: Oxford Univ Press, 1993.

[E1]The Black Death of the fourteenth century caused more deaths—perhaps 25 million in Europe and another 37 million elsewhere—but these deaths occurred over a three-year period. The great plague of Justinian, which began in 542 CE, may have caused 100 million deaths, but it extended over a period of 50 years. The death rate from "the flu" exceeded both, since almost all the 21 million deaths occurred in 120 days!

[E2]The German Army was receiving reinforcements from the Russian front after the surrender of the Bolshevik government. Their quick surrender after gaining power was repayment for Germany's aid in providing the secret sealed train that transported Lenin from Switzerland to Russia, to augment the revolution against the Tsar.

CHAPTER 8

POLIOMYELITIS

WHY DID FRANKLIN DELANO
ROOSEVELT GET INFANTILE
PARALYSIS AS AN ADULT?

O CCASIONAL CASES OF INFANTILE PARALYSIS, OR *POLIO-MYELITIS*, have occurred since ancient times. We know this from a number of historical remnants, such as a bas relief of an Egyptian priest showing the typical atrophy of a leg paralyzed since infancy, and a few case reports by physicians.

Polio was probably present in the Middle East during Biblical times, since a priest named Ruma from the XVIIIth dynasty of Egypt (1580–1350 BCE), is depicted in a stele as having an atrophic leg with a contracture of the calf muscles producing a foot drop, changes typical of childhood poliomyelitis. This dynasty ruled in Egypt after the expulsion of the Hyksos, a period during which the Israelites probably were in Goshen, under Egyptian rule. Polio could have been a cause for some of the instances of "crookback," a deformity mentioned in the King James version of the Old Testament.

However, only isolated cases were seen until late in the nineteenth century, when epidemic outbreaks of the disease began to occur and it began to affect adults. The disease had until then been called infantile paralysis, a correct description of the onset of almost all cases before that time. These changes in the epidemiology of poliomyelitis illustrate the phenomenon of a deleterious "side-effect" resulting from generally beneficial public health measures: Twentieth-century poliomyelitis epidemics were the result of actions taken to prevent and virtually eliminate such feared diseases as typhoid fever.

THE CAUSE OF POLIO EPIDEMICS. Viral diseases that produce immunity, as polio does, often become rare or disappear entirely from a given geographic area after all susceptible people have encountered the virus and either died or become immune to it. When a virus is reintroduced after the arrival of a new population without immunity, severe epidemics can occur. Adult polio was rarely seen until sanitary improvements, beginning the in the eighteenth century, limited exposure to enteric organisms. Typhoid became infrequent, even rare, thanks to improved sanitation and other public health measures, but these same advances now caused large numbers of infants to reach late childhood or even adulthood without exposure to another enteric organism, the polio virus. Epidemics could then develop since there would be large numbers of unimmunized, susceptible older children and adults in a community when the virus was reintroduced. Paralysis develops much more frequently when infection first occurs after infancy.

Polio, or at least the paralysis it caused, was often blamed on some form of trauma until microbiology revealed a viral etiology. In the Second Book of Samuel (4:4), a passage is often quoted as indicating the ancient existence of poliomyelitis. This is the story of Mephiboseth, who became lame following an accident when he was five years old. "And Jonathan, Saul's son, had a son who was lame of his feet. He was five years old...." The lameness was blamed on an earlier episode "... and his nurse took him up, and fled: and it came to pass, as she made haste to flee [from the Philistines], that he fell, and became lame. And his name was Mephiboseth." In this context, in the first edition of the classic *Principles and Practice of Medicine* (1892), William Osler mentions this passage in discussing the cause of poliomyelitis, which was not yet known: "Since the days of Mephiboseth, parents have been inclined to attribute this form of paralysis to the carelessness of nurses in letting children fall, but very rarely is the disease induced by traumatism...."

Some paleopathologic evidence suggests the existence of cases of paralytic polio in ancient times. In the nineteenth century, a neolithic skeleton found in Sussex, England shows undeveloped bones of the left humerus and radius, as did a similar Bronze Age skeleton found in Norfolk. Similar findings from other regions are considered examples of polio, but all of these "withered arms" could be the result of childhood polio or they could have resulted from failure of development following brachial plexus injury at birth. A club-foot deformity found in the Hopewell Indian mounds in Ohio is also considered suggestive of a disease such as polio, but that conclusion also is questionable. Clubfoot is often a congenital deformity, present at birth. Cases of clubfoot described in the works of Hippocrates and in medical works of later centuries, in which the deformity appeared later in childhood, are more likely the result of polio. Even more convincing is an Italian jar dating from 4th century BCE depicting a bearded man with a withered leg supporting himself with the leg entwined around a staff, using it like a brace; his deformity is characteristic of the effects of early childhood polio.

Polio then, must have existed as a sporadic disease through the centuries, primarily or almost exclusively affecting young children. At least one famous author was affected: Sir Walter Scott (1771–1832), at the age of 18 months "was discovered to be affected with the fever..." which was thought to be due to teething, but, as he recorded, "...On the fourth [day]...I had lost the power of my right leg." Later, Scott wrote, "The impatience of a child soon inclined me to struggle with my infirmity, and I began by degrees to stand, to walk, and to run. Although the limb affected was much shrunk and contracted, my general health, which was of more importance, was much strengthened by being frequently in the open air, and, in a word, I, who in a city had probably been condemned to hopeless and helpless decrepitude, was now a healthy, high-spirited, and my lameness apart, a sturdy child...." Scott, however, remained permanently lame. Because most cases of polio began in infancy or early childhood, with the onset occurring between 3 and 36 months, such an association with teething was made often.

Polio is caused by an *enterovirus*, one of many organisms that enter the body via the gut, and it is spread by fecal contamination of water and food supplies. Before the nineteenth century and the impetus of bacteriology, sanitation was primitive or nonexistent virtually everywhere. Diseases were often thought to be caused by miasmas, or odors, and efforts to eliminate these odors had some beneficial, albeit accidental, effect. These miasmas were thought to contain chemical poisons, such as those in snake venom, or *ferments* (enzymes) that could produce destructive poisons in tissues. These agents were sometimes described as "virus," a Latin word meaning poison, venom, or stench. The changes these agents caused in tissues, called sepsis, were thought to be similar to the putrid changes that occur after death. Therefore, agents that could prevent or minimize such tissue damage were called *antiseptics*.

The observations on hygiene made during the Crimean War by Florence Nightingale, and similar observations made during the American Civil War, led to sanitary movements in many American and European cities. It is hard for modern people to appreciate how ubiquitous "filth" was, when wastes were thrown in the street in most cities and remained until the rain washed them away. Personal bathing was a luxury not desired by most people. When in public, fastidious, fashionable ladies held scented handkerchiefs in front of their noses to ward off the offensive, disease-producing odors.

The modern medical literature on polio began when Michael Underwood (1737–1820), a London obstetrician and pediatrician, became the first to associate fever with the onset of lameness. The initial edition of his book, *Treatise on Diseases of Children*, which appeared in 1784, did not mention a disease suggestive of polio, but the second edition, published in 1789, contained an article on "Debility of the Lower Extremities." In it Underwood mentions a form of paralysis that "usually attacks children previously reduced by fever; seldom those under one, or more than four or five years old." Referring to the legs, he advocated braces similar to those used in the twentieth century: "when both [legs] have been paralyzed, nothing seems to do any good but irons to the legs, for the support of the limbs, and enabling the patient to walk."

In succeeding years, reports suggestive of polio began to appear with increasing frequency, stressing the very early age of onset. Giovanni Battista Monteggia (1762–1815), describing cases of paralysis affecting children, noted that, "it occurs in children who are nursing, or not much later...." In an 1840 monograph, Jacob von Heine (1800–1879), a German orthopedist and exponent of physical medicine from Stuttgart, listed prominent features of a disease causing paralysis in young children and described the onset as occurring between 3 and 36 months. By the mid-1830s, reports of polio cases occurring simultaneously began to appear. The famous British neurologist, Sir Charles Bell (1774–1842), described several cases in children three to five years old on St. Helena Island in 1832. A Dr. John Badham reported four cases occurring in Nottinghamshire, England, in 1835. Later in the nineteenth century, outbreaks grew, usually ten to twenty cases. Then, in 1887, an outbreak in Stockholm resulted in 44 cases of paralysis and similar outbreaks were reported in Italy, France, and Germany. Twenty-six cases occurred in Boston in 1893. In 1894, the first large outbreak occurred in the United States—132 cases in Rutland, Vermont. Virtually only young children were affected in these outbreaks, and the disease was still called "infantile paralysis." The famous French neurologist, Jean-Martin Charcot (1825–1893), was the first to note that pathology in the spinal cord affected the gray matter anteriorly, where the motor cells of the cord are located, and that the affected zones in the spinal cord corresponded to areas of the muscle paralysis. A new name for the disease emerged: "*acute anterior poliomyelitis*" based on the Greek word for gray, polio.

Karl Oskar Medin (1847–1927), a prominent Stockholm pediatrician, saw one or two cases of infantile paralysis per year for 15 years, but in 1887 he saw an epidemic of forty-four cases. In 1905, the first substantial epidemic of polio occurred in Scandinavia, where it affected 1,031 children. It was described by Ivar Wickman (1872–1914), the first physician to recognize nonparalytic cases of the disease.

Increasingly large epidemics followed in New York in 1907 and 1911, and in other American cities in 1910, 1911, and 1912. In 1911, in Sweden, an outbreak of 3,840 cases was the largest up to that time. As outbreaks began to occur in the United States, fear mounted, and the U.S. Public Health Service assigned Dr. Wade Hampton Frost (1880–1938) to investigate it. Frost studied epidemics in Mason City, Iowa, Cincinnati, Ohio, and Buffalo and Batavia, New York, that occurred between 1910 and 1912. He noted that many more people were exposed and infected with poliomyelitis than actually showed signs of illness and, after his descriptions, the concepts of widespread asymptomatic infection and of cases of nonbacterial (aseptic) meningitis, called "nonparalytic polio," became widely accepted. Frost reviewed research concerning the means of polio spread, emphasizing the existence of asymptomatic carriers of the virus who shed the infective agent in their secretions. Although the disease was shown to spread by infecting nasal passages, he emphasize that the epidemiologic characteristics of the disease were those of an agent spread by intestinal infection.

In 1916, the largest epidemic to date produced panic in the northeastern United States, causing 9,000 cases in New York City alone. Following 1916, huge epidemics occurred in the United States during most summers. Although the disease still primarily affected young children, a shift in age incidence was developing. In 1890, of an epidemic in Philadelphia (241 cases), 1.4 percent were 10 years of age or older. In 1899, in New York, 115 cases were recorded, of which 0.9 percent were 10 or older. As the table shows, in subsequent years, the percentage of older children and adults affected during summertime outbreaks rose remarkably.

Percentage of Reported Cases of Poliomyelitis in New York City, Over 9 Years of Age.

1899	0.9%
1916	5%
1931*	16%
1938	26%
1940	35%
1944	37%
1947*	48%

Years marked by * were years of major epidemics.

Once the viral agent of polio was demonstrated in animals, and antibodies to it found in patients' serum, it became practical to do studies of the distribution of neutralizing antibody in serum. In 1949 and 1950, a study was done that explained why epidemics and cases affecting older individuals occurred in some areas and not others. This study compared the populations of Cairo, Egypt, and

Miami, Florida, cities situated at the same latitude, but with widely differing standards of sanitation and hygiene. In Cairo, infants were born with antibody acquired *in utero* from their mothers, since virtually all adults had neutralizing antibody in their serum. The infants lost the antibodies by about six month of age, as typically occurs with maternally acquired antibodies. By one year of age, about 50 percent again had antibodies, meaning that they had been infected with the virus and produced their own antibodies. By age three years, virtually all children in Cairo had antibodies to poliovirus and thus were immune to new infection with the disease.

The pattern in Miami was very different. Very few infants were born with antibodies, and fewer than 10 percent showed their presence before about age three; around ages five to seven, only about 50 percent had neutralizing antibodies, and even in older adults, only about 70 percent showed this evidence of prior infection by polio virus. Thus, if poliovirus was introduced into the Cairo population, no on would get sick from it because everyone had immunity from exposure in early childhood. But in Miami, a large population of susceptible individuals, both children and adults, existed; introduction of the virus could result in a major epidemic of the disease. And, in older children and adults, poliovirus is much more likely to cause paralysis than in infants.

The 1916 epidemic of polio was blamed on "filth," "want of proper attention to cleanliness," and overcrowding, those factors then blamed for almost all epidemic diseases. But in this case, the opposite was really true. In retrospect, data concerning that epidemic show that those areas of the city that were most overcrowded had the highest overall infant mortality, and the most deaths from infantile diarrhea, also had the lowest incidence of paralytic polio per 1,000 population. On the other hand, the wealthiest areas with the lowest population density had the most paralytic disease per 1,000 population. These wealthier areas also had the highest frequency of older children and adults becoming affected by the disease. However, such facts were not obvious: Manhattan, with the largest population, had the most cases of polio, but it also had the highest population density and thus the fewest cases per 1,000. Not until the Cairo-Miami studies were these surprising epidemiologic facts understood.

During the early years of the twentieth century, definitive pathological studies done during epidemics established modern knowledge of the nature of the viral etiology of poliomyelitis. At a landmark medical meeting in Vienna, on December 18, 1908, Drs. Karl Landsteiner (1868–1943) and his assistant, E. Popper, described experiments on the spinal cord of a nine-year-old boy who had died of polio. Bacterial cultures were negative, but ground spinal cord tissue injected into two monkeys produced spinal cord lesions indistinguishable from those of the boy. (Fortunately, Landsteiner and Popper chose two Old World monkey species, *Cynocephalus hamadryas* and *Macaca rhesus*, for their experiment; New World monkeys are resistant to infection with that virus.) The researchers also injected guinea pigs, rabbits, and adult mice, all of which failed to develop any disease. Their proof that polio was caused by a viral agent that could pass through filters capable of holding back bacteria was the key initial step in the sequence leading to the development of polio vaccines.

Attempts to find a causative organism at the Rockefeller Institute in New York City led to the confirmation of the Viennese study; injection of nervous tissue from a fatal human case into a susceptible monkey species reproduced both flaccid paralysis and spinal cord pathology. Flexner's later studies of monkeys at the Rockefeller Institute established that the disease-producing virus could be inactivated by serum from both convalescent monkeys and humans, thus laying the foundation for development of a vaccine. The demonstration that suckling mice were susceptible to the virus also greatly accelerated acquisition of knowledge and made it possible to test large numbers of sera for neutralizing antibodies. The discovery that viruses could be propagated in tissue culture (Nobel Prize-winning research) was yet another major step in the development of the vaccine.

The details of the production and testing of vaccines is beyond the scope of this chapter; in brief, the Salk killed-virus vaccine became generally available in 1955, and the Sabin live-virus vaccine was licensed in 1961. The average annual number of cases of polio reported in the United States between 1951 and 1955 was 37,864, with about 500 deaths. During these epidemics, a high proportion of the cases involved permanent paralysis of one or more extremities; patients with "bulbar polio" were kept alive, when possible, in mechanical ventilators called "iron lungs." Between 1961 and 1965, total cases dropped to 570; no cases have been reported since 1965.

The epidemic of 1916 was the first for which something approaching complete records is available, with 27,000 cases in 16 reporting states. Extensive epidemiologic studies in New York were made, and efforts at quarantine were instituted. All children under 16 were placed in a restricted category and not allowed to leave the city from July 18 until October 3, unless a certificate was produced verifying that the premises they occupied were free of polio. This measure was instituted despite data showing only rare cases where more than one patient was affected in the same household, evidence that human-to-human transmission probably did not occur. The measure may have had some benefit, however, since it was later discovered that asymptomatic people could be carriers of the virus, and members of the same household were more likely to be carriers, thus capable of infecting others, even if they themselves were well. New Yorkers fled the city during the epidemic, but were not welcomed elsewhere: In other towns, signs greeted them saying, "New Yorkers Keep Out."

In New England, a 1931 epidemic resulted in screaming headlines, pictures of mortally ill children in respirators, and frantic warnings to parents to protect their children from exposure to crowds. Similar panic occurred during almost every subsequent epidemic. In 1955, one of the last big outbreaks of polio occurred in Boston. A large number of patients with bulbar polio, which paralyzes respiratory muscles, were being kept alive on the Drinker "iron lung" respirators in the contagious-disease building of the Boston City Hospital. On August 18 and 19, during this outbreak, hurricane Diane hit Boston. Electric power in the contagious-disease building was knocked out and emergency back-up power was woefully inadequate. House staff physicians on duty at Boston City Hospital immediately realized that patients in the respirators were in mortal danger. They dashed frantically through the torrential rain, jumped a fence to shorten the distance to the polio unit, and then spent a long night taking turns manually working the respirator bellows. While wind, rain, and thunder howled outside, everyone available took turns pumping the iron lungs by hand, usually with machines lined up toe-to-toe so that one person could work the two bellows at a time. Polio patients who were not in respirators got out of bed to help, relieving staff members at least briefly. All patients survived.

Many physicians were surprised at the rapidity with which severe muscle atrophy and deformity could develop following polio infection. Because the painful spasms of unaffected muscles dominated the clinical picture, physicians did not realize how rapidly a muscle could become permanently contracted if the patient was allowed to lie with joints flexed to relieve pain. Much of the resulting deformity and disability was later prevented as knowledge improved. Physicians caring for polio patients also became expert at handling the multitude of other complications that appeared in patients with extensive paralysis, including metabolic and electrolyte abnormalities such as hypercalcemia, as well as infections of the lungs, urinary tract, and gut.

During the 1920s, Sister Kenny, an Australian nurse, found that hot packs helped relieve the painful muscle spasm of the early phase of the disease and prevented contractures. This treatment became known as the Sister Kenny Method and was widely adopted. Although Sister Kenny was admired for her accomplishments in changing physical therapy practices in polio, she became a controversial figure when she refused to believe that any actual nervous system disease or paralysis occurred.

FRANKLIN D. ROOSEVELT AND POLIOMYELITIS. In 1921, polio devastated Franklin Delano Roosevelt, a prominent 39-year-old politician, former assistant secretary of the Navy in President Wilson's cabinet, and unsuccessful vice-presidential candidate the previous year. Roosevelt recovered sufficiently to become one of the three American presidents usually ranked as "great" by historians. His illness illustrates the clinical features of the disease. His response to it illustrates how a strong, resourceful personality reacted to severe illness, overcame the effects of permanent disability on a promising political career, and made himself, in effect, a practitioner of a new field of medical specialization.

Roosevelt lived a sheltered childhood, growing up as a pampered only child in a wealthy family. Because he was educated by tutors at home, he was not exposed to many of the diseases usually shared by children, and so he never acquired immunity to them. As a young teenager, he was sent to Groton, an exclusive preparatory school, and then on to Harvard undergraduate and law schools. Thus he was rarely exposed to the infections ubiquitous in less affluent surroundings. In 1910, his appealing personality and famous name gained him election to the New York State Senate as a Democrat in a heavily Republican area. In 1912, during his reelection campaign, he came in contact with large numbers of people and, as a result, developed typhoid fever. The illness hampered his campaign, but he recovered and won reelection. His only other notable illnesses were appendicitis and subsequent appendectomy in 1915 and, after a tour of the World War I Western Front during the influenza epidemic in 1918, pneumonia.

During the presidential election of 1912, FDR was an early supporter of Woodrow Wilson, the Governor of New Jersey. In March 1913, his support was rewarded by his being made Assistant Secretary of the Navy, a post he held throughout the war years. Vigorously healthy himself, FDR led a national campaign for physical fitness during the war; a photograph used to promote his fitness campaign shows Roosevelt leading a group in calisthenics. He even arranged for members of President Wilson's cabinet to take physical training in a park along the Potomac, with disastrous consequences for Franklin Lane, Secretary of the Interior, who had a fatal heart attack while performing the exercises.

After the war, and despite his youth, Roosevelt's national prominence (partly based on name association with his famous cousin and former president, Theodore) led to his nomination as the vice-presidential candidate on the Democratic Party ticket. He ran with Governor James Cox of Indiana in a hopeless campaign against Warren Harding, Senator from Ohio, and his reserved Vermont running mate, Calvin Coolidge. Campaign photographs show Roosevelt marching in political parades besides Cox and giving stump speeches, his youthful vigor and strength clearly evident.

After his unsuccessful vice-presidential campaign, FDR returned to New York City and turned his energies to a corporate law practice, meanwhile planning his run for the governorship of New York as a stepping-stone to the presidency. He volunteered to be president of the Boy Scout Foundation of Greater New York and, in that capacity, on July 27, 1921, he visited a scout camp at Lake Kanowahke, near Bear Mountain on the Hudson River. Photos show him marching and posing with a large group of scouts.

A few days later, he helped a friend pilot a yacht, the *Sabalo,* from New York to his family's summer retreat at Campobello Island off the coast of Maine. There, Roosevelt engaged in strenuous activity, playing with his children, fishing, sailing, swimming, and jogging. Between recreational activities, he met with his political aide, Louis Howe, to plan his campaign for the governorship. On Wednesday, August 10, FDR spotted a small forest fire on a nearby island, sailed over with his family to put it out, then swam in the icy waters of a nearby lake. That evening he felt too tired to dress for dinner, was achy and chilly, and retired early. The next day he had a temperature of 102° and noted that his left leg dragged when he got out of bed; soon he could not move it at all. By that afternoon, he was unable to move either leg. On Friday, August 12, he was paralyzed from the waist down. A weakness of the thumb muscles of his right hand subsequently developed, making it very difficult for him to write.

Although the incubation period for polio is usually 8 to 10 days, this can vary between 5 and 35 days. The two-week interval between Roosevelt's attendance at the Boy Scout encampment and the onset of his symptoms was well within that period.

Ironically, Roosevelt's sheltered childhood had been a prime cause of his developing polio as an adult. Very young infants exposed to the poliomyelitis virus rarely develop paralysis. Rather, the disease usually runs a far more benign course of fever and general malaise. However, when the disease is first encountered as an older child or as an adult, the infection is far more serious and usually results in paralysis. The same public health measures that protected children from the many deadly infections spread by contaminated water or food also shielded them from exposure to the polio virus. Because FDR had not acquired immunity to polio as a child, his exposure to the boy scouts at the encampment, some of whom were probably carriers of the virus, resulted in his falling prey to the paralytic form of polio.

Typical of the early phases of polio, Roosevelt suffered a great deal of pain, because sensory pathways are unaffected by this viral disease of the spinal cord. However, the anterior horn (motor) cells are selectively attacked; unaffected or less affected muscles typically develop spasm, and the resulting cramps are quite painful. Dr. Bennett, the local family physician, at first diagnosed a cold, but soon began searching nearby resorts for a specialist in nervous system diseases. He found Dr. William Williams Keen of Philadelphia, a pioneer neurosurgeon who had helped to care for President Cleveland during his secret operation for cancer on the yacht Oneida in 1893. Keen, now in his eighties, drove to Lubec, Maine, and took a launch to Campobello where he spent the night.

Keen's diagnosis was, "a clot of blood from a sudden congestion...in the lower spinal cord, temporarily removing the power to move though not to feel." Keen recommended heavy massage, which aggravated the pain of the sore, spastic muscles. A few days later, in a letter to Eleanor Roosevelt, Keen changed his diagnosis to "a lesion of the spinal cord" and became more pessimistic about the prognosis. He enclosed a bill for the then staggering sum of $600, and the Roosevelts never forgave him for either the misdiagnosis or the bill. Five years later, however, in a letter to Roosevelt, Keen commented on Mrs. Roosevelt's strenuous efforts to provide 24-hour care during this period, calling her "one of my heroines." Indeed, she devoted herself fully to the care of her husband, following doctors' suggestions to the letter. The summer became a nightmare for everyone, which Eleanor later referred to as "a trial by fire."

Roosevelt remained in severe pain. After ten days, the family located Dr. Robert W. Lovett, an orthopedist and specialist in poliomyelitis, vacationing in Newport, Rhode Island. He immediately came to Campobello, changed the diagnosis to polio, stopped the massage, and warned the family of the psychological impact of polio, particularly the severe depression that usually developed. Members of the family forced themselves to remain cheerful and optimistic in each other's presence, a brave pattern they maintained throughout Roosevelt's illness.

Arrangements were made for his transfer to Presbyterian Hospital in New York City, where he was placed under the care of another orthopedist, Dr. George Draper, a friend since their days as classmates at Harvard. In trying to keep the truth about Roosevelt's condition from the public, his aide, Louis Howe had FDR strapped to a stretcher, transferred from his second-story bedroom down a steep hill to a fishing boat, then moved to an iron-wheeled baggage cart and painfully jostled over cobblestones to a train. Meanwhile, waiting reporters were diverted to a launch landing passengers at the other end of the dock. When they finally caught up, FDR was lying comfortably covered in his berth, waving through the window and smiling.

Howe's press release mentioned little except that FDR was recovering from an attack of infantile paralysis and that the use of his legs was affected. The *New York Times* reported some temporary paralysis below the knees, but that Roosevelt was recovering and "will definitely not be crippled." The day after that article appeared, in typical FDR style, Roosevelt wrote a note to Times publisher, Adolph S. Ochs, saying that, "while the doctors were ... telling me ... that I was not going to suffer any permanent effects ... I had, of course, the usual dark suspicion that they were just saying nice things ... but now that I have seen the same statement officially made in *The New York Times*, I feel immensely relieved because I know it must be so."

Roosevelt was discharged from the Presbyterian Hospital on October 28, and went to the family home in Manhattan. The conclusion of the discharge summary was "not improving." During this period, his knees were allowed to remain bent (probably with a pillow under them to relieve some of the pain of the muscle spasm). As a result he developed shortening (flexion contractures) of the hamstring muscles, a complication usually avoided once physicians learned more about treating polio patients. His legs had to be forcibly straightened so that he could stand. Eventually, plaster casts were applied with wedges inserted behind the knees. The wedges were progressively enlarged to gradually straighten the knees, painfully stretching the contracted muscles. FDR described this agonizing process as "like being on a rack," although he bore the pain stoically and eventually became able to straighten his knees.

Despite pain, FDR faithfully carried out strenuous exercise programs in an attempt to strengthen his weakened muscles. He made little progress, however, and his paralysis remained extensive; he had difficulty in sitting upright without assistance. Weakened ankle muscles resulted in a foot-drop that required supporting his feet with plaster casts. In spring 1922, he went to Boston to be fitted with heavy steel braces that extended from his feet to his hips, with shoes attached to correct the foot-drop. While wearing them, he could stand upright, but once standing it was impossible for him to maintain his balance, even using a heavy cane. It took strong men to physically lift, carry, and then support him to prevent his falling. After several years of hard work strengthening his arm muscles, he finally was able to propel himself crablike along the floor using his now powerful arms, and he could wrestle with his children while prone.

A close friend, Vincent Astor, suggested the use of his "swimming tank," and Roosevelt found that he could do more with his legs while in warm water. As a result, he traveled to Florida each of the next four winters, lived on a houseboat, and sought warm patches of water in which to swim and fish. Summers were spent in Marion, Massachusetts, working on special exercises with Dr. William McDonald, a general practitioner with considerable success treating polio victims. McDonald insisted that patients be self-sufficient, even if it meant dragging themselves painfully up stairs, which Roosevelt did.

Another friend, George Foster Peabody, introduced Roosevelt to a spa he owned in western Georgia, where the mineral-laden water gushing from a rock remained at a constant 88°. Roosevelt first went to Warm Springs on October 3,

1924; finding that he was able to stand unaided in the warm water, he became enthusiastic about the therapeutic potentialities of the spa. A reporter from Atlanta learned about Roosevelt's presence at the spa, and an article he wrote about it soon resulted in other hopeful polio victims visiting Warm Springs. The older guests of the ramshackle Merriweather Inn objected to their presence; after all, polio might be contagious, and at any rate, the sight of crippled people was displeasing. As a result, in 1926, FDR arranged to buy the Inn from Peabody for $195,000, using money he had inherited from his father. In 1927, he converted it to a facility for the care of polio victims. People who could pay for their care did so, but no one was turned away. Roosevelt received contributions from wealthy friends to help maintain the facility, but he went into debt running it. A gift from Edsel Ford paid for construction of a shed to cover the pool so that it could be used in any weather.

The field of rehabilitation medicine was in its infancy during Roosevelt's time; most of the impetus for its later development arose from the large number of disabled military personnel from World War II. Roosevelt played a major role in establishing the field. By acting as a practitioner himself, he learned a great deal about exercise programs as part of his own treatment, and he taught these exercises to other patients at Warm Springs. Roosevelt also taught anatomy and the function of muscle groups affected by polio, and designed specific exercises for each patient; the other patients called him "Doctor Roosevelt" and he liked that.

Because the American Orthopedic Association (AOA) was the professional organization concerned with establishing the field of rehabilitation medicine, Roosevelt wanted their endorsement to establish the authenticity of his program at Warm Springs. When he learned that the AOA annual convention was scheduled to take place in nearby Atlanta, he wrote asking for permission to address the group, explain his therapeutic program and the beneficial results being obtained, and ask for "technical guidance and help." He was turned down. When he called for an explanation, an officer of the Association told him could not address the group because he was not a physician.

A furious FDR ordered a car, drove to the convention, and buttonholed as many delegates as possible, prowling the corridors of their hotels in his wheelchair. As a result of his lobbying efforts, a resolution was introduced to approve the establishment of a committee of three orthopedists to evaluate the program at Warm Springs.

Following the advice of this committee, Roosevelt brought in Dr. LeRoy W. Hubbard, a New York orthopedist experienced in the care of polio victims. Hubbard was accompanied by Helen Mahoney, a nurse who had learned physical therapy while working with polio victims in the epidemic of 1916. She was a tough, hard-working, hard-driving person, who worked closely with Roosevelt. Her personality was so intimidating that, although FDR called everyone by his or her first name or a nickname that he invented, he never dared call her anything but Miss Mahoney.

The team of Roosevelt, Hubbard, and Mahoney gradually established a major center to treat polio victims, regardless of their ability to pay. With assistance from Basil O'Connor, a former law partner, a public foundation was organized to support the center. Their fund-raising effort evolved into the National Foundation for Poliomyelitis. Later, as president, annual "Birthday Balls" were held on FDR's birthday to raise money for the foundation, and people all over the country sent coins to the White House to support the research in a program called the March of Dimes. When this research, largely supported and guided by the foundation, led to the virtual elimination of new cases of polio, its name was shortened to "The National Foundation," and it base was broadened to conquer new problems. Recently, the name was officially changed back to the March Of Dimes.

Roosevelt's legacy in fighting this disease was almost as great as his political legacy. At the time he started his program at Warm Springs, disability was considered a shameful embarrassment to a family, and people with deformities or who required wheelchairs or crutches were kept out of sight to avoid offending the sensibilities of others. Handicapped people were hidden at home or in custodial institutions or "homes for incurables," grim places that resembled penal institutions, with strict rules and discipline, as if a physical handicap was the result of some moral failing. The mission statement of the Society for the Ruptured and Crippled in New York City exemplifies the prevailing attitude: This philanthropic organization had teachers who would "stimulate and train neglected minds and stagnant brains into an activity that will transform from ignorance and vice into moral purity and beauty..."

Conversely, at Roosevelt's Warm Springs, efforts were made to keep people happy, and fun was considered an essential part of therapy. An excellent staff was developed, with emphasis on functional training. The surroundings were beautiful and meals were festive, often held with good china and tablecloths, served by waiters in dinner-jackets. Movies, bridge tournaments, theatricals, excursions, and spontaneous activities were encouraged. Roosevelt hired local high school students to serve as "push-boys;" always within ear-shot, they were available to move wheelchair patients wherever they might want to go. Girls from a local college were hired as assistant physical therapists; having young people around added to the pleasant atmosphere. In a real sense, Roosevelt was the main therapist, creating at Warm Springs a center with an entirely unique approach to polio and similar problems. As an alumnus of the institution put it,

PLATE 1

THE CHOLERA IN EGYPT: QUARANTINE EXAMINATION AT BRINDISI.

Passengers on a ship undergoing quarantine examination at Brindisi during the Egyptian cholera epidemic of 1883. Cholera frequently spread from its persistent reservoir in India causing repeated pandemics; ships that traveled from India through the Suez Canal after it opened on November 17th, 1869 repeatedly brought cholera to Egypt. Cholera spread to other ports, such as Hamburg, and the severe epidemic of the disease in Germany in 1883 lead the Kaiser's government to send Dr. Robert Koch (who had recently announced the discovery of the tubercle bacillus) with a group of scientists to Egypt to find the etiologic agent. In August, 1883 they identified the causative organism in material from the intestines of fatal cases in Alexandria. (Source: Wellcome Library, London.)

PLATE 2

General Napoleon Bonaparte visiting his troops afflicted with bubonic plague at Jaffa, Egypt, in 1799. He is shown in the courtyard of the hospital, touching the swollen glands (buboes) in the armpit of a soldier. The gesture mimics the supposed healing effects of the "king's touch," long after such an effect was no longer believed, and several years before Napoleon declared himself emperor. After they defeated the Mameluke army near the pyramids, bubonic plague severely affected and weakened the French troops in Egypt. The defeat of the French Navy by Admiral Nelson at the mouth of the Nile doomed them and Napoleon abandoned the entire army, sneaking away on August 23, 1799, shortly after this scene occurred. (Source: National Library of Medicine, NIH.)

PLATE 3

A group portrait of six rat-proofing volunteers posing with the rat traps, cages, and collection buckets used during the plague epidemic in New Orleans that lasted from 1914 to 1920. Outbreaks of bubonic plague in several American cities in the twentieth century led to extensive measures to control the rat population. Public Health Service campaigns to control plague were instituted in several cities including in San Francisco during a series of plague epidemics that occurred there between 1900 and 1924. Currently the few cases of plague that occur in the U.S. each year have been acquired from close contact with small field mammals such as marmots and prairie dogs in the southwestern states. (Source: National Library of Medicine, NIH.)

PLATE 4

Malaria control was necessary in the Southern U.S. in the 1930's during the construction of the TVA dams and other flood control projects. The elimination of mosquitoes was much more difficult than in the Panama Canal Zone since a much larger area with innumerable breeding sites for the insects had to be treated. Crop-dusting planes were used and mosquito breeding sites were treated from the air, as shown in this picture. (Source: National Library of Medicine, NIH.)

PLATE 5

Preventing spread of yellow fever during construction of the Panama Canal. A screened bed to prevent mosquitoes from feeding on a yellow fever or malaria patient in the "old hospital" (the Ancon Hospital) in the Canal Zone in Panama. Later the hospital was renamed the Gorgas Hospital in honor of Dr. William Crawford Gorgas (later Brigadier General and Surgeon General of the Army), whose anti-mosquito campaign successfully eradicated yellow fever and malaria from the area and made successful completion of the canal possible. These mosquito borne diseases had crippled the French attempt to build the canal under DeLesseps so severely that they abandoned the project in 1889 and they almost defeated the American effort also. After U.S. army doctors, led by Walter Reed, convincingly demonstrated the role of the mosquito in the transmission of yellow fever in Havana in 1898, preventive measures controlled the diseases there. Successful preventive measures were subsequently instituted in Panama and protected the workers sufficiently to permit construction of the canal. The screened bed shown here not only protected patients from the annoyance of the mosquitoes but prevented the mosquitoes from picking up the virus and spreading it to other people. (Source: National Library of Medicine, NIH.)

PLATE 6

Section of the bronze doors at the entrance to the rotunda of the U.S. Capitol building known as the Columbus Doors. The doors are the work of Randolph Rogers and contain a series of historical episodes that Rogers based on the narratives in Washington Irving's *Life and Voyages of Christopher Columbus* (1835). This panel depicts Columbus' arrival in the New World; on the right one of Columbus' sailors is carrying off a native girl, the actions that are thought to have resulted in the appearance of syphilis in the Old World shortly after Columbus' men returned home. Columbus himself does not seem to approve. The spirochetal disease(s) of the natives were benign and ubiquitous, primarily skin infections that were acquired very early in life. When Europeans acquired this new infection it affected them much more severely and was spread primarily sexually, hence the significance of the sailor's actions. Completed in 1857 and cast by the Royal Bavarian Foundry (which is rumored to still own the models) in Munich in 1860, they were installed in 1863. The doors were initially intended to be placed at the entrance to the new House Wing near Statuary Hall but were moved to their current position of honor at the main entrance to the Rotunda when the building was remodeled in the mid-twentieth century. (Picture from the author's collection.)

PLATE 7

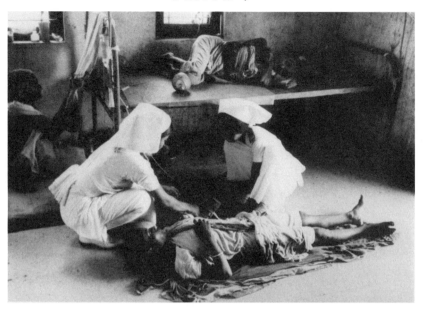

Emergency rehydration of a cholera patient at a World Health Organization dispensary near Calcutta, India, late in the twentieth century (exact date unknown). Two nurses are seen attaching an intravenous drip containing rehydration fluids to a female patient lying on the floor; two other female patients are awaiting treatment. Fluid replacement is life-saving in patients suffering from cholera. When it is available, the mortality of cholera is greatly diminished; oral methods of rehydration have been developed because of the limitations in the availability of intravenous fluids in the areas most frequently affected by cholera. The picture was taken in India, the initial site of most outbreaks of cholera (Asiatic cholera) and of the worst epidemics of the disease. (Source: W.H.O. via the National Library of Medicine, NIH.)

PLATE 8

AT THE GATES.
Our safety depends upon official vigilance.

"At the Gates," a cartoon that appeared in Harper's Weekly late in the 19th century (date uncertain) illustrating the effectiveness of the angel of cleanliness and quarantine blocking the entry and spread of epidemic diseases; the diseases illustrated are cholera, yellow fever and "small-pox." In the background the masts of ships can be seen, pointing to the usual methods of spread of these diseases by maritime commerce. Quarantine was the most effective measure when assiduously applied. Cleanliness was thought to eliminate the decaying vegetable and animal matter that produced "effluvia" and "malarias", toxic air-borne miasmas that contained the poisons that spread disease. Even before the knowledge of bacteriology revealed the reasons for the effectiveness of these measures, cleanliness helped prevent spread of disease, as did improved disposal of wastes, the main result of the sanitary campaigns of the late 19th century. (Source: National Library of Medicine, NIH.)

PLATE 9

Bubonic plague in the twentieth century: A medical officer examining a ship's crew for bubonic plague on arrival in the Thames. Plague had reappeared in England in 1902–3; it was again a problem from 1906–18, both times apparently brought in by ship and spreading from waterfront areas. Quarantine measures established along the Thames River included examination of everyone aboard incoming ships for buboes, swollen glands that are manifestations of plague; ships were kept from landing until all evidence of the disease had gone. "Watercolour" drawing by F. de Haanen, 1905. (Source: Wellcome Library.)

PLATE 10

On the left is a portion of a bas relief thought to be from the XVIIIth dynasty in Egypt (1580–1350 BCE.) It shows a priest named Ruma at a sanctuary of the goddess Astarte at Memphis who had an atro-

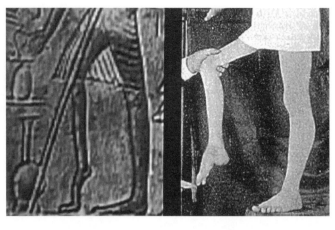

phied leg and "foot-drop" resulting from the muscle weakness, typical changes resulting from childhood poliomyelitis. On the right is a picture of a child who developed polio during one of the early epidemics of that disease in the U.S. in the 1890s. He shows the same changes. It is from the classic textbook *Pediatrics* by L. Emmet Holt.

PLATE 11

Photo showing future president Franklin D. Roosevelt march-ing at a Boy Scout encamp-ment at Lake Kanowahke, near Bear Mountain, NY. before he developed poliomyelitis. It is the last picture showing Roosevelt walk-ing without aid.

He was visiting the Scouts as President of the Boy Scout Foundation of Greater New York. (Source: Franklin D. Roosevelt Library.)

PLATE 12

A second photo taken on July 27, 1921 showing Franklin D. Roosevelt among a group of Boy Scouts at the encampment near Bear Mountain. In view of the known incubation period of polio, it is extremely likely that he became infected with the virus on this occasion as a result of exposure to the scouts, some of whom probably were carriers of the virus. He became ill two weeks later. (Source Franklin D. Roosevelt Library.)

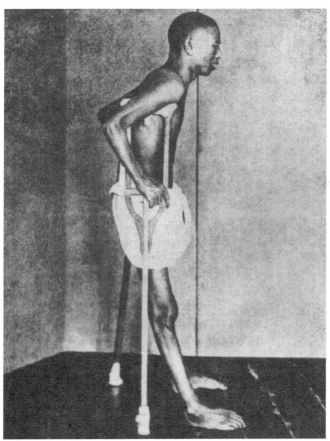

PLATE 13

A patient with beriberi who needs the aid of crutches to stand because of nerve damage, a typical feature of the disease. The picture was originally published in a book by Dr. Casimir Funk whose studies relating to beriberi led to his coining the word "vitamine," combining the term for "life" with "amine." Later the final "e" was removed when it was realized that not all these vital substances were amines. The patient is apparently Asiatic, possibly Japanese since they were among the groups most severely affected by the disease when the method of polishing the rice grains was changed in the late 19th century. (Source: National Library of Medicine, NIH.)

PLATE 14

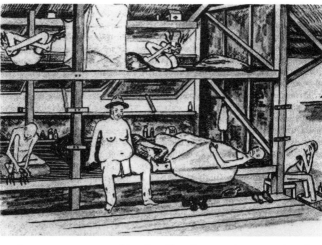

Cartoon drawn by an American soldier while a prisoner of war in a Japanese camp during World War II. It shows the main manifestations of beriberi: jagged lines like lightening strikes pointing to the legs and feet represent the severe pain from the neuropathy; some men are touching the affected area and one is soaking his feet in a tub, actions which decreased the pain somewhat. Two men obviously have heart failure from the effects of lack of thiamin (vitamin B1) on heart muscle; they show massive edema of the legs and body; one is too weak to sit up. Malnutrition, primarily manifest as beriberi, was the main cause of death among American and British/Australian/New Zealand POWs during World War II. (Originally published in *Internal Medicine in World War II*, Ed. Col. Robert S. Anderson, Volume 3, edited by W. Paul Havens, published by the Office of the Surgeon General, Department of the Army, Washington DC, 1968, p 273.)

PLATE 15

Painting representing the experiment testing various treatments for scurvy performed by Dr. James Lind in a hold made into a "clinical research unit" aboard the HMS Salisbury in May, 1747. This scene can be considered the birth of scientific, controlled clinical research. Lind is shown feeding orange or lemon juice to a patient; actually two of the twelve sailors received orange and lemon juices and they soon recovered enough to nurse the patients receiving the other suggested treatments for scurvy being tested. The patient shows typical manifestations of severe scurvy, weakness and multiple small hemorrhagic spots on his legs. (From a painting by Robert A. Thom in volume four of "A History of Medicine in Pictures" published by the Parke, Davis & Company in 1960.)

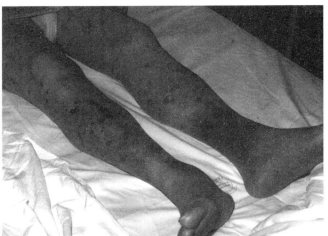

PLATE 16

Photo of legs of a man with "bachelor's scurvy" showing extensive skin hemorrhages typical of the disease. The term bachelor's scurvy arose in the twentieth century since most cases of scurvy seen then occurred in individuals who shopped infrequently and rarely ate fresh vegetables or salads, mimicking the cause of scurvy in sailors who did not have access to fresh food. (Photo by author.)

PLATE 17

Giving the daily lime juice ration to British sailors, after the recommendations of Joseph Lind were finally instituted because of the influence of Dr. Gilbert Blane when he became a commissioner of the Board of Sick and Wounded Sailors. The regular use of lime or lemon juice prevented scurvy in the British Navy and sailors were able to keep ships at sea for long periods, such as during the blockade of France during the Napoleonic Wars. Lind's work was credited with doubling the manpower of the British Navy. This watercolor painting by E.L. Moss actually shows the daily distribution of lime juice aboard the ship *Alert* during an 1875 polar expedition to the arctic; note the caged pigeons probably sent out to look for dry land. Despite the use of the lime juice, scurvy interrupted the expedition, probably because the West Indian limes used were not good sources of vitamin C; lemons were good sources but the British used the terms lemon and lime interchangeably, leading to confusion and the wrong choice for outfitting the expedition. (From Carpenter KJ, *The History of Scurvy and Vitamin C* New York: Cambridge Univ. Press, 1986; original from the Scott Polar Institute, Cambridge, England.)

PLATE 18

"Exquisite taste with an enlarged understanding," illustrating the typical patient with gout: an older man enjoying his wine and rich food, with the painful foot wrapped in linen and elevated on a "gout stool," crutches behind him. His smile is inappropriate since acute gouty arthritis is an extremely painful affliction, but it was a frequent source of mirth in cartoons that often depicted the association of the disease with affluence and the ingestion of wine, as in this instance. Original is a drawing by E.Y. Esq, engraved by G. Hunt, and printed by G. Hunt, London. (Courtesy of the Boston Medical Library in the Francis A. Countway Library of Medicine, Harvard Medical School, Boston.)

"He helped to change the way the American society viewed the handicapped, and he helped to alter the way the handicapped see themselves."

Roosevelt did not want to return to politics until he was strong enough to walk without assistance, but progress was slow. Thinking that political life would be the best therapy, Eleanor and Louis Howe got New York Governor Al Smith to ask Roosevelt to place his name in nomination for the presidency at the 1924 Democratic National Convention, after convincing him that it was important for Smith, a big-city Tammany politician, to have support from wealthy, upstate patricians. FDR reluctantly accepted, and he attended every session of the convention. His son, James, brought him in a wheelchair early, before other delegates arrived. Roosevelt used an inconspicuous entrance close to his own seat and walked with a crutch on one side and James' arm on the other to a special large armchair that helped him stay upright. After each session, he remained in his seat until the other delegates left, although visitors who remained in the galleries would cheer him on in his struggle to walk.

Although fearing to lose balance and fall, Roosevelt was determined to walk unaided to the podium to deliver his carefully rehearsed "Happy Warrior" speech that would nominate Smith. (This speech would be the first of many to be carried on radio.) James assisted him to the back of the speaker's platform. After being introduced, the applause tapered quickly as he struggled forward. Wearing braces, FDR slowly and grimly walked the roughly 15 feet to the podium, alternately advancing each crutch, carefully shifting his weight and swinging the opposite leg forward, then repeating the process, sweating profusely from the effort. James stayed close behind, ready to catch him if he lost his balance, while the hushed auditorium watched, remembering his vigorous vice-presidential campaign four years earlier. When he finally reached and grasped the podium, he looked up, threw his head back, and broke into his famous broad grin. The convention hall erupted in cheers. Those who were present always remembered that moment.

Although the speech did not gain Smith the nomination—the convention deadlocked for a 103 ballots—it firmly reestablished FDR as a national figure; his return was considered the high point of the convention. At Warm Springs, he continued his own demanding therapeutic exercise program and made gradual progress. When he first discovered the health spa at Warm Springs, Roosevelt could stand unaided buoyed by warm water up to his chin. By 1928, he could stand in water up to his armpits. He always believed that he would have eventually been able to walk again if he could have continued the exercise program, but the tiny progress he made over many years shows that his innate optimism overcame his judgment. Roosevelt never accepted the hopeless prognosis given him by the physicians, clinging to the belief that hard work would gradually strengthen the atrophic muscles and allow him to walk again.

Roosevelt successfully nominated Al Smith for the presidency at the Democratic National Convention in 1928. Although controversy arose among the Roosevelt family and advisors regarding the advisability of his running for the governorship of New York, telegrams and phone calls poured in to Warm Springs pressuring Roosevelt to accept the nomination. Howe felt that the timing was wrong: It was a Republican year, and he urged Roosevelt to resist. The governorship was a two-year term, and Roosevelt believed that two more years of therapy would enable him to get rid of the braces, but now Smith needed his help to carry the pivotal state of New York. On the day before the nominating convention for the governorship, Roosevelt made himself unavailable to calls from Smith, going on a picnic and then giving a speech at a nearby high school. But Eleanor arranged for Smith to reach FDR by telephone; Roosevelt had to be carried down the stairs of the high school and taken to a local drug store, where he talked on a pay phone with his braced legs sticking out of the booth. He finally agreed that if nominated, he would accept.

Roosevelt's health was an issue during the campaign, and he met it forthrightly, giving more campaign speeches and public appearances than anyone before. Arrangements for these appearances were not always appropriate, and once he had to haul himself up a fire escape in the back of a building to get to the podium without his disability being too obvious to the public. On one occasion, he listed all the towns in which he had spoken during the previous several days, including a talk in Schenectady earlier that same evening, concluding, "Too bad about this unfortunate sick man, isn't it?"

Al Smith was buried at the polls, even losing New York. However, Roosevelt was narrowly elected to the governorship by 25,564 votes. He was reelected to a second two-year term, after having neglected his therapy to work hard and effectively as governor. By 1932, he was clearly the leading contender for the Democratic presidential nomination. He broke tradition, flying to Chicago to accept the nomination personally, pledging a "new deal for the American people" in his speech. He was elected, and remained president until his death.

While Roosevelt was president, it was an unspoken rule among reporters covering the White House that photographs were never taken of him being carried, or painfully attempting to walk supported by an aide and wearing heavy steel braces hidden by his clothes. He was only photographed after he was assisted to a well-braced standing position. He sat for most photos, while reporters stood around his desk; his uptilted chin, grin, and long cigarette holder became famous from innumerable pictures and cartoons.

Although the public knew he was disabled, the full extent of his disability was concealed by the press. Because the news conferences he held twice weekly before the war were conducted in his office, he was seated at his desk when reporters entered and left the room. As a result even experienced, hard-boiled newsmen were startled on the rare occasions when they did see him being carried into a room, or propelling himself in his wheelchair. Foreign affairs reporter John Gunther recalled that, "in the 1930s ... in Europe, I repeatedly met men in important positions who had no idea the President was disabled."

During his presidency, Roosevelt traveled more extensively than any previous chief executive—usually by private train, since he did not like flying. During his twelve years as president, he logged 544,000 railroad miles in over 400 separate trips, even though he had great difficulty maintaining his balance while sitting on a train. At his orders, the train's speed stayed under 35 miles an hour during the day to minimize jostling and swaying; at night, while FDR was in bed, the engineer made up for lost time.

The code of silence that effectively prevented mention of his disability in public was violated on one occasion when Eleanor Roosevelt, during one of her many trips as First Lady, was lecturing in Akron, Ohio. Questions were submitted to her in writing, and there were gasps of surprise and embarrassment when she read aloud one question, "Do you think your husband's illness has affected his mentality?"

The room was quiet as she paused, and then in her characteristic, crackling voice she answered, "I am glad that question was asked. The answer is yes.... Anyone who has gone through great suffering is bound to have a greater sympathy and understanding of the problems of mankind." There was a standing ovation.

The lack of mention of Roosevelt's disability in the press has been referred to as "the splendid deception." Ordinarily he did not let visitors to the White House see him in his wheelchair, and when he reviewed troops during the war, he was usually seated in his car or standing with support. But when visiting wounded men in hospitals, which he did every chance he got, he purposely had himself lifted into his wheelchair and wheeled slowly around the wards, especially where there were amputees.

One notable occasion reveals how FDR liked to think of himself as a specialist in rehabilitation medicine. While in Hawaii during the key conference with Admiral Nimitz and General MacArthur about Pacific strategy, he inspected every war installation on the island and visited the 5,000-bed naval hospital on top of Aiea Heights above Pearl Harbor. At one point, he was wheeled into the room of a Marine lieutenant who had been wounded by mortar fire on Saipan; his leg had been partly blown off; he had put on a tourniquet and awaited help. None came, and despairing of being found, he took out his combat knife, completed the amputation, then dragged himself to safety. When FDR entered the man's room, he said, "Good morning doctor. I understand you are quite a surgeon. Well, I happen to be a pretty good orthopedist myself, so what about a consultation."

BIOWARFARE AND POLIOMYELITIS. The history of poliomyelitis describes a disease of ancient lineage that did not become a cause of greatly feared epidemics until human actions modified its natural history. The epidemics of poliomyelitis resulted from the unintentional consequences of public health measures that were enormously beneficial. Although polio is not transmitted to any great extent from person-to-person, it is transmitted through contaminated of food and water supplies, a feature that could encourage the purposeful transmission of disease.

Fortunately, a large proportion of the world's population has been actively immunized with vaccines that should produce lifelong immunity. However, that immunity is not yet worldwide. Therefore, it is not possible to rule out the use of polio virus for biowarfare in some parts of the world.

ADDITIONAL READING

Alsop J. FDR, 1882–1945: A Centenary Remembrance. New York: Viking Press, 1982.
Asbell B. FDR's extra burden. Am Heritage 1973;24:21.
Bishop J. FDR's Last Year, April 1944–April 1945. New York: W. Morrow, 1974.
Chase A. Magic Shots. New York: Wm. Morrow & Co, Inc, 1982.
Daniel TM, Robbins FC, eds. Polio. Rochester, NY: Univ of Rochester Press, 1997.
Frost WH. Epidemiological studies of acute anterior poliomyelitis. U.S. Hygiene Laboratory Bulletin 1913, No. 90.
Frost WH. Poliomyelitis (infantile paralysis), what is known of its cause and modes of transmission. Public Health Reports. 1916;31:1817.
Gallagher HG. FDR's Splendid Deception. New York: Dodd, Mead, 1985.
Graham OL Jr, Wander MR, eds. Franklin D. Roosevelt, His Life And Times: An Encyclopedic View. Boston: G.K. Hall, 1985.
Hare R. The antiquity of disease caused by bacteria and viruses, a review of a problem from a bacteriologist's point of view. In: Diseases in Antiquity. Brothwell D, Sandison AT, eds. Springfield, IL: Chas C. Thomas, 1967.
Hoy S. Chasing Dirt, The Pursuit of Cleanliness. New York: Oxford Univ Press, 1995.
Lash JP. Eleanor and Franklin; The Story of Their Relationship, Based on Eleanor Roosevelt's Private Papers. New York: Norton, 1971.

Marks G, Beatty WK. *Epidemics.* New York: Scribner, 1976.

McIntire RT. *White House Physician.* New York: G.P. Putnam's Sons, 1946.

Nathanson N. The eradication of poliomyelitis in the United States. *Rev Infect Dis* 1982;4:940.

Paul JR. *A History of Poliomyelitis.* New Haven: Yale Univ Press, 1971

Rogers N. *Dirt and Disease, Polio Before FDR.* New Brunswick, NJ: Rutgers Univ Press, 1992.

Spink WW. *Infectious Diseases, Prevention and Treatment during the Nineteenth and Twentieth Centuries.* Minneapolis: Univ of Minnesota Press, 1978.

Tang HLE. The pathology of leadership. In: William Henneman Medical Books, *Franklin Roosevelt: A Puzzling Diagnostic Problem.* London: Cox Wyman, Ltd. 1969.

Tomes N. *The Gospel of Germs: Men, Women, and the Microbe in American Life.* Cambridge, MA: Harvard Univ Press, 1998.

PART TWO

———————⁂———————

Noninfectious Diseases

CHAPTER 9

BERIBERI

AN EPIDEMIC AFFECTING
RICE EATERS

N OT ALL EPIDEMIC DISEASES ARE THE RESULT OF INFEC-
tious agents. Sometimes, technologic advances in food processing that
may improve shelf life or appearance may also change the nutritional content of
a staple food product. Beriberi and pellagra are two diseases that resulted from
such "improvements." Other Industrial Age developments led to rickets becoming an epidemic disease in Europe during the seventeenth and eighteenth centuries, and a political-commercial treaty triggered an outbreak of gout in the
eighteenth century. These epidemics of metabolic diseases, brought on by historic human actions, are the subject of the following chapters.

Beriberi had been an infrequent, sporadic disease in the rice-eating areas of
the world until late in the nineteenth century, when it erupted into a severe,
widespread, persistent epidemic, killing tens of thousands. It was the main cause
of death among American and British prisoners of the Japanese during World
War II. The disease persists in the United States today among people with certain forms of malnutrition, especially alcoholics, whose alcohol consumption
may make them deficient in vitamin B1 (thiamin).

The nineteenth century epidemic was a by-product of the Industrial
Revolution and the invention of new methods of rice milling. Although initially
infection was the favorite theory of cause (as was the case with all epidemic diseases at that time), extensive research early in the twentieth century in the Far
East, Europe, and the United States uncovered the link between thiamin deficiency and beriberi. Effective means of prevention were available by the 1930s.

The causes of epidemic beriberi resemble those phenomena that led to the pellagra epidemic in the United States, which occurred almost simultaneously. In both cases, new food processing technology was a key factor: Investigators of the cause of pellagra also had to disprove an infectious etiology before convincing evidence of a nutritional cause was accepted. The studies that brought understanding of the causes of beriberi and pellagra led to several Nobel Prizes.

THE DISEASE.   Beriberi is a complex disease with two main manifestations. One is a form of polyneuritis (damage to multiple nerves) that causes pain and loss of muscle function (paralysis); this is known as the "dry" or paralytic form of beriberi. Typically, the affected individual will drag a foot along the ground when walking ("foot drop") because of weakness in the muscles that hold the foot at right angles to the ankle. More extensive paralysis can develop so that, ultimately, the patient is bedridden and too weak to eat; death soon follows.

In other cases, beriberi affects the heart, in a form of myocarditis (or more accurately, a myocardiopathy). This is the "wet" or edematous form of beriberi. The weakness of the heart muscle causes the heart to enlarge (dilate), and an unusual type of heart failure develops. Because the defect in nutrition impairs metabolism in all tissues, there is an initial increase in cardiac output, a form of compensation to deliver more oxygen to the inefficient tissues. The extra load on the heart contributes to the development of heart failure; because this occurs while the heart is still increasing the amount of blood it pumps, the syndrome is known as "high output failure." This heart failure causes accumulation of fluid in the tissue, or *edema*. Because patients developing beriberi usually have multiple causes of malnutrition that can cause edema, such as protein deficiency, the edema can become massive. Patients who develop heart failure usually die quickly. It is not clear what determines which patients contract polyneuritis and which contract the cardiac form of the disease.

Many derivations have been suggested for the word beriberi, including the Singhalese word for weakness (*blayrhee*), because of the paralysis resulting from the polyneuropathic, "dry," paralytic form of beriberi; or, it may derive from a Hindu word for swelling (*bharbari*), referring to the edema that results from the heart failure seen in the "wet" or edematous form of the disease.

A deficiency of a micronutrient, vitamin B1 or *thiamin*, was eventually found to be the cause of beriberi, and the properties of that vitamin, when known, helped to explain some observations on the frequency of the disease made earlier in the study of the epidemic. For example, it was found that about 70 percent of the thiamin in rice is removed when the crude grains are milled and, because the thiamin is soluble in water, much of what is left after milling is removed by washing. Additional losses occur as some thiamin is dissolved into the cooking water. This fact explained why, in one study, a low incidence of beriberi was found among the monks in a monastery but a high incidence of the disease was present among the nuns in a nearby convent, although both groups ate the same test diet containing polished rice. It turned out that the more fastidious nuns washed the rice before cooking it.

In Japan, because polished, white rice was considered more attractive and desirable than the darker rice, beriberi was more common among the well-to-do than the poorer classes, who could not afford the polished rice. This preference for polished rice led to variations in the incidence of the disease that puzzled investigators for a long while. For example, impoverished rickshaw boys in Japan seemed to be immune, and in a Brazilian study done in the late nineteenth century, it was found that slaves did not get beriberi, whereas wealthy slave-owners did.

HISTORY OF BERIBERI. A disease resembling beriberi is found in Chinese medical writings 1200 years ago, and knowledge of the disease existed in Japan for about as long. In those countries, it was known as *kakké*. As early as 1611, people were described as having paralysis of the hands and feet—in retrospect probably beriberi—and the Governor-General of the Dutch East India Company described such paralysis. In 1642, Bontius, the first European physician to write about the disease, described cases of beriberi in Batavia, the capital of the Dutch East Indies (now Djakarta, capital of Indonesia). However, the incidence of beriberi skyrocketed after 1870, reaching epidemic proportions in many areas of the Far East. Records of the Japanese and Dutch navies reflect the epidemic nature of the disease during this period.

In 1873, a Dutch naval surgeon, Van Leent, noted an alarming 70 percent rate of beriberi among the Javanese sailors serving in the Dutch East Indies fleet, whereas among the European sailors it was less than 1 percent. He attributed the disease to diet; when he arranged for the Javanese to receive the same diet as the Dutch sailors, the disease disappeared.

Around 1870, 75 percent of the patients in the Tokyo naval hospital had *kakké*. Between 1878 and 1892, the Japanese navy recorded an average one-third of the enlisted men sick with *kakké* each year. In 1878, on a training voyage to New Zealand, 161 of 278 sailors developed *kakké* and 25 died. Concerned about the disease among his men, Japanese Admiral K. Takaki, scrutinized their diet, suspecting a deficiency of protein. The following year, he had the diet modified, adding more meat and milk, and reducing the amount rice. That year, only 14 cases appeared in his fleet, with no deaths. In 1887, the entire Navy received

Takaki's diet and while there had been over a thousand cases of *kakké* a year until then, that year there were only three. The Mikado made Takaki a baron.

Epidemic beriberi in the Far East was particularly severe among prisoners in many countries; in the Dutch East Indies, a three-month prison sentence was actually a death sentence. Prisoners in the Japanese navy had the highest incidence of beriberi, as did those in civilian Japanese prisons. In 1885, Takaki arranged to replace part of their rice ration with barley, and beriberi decreased markedly. Most Japanese medical authorities continued to doubt that the disease was nutritional, believing that this dietary change eliminated some rice-borne toxin from the diet.

The outbreaks of beriberi in the Japanese navy in 1870, and in Dutch East Indies around the same time, signaled the start of a major epidemic of this previously sporadic disease. Beriberi quickly became widespread, but not universal, in all rice-eating populations of the Far East. Early reports emphasized its effect on native troops working for the Dutch colonial administrators in what is now Indonesia; in 1908, 12 percent of the Philippine Scouts working with the U.S. army after the Spanish-American War were hospitalized with beriberi.

The Russo-Japanese War of 1904–1905. Beriberi had a major effect on the course of the Russo-Japanese War of 1904–1905, the first major war fought by the Japanese against a western power. The disease severely affected the Japanese army, but not the much larger but incompetently led Russian army. Estimates of the number of cases in the Japanese army range from 90,000 to 200,000 in a total combat force of about 400,000, and this, combined with heavy battle casualties, severely weakened the Japanese force. Although they had won just about every battle on sea and on land, dwindling manpower drawn from a much smaller population (45 million Japanese versus Russia's 136 million) finally forced them to agree to peace, thus gaining less territory than they sought when they attacked. (Japan did gain control over Korea.) Late in the war, when the Japanese army added barley to the rice as the standard ration, cases of beriberi decreased.

Of the total Japanese combat force of 400,000, about 20 percent died, a relatively high figure for a war in the second half of the nineteenth century. (By comparison, during the American Civil War, 13 percent of Union forces died of either disease or combat wounds.) In the Japanese army, 21,802 deaths were attributable to disease: 3,956 deaths from beriberi, 4,073 deaths from typhoid, 1,804 deaths from dysentery, and 11 deaths from typhus. Combat-related deaths totaled 58,387; thus, the ratio of deaths from disease to those from combat wounds was 0.37. This was the first time that disease caused fewer deaths than combat in a major war. In analyzing this statistic, however, it is important to note that total deaths were relatively great, and deaths in battle were extremely high because of the Japanese tactic of charging entrenched defenses relentlessly until their manpower gave out. Disease was still a very important cause of loss of manpower, however, and beriberi was a major contributor to the Japanese losses.

In the Japanese army, the numbers of deaths caused by typhoid and beriberi were about equal, while in Japan's civilian population during the war years, twice as many deaths occurred from beriberi as from typhoid.

Beriberi among World War II POWs. Beriberi was the main cause of death among American and British prisoners of war of the Japanese during World War II, a fact that may bring this disease "closer to home" for some of us. It was especially severe among the men who surrendered at Corregidor after the Battle of Bataan and survived the infamous "death march." Beriberi appeared within approximately three months in the prisoner-of-war camps in the Philippines, exactly the interval it took for it to appear in the inmates of the Dutch East India prisons half a century earlier. Similarly, beriberi was the main cause of death among the British prisoners who surrendered at Singapore and were kept in POW camps in Burma. These men were forced to work on the railroad the Japanese were building to enable them to attack Thailand, a subject made famous by the movie "Bridge over the River Kwai."

By the time of World War II, the etiology of beriberi had been established and the properties of the vitamin deficiency that was its basis were known. A British physician, C.R. Burgess, who did important studies of beriberi after the war, was one of the POWs of the Japanese in Singapore. He was very concerned about the development of beriberi in the prison camp. He got a message to a former technician, who was Chinese and still at liberty, to smuggle into him a copy of a book on thiamin from Singapore Medical College, where they had worked together. The book, *Vitamin B1 and It Use in Medicine,* by R. R. Williams and T. Spies, provided tables of the thiamin content of a whole range of foods, as well as information about its properties. For example, it mentioned that thiamin, being soluble in water, is removed from rice by washing. Burgess then minimized the washing of the polished rice made available for prisoners, minimized the volume of cooking water, and used any water left over for soups; he had the prisoners eat the rice polishings when they were available, and instituted other measures to minimize the occurrence of beriberi.

Interestingly, beriberi continued to be a problem in military units in the Far East long after World War II; not long ago it broke out in the Thai army, among officers but not among enlisted men. The officers were being given the more desirable polished rice, while the enlisted men were given cruder, unpolished (but more nutritious) rice. Affluence, it seems, is not a protection against disease resulting from technological advances.

Occasional cases of beriberi still are seen in the United States, mostly among alcoholics, whose requirement for thiamin is increased by the need to metabolize ethanol, accompanied by a poor diet. The entire syndrome of beriberi is seen in such patients, along with the cognitive manifestations of lack of thiamin needed for brain function. As a result, patients with thiamin deficiency are occasionally encountered in mental hospitals.

SEEKING THE CAUSE OF THE EPIDEMIC OF BERIBERI. Because the epidemic of beriberi appeared late in the nineteenth century, about the same time that the science of bacteriology began, studies seeking the cause of a new epidemic disease immediately focused on a possible microbial etiology. However, dietary factors began to receive attention after an accidental observation in chickens.

The concept of *miasmas* (poisonous vapors emanating from decaying organic material) still dominated medical thinking in the 1870s and 1880s. Miasmas were thought to be the etiology of beriberi; an alternate theory of its etiology postulated the presence of a toxin produced by rice contaminated by an agent, such as a mold. This theory was analogous to the known causes of outbreaks of epidemic lathyrism in India and ergotism (also called St. Anthony's fire) in Europe, which is caused by an ergot-producing fungus (*Claviceps purpurea*). A similar theory was also prominent in the thinking about the etiology of pellagra, as is discussed in the next chapter.

Observations of the incidence of beriberi among different population groups seemed to support the toxin concept. For example, of the 16,716 people with beriberi admitted to government hospitals in Malaya in 1909, 97.6 percent were of Chinese origin, whereas only 0.5 percent were Tamils, impoverished immigrants from Southern India. Yet both groups depended on rice as their main source of food. The difference was that the Tamils consumed cured or parboiled rice, in which the harvested grains are soaked in heated water and lightly milled to the remove husks, whereas the Chinese ate only finely milled, polished rice. Other physicians in Southeast Asia made similar observations, and all concluded that some toxin was present in polished rice. But all attempts to find such a toxin, or a contaminating microorganism that might be producing a toxin, were unsuccessful.

The processing of rice before cooking by different rice-eating populations was an important factor in whether beriberi appeared. The first step always involves the removal of the husk. Some groups then remove the thin outermost layer of the rice grain, known to botanists as the pericarp or "silverskin," by pounding the grains in a wooden mortar and pestle. The rice is then tossed in the air, allowing the wind to carry away the thin, light pericarp. This process usually carried off some of the next layer of the grain, the subpericarp or aleurone, which contains most of the fat and some of the protein, but left almost all of the innermost layer. This innermost layer primarily consists of starch, but also retains the germ or embryo at one end of the kernel. The embryo is packed with micronutrients (vitamins), and it is particularly rich in enzymes and their co-factors, which are needed for the germination and growth of the rice plant.

In parboiled rice (also known as cured or converted rice), the harvested grain is soaked in water and then heated until the husks burst. Light rubbing by hand removes the remnants of the husks, and the grain is ground coarsely, generally using water-driven stone mills.

Steel rollers for milling grain were invented about 1870. Their use permitted large amounts of rice to be milled rapidly using steam power. The resulting product, called "polished" rice, was both attractively white and had the important virtue of not spoiling as readily as rice prepared by other means, since the germ with its enzymes that cause the decay was removed. The ability to store rice without spoilage led to a greater yield of calories and protein from each harvest, thus providing more food to feed large numbers of people. As a result, this useful new food-processing technology was widely and quickly adopted in much of the Far East, particularly in crowded, urban, and poor regions. The cheaper product was commonly used for institutional diets, such as in prisons.

One of the early investigators of the cause of the epidemic of beriberi was a young Dutch military physician, Christian Eijkman, who had been assigned to the project by the Dutch government. Eijkman believed the classic theory that a toxin in the polished rice was responsible, or that organisms in the intestinal flora produced such a toxin from the rice. He reasoned that an antidote to that toxin must have been present in the pericarp of the unpolished rice, thus preventing people who used that product from getting the disease.

Among the Europeans, the Dutch were most troubled by beriberi because they had extensive and lucrative holdings in the East Indies. At that time, commissions were established to find the cause of several diseases, most notably cholera. Robert Koch and Louis Pasteur led the investigation of the microbial etiology of important diseases. Koch led a commission sent to Cairo to study an outbreak of cholera there and found the causative bacterial agent. Dr. Cornelius Pekelharing from the University of Utrecht was head of the commission set up by the Dutch to study beriberi; he started by going to Koch's laboratory in Berlin to improve his knowledge of bacteriology. Dr. Christian Eijkman had been sent home from Java to recover from severe attacks of malaria. Before returning to

Java, he also went to Koch's lab and met Pekelharing there. Ultimately, Eijkman took over Pekelharing's responsibilities in Java, although he was only thirty years old. He continued seeking a microbial cause of the disease, which Pekelharing had believed to be a round (coccoid) bacterium.

Eijkman injected blood and tissue extracts from autopsies on beriberi patients into rabbits, but none of them developed manifestations of beriberi. Believing that he needed larger numbers of animals on which to experiment, he switched to chickens, which were cheaper and more readily available. An assistant obtained leftover cooked rice from the army hospital adjacent to their laboratories to feed them. The chickens began to develop paralyses and showed peripheral nerve damage at autopsy, the findings Eijkman hoped to produce in his animals after injecting them with a causative organism. Strangely, however, these abnormalities developed whether or not the chickens were injected with the suspected bacteria, and they took six weeks to develop, surprisingly long for a bacterial disease.

On November 21, 1889, a new cook took over at the hospital, and he thought it was improper to give "military rice to civilian hens." Eijkman and his assistant were forced to reinstitute feeding the chickens cheap, crude rice, which they bought and milled themselves. After a few weeks on this diet, Eijkman noticed that the sick chickens had improved and no longer showed evidence of the peripheral neuritis. (Fortunately, he didn't give up on the chickens because of the inconsistent results and switch back to using rabbits, the favorite laboratory animal of most investigators.) Eijkman tested his observation by thoroughly polishing some of the rice himself; polyneuritis again developed in his fowl. When he then fed them the germ and pericarp that had been removed during the polishing, they were again cured.

These observations were a critical step in elucidating the etiology of beriberi. Subsequent studies of the "antineuritic factor" in the rice, using Eijkman's experimental model, soon led to an identification of the substance missing from the diet of the chickens. This observation led to the control and prevention of beriberi. Later, in 1929, Eijkman was awarded the Nobel Prize, despite the fact that, after he returned to Holland, he went back to thinking that the disease was infectious, postulating that the role of diet containing the rice polishings was to increase resistance to the infectious agent or its toxin. Late in his career, Eijkman gave a lecture about his earlier theory entitled "*Simplex Non Veri Sigillum*" (Simplicity is no sign of truth).

When studying the association of polished rice with beriberi, Eijkman compared the occurrence of the disease in prisons that used different rice preparations. The incidence of beriberi varied significantly: In fifty-two prisons that used rice from steam-run mills, thirty-seven had scores of inmates with beriberi. Of thirty-seven prisons that were supplied with crude rice that was then milled by hand by the prisoners, thirty-six were free of the disease, while one had some prisoners with beriberi, all of whom had been transferred from another jail. A half-milled rice product was used in twelve jails, five of which had prisoners with beriberi, but the incidence was less than 1 percent.

After Eijkman was transferred back to Holland, another young Dutch military physician, Gerrit Grijns, succeeded him in running the laboratory in Batavia. (Later, a new lab was built and called the Eijkman Institute.) Shortly after the beginning of the twentieth century, Grijns made a key intellectual leap, proposing a new, basic theory of nutritional deficiency disease. He pointed out that the disease affected peripheral nerves, and that the minimal blood flow to these nerves suggested that they had very little metabolic activity. He then reasoned that if a substance was necessary for maintenance of peripheral nerve tissue, but not indispensable for the metabolism of large organs, such as muscles, it could logically be assumed that the amount required was very small. Therefore, it would not be surprising that the existence of such a substance had escaped detection by the usual chemical analyses of the time. Grijns was thus the first to postulate the existence of small amounts of certain organic substances necessary for health; we now call them "essential micronutrients," whereas he called them "protective substances."

Casimir Funk was a Polish biochemist who had obtained his doctoral degree at age 20 in Geneva and then worked at the Pasteur Institute in Paris and in Berlin. In 1911, he was working at the Lister Institute in London, studying the anti-beriberi factor extracted from rice polishings. He isolated what was thought to be the factor that prevented or treated the paralysis in Eijkman's chickens. Because it was an amine and a protective substance necessary for life, he coined the term *vitamine*. In 1920, after another essential micronutrient had been found which was fat-soluble and thus not an amine (later it was called vitamin A), it was suggested that the final "e" in vitamine be dropped, and the word became vitamin. Later, it was realized that the essential nutrient actually isolated by Funk was nicotinic acid amide, subsequently found to be the anti-pellagra vitamin rather than the specific substance lacking in beriberi, which had been designated vitamin B. Later, it was renamed vitamin B1 and a variety of chemical names were suggested for it; an international committee finally agreed on the name thiamine in 1951.

This is not the place to document all the steps in the isolation, chemical characterization, and ultimately the synthesis of thiamin. However, one key worker in the field is worthy of note, an American named R.R. Williams. He began studies of beriberi in Manila in 1909, but returned to the United States later and became chemical director of the Bell Labs in New Jersey. Because beriberi had nothing to do with his responsibilities at Bell Labs, Williams continued to look for vitamin B_1 nights and weekends. He worked in a basement lab at the New York Hospital and also experimented on pigeons he kept in his garage at home. Crystals of the vitamin were obtained from yeast in 1931 by A. Windaus, a chemist at the University of Göttingen, Germany, working with chemists at the I.G. Farben Industrie in Berlin. By 1933, Williams had obtained enough purified, crystalline vitamin to work out its atomic composition and molecular structure. This work allowed the vitamin to be synthesized, and it became available as a medication and preventative for beriberi.

Once synthetic thiamin became available, many lives were saved. In 1937, when the crystalline vitamin was available, some was sent to Singapore, which had large numbers of beriberi cases at the time. Most were cardiac manifestations, the form of beriberi that was universally fatal, and patient usually died within 12 hours after admission to the hospital. Administering small doses of the crystalline thiamin, the hospital staff began to save patients; when the dose was raised to 5 to 8 mg, all 10 of the group so treated survived, showing improvement in blood pressure and heart rate within one to two hours after receiving a dose. The prognosis of beriberi was permanently changed, as long as treatment was available.

The growing science of nutrition developed evidence for the existence of many micronutrients, including trace metals, and the supplementation of commonly used foods with these essential nutrients has made vitamin deficiency diseases rare in the United States. The public imagination became as stirred by this dramatic development as by the triumphs of bacteriology, but this enthusiasm has also led to the development of what should be called "nutritional quackery." Millions are spent annually on food products and dietary supplements containing substances for which no evidence of need exists, and "vitamins" have become a panacea and sold for all sorts of imaginative purposes, even to be applied to hair or other body appendages.

The history of beriberi provides one of many examples of the principle that disease can be controlled if an essential step in the pathogenic sequence can be found and eliminated without a complete understanding of the cause.

ADDITIONAL READING

Anderson RS. *Internal Medicine in World War II, Vol. III, Infectious Diseases and General Medicine*. Washington, DC: Office of the Surgeon General, Department of the Army, 1968.

Blankenhorn MA, Vilter CF, et al. Occidental beriberi heart disease. *JAMA* 1946;*131*:717.

Bontius J. Concerning paralysis of the type the natives call beriberi. In: Major RH, ed. *Classic Descriptions of Disease*. Springfield, IL: Chas C. Thomas, 1932.

Carpenter KJ, Sutherland B. Eijkman's contribution to the discovery of vitamins. *J Nutr* 1995;*125*:155.

Carpenter KJ. *Beriberi, White Rice and Vitamin B. A Disease, a Cause and a Cure*. Berkeley, CA: Univ of California Press, 2000.

Funk C. On the chemical nature of the substance which cures polyneuritis in birds, induced by a diet of polished rice. *J Physiol* 1911;*43*:395.

Funk C. The etiology of deficiency diseases. *J State Medicine* 1912;20:341.

Harrow B. *Casimir Funk, Pioneer in Vitamins and Hormones*. New York: Dodd Mead, 1955

Hibbs RE. Beriberi in Japanese prison camps. *Ann Internl Med* 1946;*25*;270.

Jensen BCP, Eijkman C. *J Nutri* 1950;*42*:3.

McCollum EV, Kennedy C. The dietary factor operating in the production of polyneuritis *J Biolog Chem* 1916;*24*:491.

Takaki K. The preservation of health amongst the personnel of the Japanese army and navy. *Lancet* 1906;*i*:1369.

Wilder RM, Williams RR. Enrichment of flour and bread: a history of the movement. *Bull National Research Council* 1944, no.110.

Williams RR. Recollections of the "beriberi-preventing substance." *Nutr Rev* 1953;*11*:257.

Williams RR. *Toward the Conquest of Beriberi*. Cambridge, MA: Harvard Univ Press, 1961.

CHAPTER 10

THE PELLAGRA EPIDEMICS
THE THREE M'S
PRODUCE THE FOUR D'S

FROM THE DAYS OF THE HUNTER-GATHERERS TO MODERN
populations, access to adequate quantities of food has always been a prime
motivation affecting human behaviors. On the other hand, such progress as the
domestication of animals and the introduction of new foods have at times
resulted in the appearance of new diseases that could develop into epidemics.
Metabolic diseases—specifically nutritional deficiency diseases—also have
appeared in epidemic form after the introduction of new staple crops or new
methods of processing traditional staples, rivaling the epidemics of infectious
diseases in incidence and fatality rates. Prime examples are the outbreaks of pellagra and beriberi. Beriberi was discussed in the previous chapter.

Pellagra is a metabolic disorder, caused by niacin deficiency, that produces
skin and mucous membrane lesions, diarrhea, and mental changes referred to as
the "three D's": dermatitis, diarrhea, and dementia. The fourth "D" is death.
The first known epidemics of pellagra occurred in Europe during the 1700s.
These epidemics followed the introduction and widespread use of new foods
from the New World, especially Indian corn (maize). Because the caloric yield
per acre of corn was much higher than that of previous cereal crops, a much
larger population could be fed from the agricultural yield of areas under cultivation. Population apparently doubled in those areas that adopted corn. However,
the new diet tended to be deficient in some nutrients needed in only minuscule
quantities and not discovered until three centuries later. When pellagra
appeared, the new disease was quickly and correctly associated with the use of
maize.

When pellagra appeared in the United States in groups of people who had become dependent on cornmeal for most of their calories, the association with corn was not considered important. The epidemic developed around 1900, a time when virtually all major epidemic diseases were being shown to be caused by microbes. The idea that an epidemic disease in certain areas of the country was associated with poverty and a monotonous diet was embarrassing; hence, the theory was not accepted and was fought politically and intellectually.

Several decades passed before it was shown convincingly that a change in the technology of food processing was responsible for pellagra. New methods of milling corn had increased the amount of usable, stable food that could be derived from a crop and shipped by railroad to other parts of the country. The cheap cornmeal supported a large population that now worked in cotton mills instead of raising its own crops. But the new milling process removed enough of micronutrients from the corn to cause an outbreak of a disease previously unknown in this hemisphere. Matters of pride and politics forced the study of possible infectious agents, thus interfering with other studies of the possible cause of the epidemic. Consequently, the disease persisted, causing millions of cases and thousands of deaths, even in the decades after the underlying cause and means of prevention had been identified by a group of investigators in the U.S. Public Health Service.

NUTRITIONAL DEFICIENCY IN EUROPE. Those of us who savor the delights of various national cuisines may find it difficult to imagine Italian food without tomato sauces, or Irish meals without potatoes, illustrating how completely foods from the New World were adopted into European culture. Columbus and other explorers of the New World introduced a variety of new foods, including avocados, chocolate (cocoa), Indian corn (maize), paprika, peanuts, peppers, pineapples, white potatoes, squash, and tomatoes. (Turkeys were also brought from the New World, but confusion concerning the birds' origin led to the adoption of a name suggesting origin in an Old World country. Another agricultural product introduced from the New World—tobacco—eventually compensated for the benefits conferred by the others products!)

A major reason for the widespread use of some of these newly introduced foods, particularly potatoes and corn, was the increased caloric yield possible per acre of cropland. These dietary changes had profound nutritional implications: Population growth was augmented because of the increased supply of food, but at the same time, growing dependence on a single crop made large groups of people susceptible to unsuspected nutritional deficiency diseases.

In Ireland, the increased food supply that followed the introduction of the potato resulted in large population increases in those areas where poverty forced the inhabitants to make it their main source of sustenance. When the potato was first introduced, at the beginning of the seventeenth century, the population of Ireland consisted of approximately equal numbers of native Irish, Scots, and English; only the Irish found the potato acceptable as the main ingredient of their diet, and hence only their numbers grew. Over the next century and a half, the Irish doubled their numbers to four million, while the English and Scots population stayed at about two million each.

When a fungus that selectively attacked potato plants was brought to Europe on a ship from Peru, its effect was most devastating in those parts of Ireland that depended on the potato for food. The "potato blight" began in the western part of the island in the fall of 1845, particularly in County Mayo, where 90 percent of the population depended on the potato for survival. Other crops were grown, but they went primarily to pay the rent-in-kind demanded by landlords, and farmers and their families lived on the potato. Ireland actually continued to export food all during the famine years. Relief measures for the starving Irish were hampered by political decisions made by the British Prime Minister, Lord John Russell, and the local governor in Ireland, Charles Trevelyan, who were afraid to create a state of "mendicancy" with too great a dependence on government largess. Deaths from starvation began in October 1846, and in the following year, epidemics of typhus and relapsing fever added to the toll. Scurvy was a major factor as well, since the potato was the main source of vitamin C for the majority of the population. Mass graves were needed to bury the dead, often without coffins. By mid-July 1847, with three million people receiving some form of government relief, the blight began to fade, allowing a small harvest consisting mainly of seed potatoes. Trevelyan was knighted for his work during the famine years; he wrote a history of the famine that ended when the small potato crop was harvested in August 1847. However, the famine actually peaked during the autumn and winter of 1847–1848, and the potato crop of 1848 was almost totally blighted. It is reported that in County Galway that winter, dead bodies lay unburied everywhere.

Emigration and deaths quickly depleted the population of native Irish during the four-year famine; estimates are that 1.5 million people emigrated, mainly to the United States and Australia, and about 1 million died. When the population stabilized after the famine, about 2 million native Irish survived—the same number as before the introduction of the potato.

PELLAGRA IN EUROPE. Spain and northern Italy also experienced a considerable increase in population per cultivated acre as a result of the introduction of a New World food source. During the second half of the seventeenth century, Indian corn, or maize, increased the yield of food calories per acre well beyond that provided by the staple rye and wheat previously grown in these areas. Although this population increase was a result of the increase in available calories, modern food analyses reveal that cornmeal is relatively deficient in the amino acid tryptophan and the enzyme cofactor nicotinic acid derived from it. Deficiency states developed when other foods, particularly meat, were unavailable to supplement a cornmeal-based diet.

In 1736, Pedro Casal, physician to King Philip V of Spain, first observed a disease in Oviedo, in the Asturias region of northwest Spain. It was known as "mal de la rosa," because of its characteristic red rash. Although Casal thought it a peculiar form of leprosy, his descriptions were extremely accurate, and the rash in the exposed areas of the neck is still known as "Casal's necklace." Although his observation was made in 1735, his work on the topic was first published posthumously in 1762. Casal associated the disease with poverty, and noted that the diet of pellagrins consisted largely of corn and little meat. The concept of a deficiency disease did not yet exist, and Casal did not consider dietary deficiency as a cause of disease. Casal suggested that pellagra was due to the contamination of spoiled corn by a toxin, and this theory remained the focus of etiologic speculation.

Corn's popularity as a staple food crop spread from Spain to southern France, Italy, Romania, Russia, and Egypt, and pellagra followed. Cornmeal was used in a variety of preparations; a favorite in Italy was *polenta* or baked cornmeal mush. Because cornmeal was the main source of calories in the spring before new crops were ready for harvest, pellagra was called "the springtime disease."

Pellagra became particularly prevalent when other crops failed. The frequency of pellagra increased during the next 200 years, occurring primarily in outbreaks that were probably relative to the availability of other foods. The obvious association of pellagra with corn resulted in many theories to explain the origin of the new disease, often called "Zeism" based on the Latin name for maize, *Zea mays*. The "spoiled corn" theory of pellagra's etiology was most popular, based on its similarity to the occurrences of "St. Anthony's fire" (erysipelas, or more commonly ergotism, which is caused by a mold toxin in contaminated rye). Repeated unsuccessful attempts were made to demonstrate an organism growing in moldy corn that could produce the symptoms of pellagra in men or animals. Nevertheless, the theory of spoilage remained popular, and publications continue to appear supporting it. Because the association of pellagra with corn was clear, "the maize disease" was eliminated in many areas by banning the use of corn. The planting of other grains was encouraged by laws prohibiting the sale of spoiled or moldy corn, and most corn became moldy during storage in the late fall and winter. Mussolini "eliminated" pellagra from Italy by banning corn and declaring that the disease no longer existed. As a result, in 1937, when an American investigator, W. Henry Sebrell, toured Italy to study the disease in some of the first hospitals established for the care of pellagrins, such as those near Padua, he was informed by local physicians that officially the disease no longer existed and that they could not discuss the subject. Political considerations interfered with the study of pellagra even then, after its cause had been established in the United States.

PELLAGRA APPEARS IN THE UNITED STATES. Few physicians today have seen a case of pellagra and some have never even heard of this disease, which devastated a large part of this country during the first half of the twentieth century. Pellagra was so widespread in the South during that period that a prominent comedian, Zero Mostel, when playing the role of a classic, filibustering Southern legislator, called his character "Senator Polltax P. Pellagra."

To American physicians of the early twentieth century, pellagra was a new disease when the first paper describing its occurrence in this country appeared. Nineteenth-century American physicians who had trained or traveled abroad knew the disease, but had not seen it in this country. In the first edition of his classic *Textbook of Medicine*, published in 1892, Osler gave an excellent description of the clinical manifestations of the disease and its association with corn, but added, "It has not been observed in this country."

Because of the observations in Europe, the association of pellagra with poverty and corn was well established for over a century before the disease first appeared in the United States. As in Europe, the cause was thought to be spoiled corn contaminated by some organism that produced a toxin—the same theory originally suggested by Casal. A mold growing on stored corn and ingested with the cornmeal was considered the most likely etiologic mechanism, and American physicians also made the analogy to the etiology of ergotism.

The first recorded case of pellagra in the United States occurred in the Mount Vernon Hospital in Alabama. The hospital was in an old fort and arsenal, originally built because of a potential conflict with Spain in 1810; it had been renovated in 1900 for use as an annex to the Bryce Hospital for Alabama Insane in Tuscaloosa. The report was written by Dr. George H. Searcy, who had accompanied Colonel Gorgas to help control the problem of yellow fever and malaria in Panama during the construction of the canal, but returned home because he developed malaria himself. Searcy was assigned to the Mount Vernon Annex to help care for several hundred of the "colored insane," particularly because of a new disease that had appeared among them. Dr. Searcy recognized the new disease as pellagra. In 1907, he reported eighty-eight cases in the *Transactions of the Medical Association of the State of Alabama,* and also published another report in the July 6 issue of the *Journal of the American Medical Association* of that year. Searcy noted that identifying the disease had led to four or five additional cases being diagnosed at the hospital, but he believed the disease had not been seen there before. Fifty-seven of the eighty-eight cases he saw during several months of 1906 covered in his reports were fatal.

In retrospect, it is interesting that Searcy's first report mentioned that no nurses had the disease, although they handled the patients frequently and slept near them in the halls. In this original report, Searcy added that the most notable difference between nurses and patients was the nurses' more varied diet. In view of the known association of the disease with corn in Europe, he took the patients off cornbread, grits, and molasses and substituted wheat bread and potatoes; new cases stopped appearing after about ten days, except in a test group of patients kept on the original diet. Because Searcy suspected that spoiled corn was the cause of the outbreak of pellagra, he submitted samples of the cornmeal from the diet kitchen for analysis. The cornmeal was found to be filthy, contaminated with numerous microorganisms.

In 1907, the same disease was recognized at the Hospital for the Insane in Columbia, South Carolina. The superintendent, Dr. James W. Babcock, brought the outbreak to the attention of the governor and a U.S. senator, both of whom were his personal friends. The local and later national press picked up the story, and publicity began to influence developments.

During the next four years, Babcock found 435 cases of pellagra in his South Carolina hospital. The Georgia State Sanitarium in Milledgeville recorded forty deaths from pellagra in 1908; by 1909, seventy-three deaths occurred, and pellagra moved into first place among causes of death in that institution, outpacing tuberculosis. The new epidemic was not limited to the southeast, however; in 1909, Peoria State Hospital in Illinois reported 135 cases with 45 deaths.

Retrospectively, it is estimated that approximately 1,000 cases of pellagra occurred nationwide in 1909; between 1907 and 1911, a total of 16,000 cases were reported in eighteen states. During 1915, when case reporting was more complete, estimates of the total number of cases reached 75,000. By the 1920s, about 100,000 cases were reported each year. Thus, from a modest beginning as an outbreak of a new disease affecting small numbers of patients in an annex to a mental hospital in Alabama, a huge epidemic developed and spread across vast areas of the country.

Was pellagra a disease new to the United States, or had it been present, but unrecognized, before? Opinions expressed at that time varied; Babcock believed he had evidence that pellagra had existed previously in the records of the South Carolina Hospital for the Insane, but that the disease had not been diagnosed. His opinion was shared by many who realized that, once a disease was diagnosed and recognized, numerous examples were then brought to the attention of physicians, or, conversely, of a newly diagnosed disease becoming "fashionable" and thus diagnosed frequently even when it was not present. However, when Searcy reviewed past autopsy records of his Alabama hospital, he found no cases that he would diagnose retrospectively as pellagra. Another staff physician, who had performed over 1,000 autopsies at Alabama mental hospitals, believed he had never before seen a case that resembled those he saw at Mount Vernon beginning in 1906. In a review on pellagra in 1941, Dr. Seale Harris, who had become a national authority on the disease, reviewed his own records and found only one patient (seen in 1902) whom he would diagnose in retrospect as having had pellagra. He concluded "I find it difficult to believe that pellagra could have been endemic in the South prior to 1906, though no doubt there were occasional cases of secondary and alcoholic pellagra."

In 1916, Dr. W.J. Kerr, a surgeon who had worked at the infamous Andersonville prison during the Civil War, suggested that pellagra had caused hundreds of deaths among Union prisoners at that camp in 1864. Others disagreed; bacillary and amebic dysentery and typhoid fever were suggested as the main diseases in the prison camps. Dr. Joseph Jones, the physician in charge of studying the disastrous medical problem at Andersonville, had diagnosed scurvy in half the inmates during the six months of his study. He attributed 25 percent of the deaths he observed directly to scurvy and 50 percent to chronic diarrhea; only a quarter of the deaths were due to infectious diseases, such as typhoid fever and pneumonia. A retrospective analysis supports the concept that malnutrition was the basis of the massive deaths of prisoners at Andersonville.[1] When prisoners were freed, their skeletal appearance roused ire in the North, and their chronic diarrhea was cured by fresh vegetables.[2] Because B vitamin deficiencies cause chronic diarrhea, and the scanty food the prisoners got was mainly cornmeal, it is likely that pellagra was a major factor.

The conditions that prevailed at Andersonville were extreme, and it is unlikely that pellagra existed to any considerable extent during the remainder of the nineteenth century. New disease or not, the incidence of pellagra markedly increased during the first few years after it was recognized and brought to medical and public attention. And, the epidemic continued to spread and increase in virulence for several decades.

In 1924, reports of pellagra were recorded from a total of thirty-six states and the District of Columbia. Not all states reported their cases to the Public Health Service in Washington. Nine southern states included in the reporting area— Florida, Georgia, Kentucky, Louisiana, Mississippi, North Carolina, South Carolina, Tennessee, and Virginia—had among them 90 percent of the total pellagra cases reported in the entire country. Other populous southern states known to have had a high incidence of pellagra, including Alabama, Arkansas, Texas, and West Virginia, were not included, because they did not report their cases. Thus, the true extent of the epidemic was greatly underestimated.

During the period from 1915 to 1925, the first decade of reporting, 27,648 deaths from pellagra were recorded. House-to-house surveys during that period, seeking to estimate the number of unhospitalized cases, concluded that at least thirty-five nonfatal cases of pellagra occurred for each death. On the basis of that estimate, a total of 967,000 cases of pellagra occurred during that decade alone. Another one million cases probably occurred between 1925 and 1930, in part because severe floods along the Mississippi decreased the food supply and aggravated nutritional deficiency. In the decade before the disease was virtually eliminated, it is likely that another one million cases occurred. Overall, therefore, the outbreak of pellagra in the United States, which lasted from about 1906 to 1940, probably resulted in at least three million cases with 100,000 deaths in those states that reported their cases, and perhaps an additional 1.5 million cases and 50,000 deaths in those states that did not report them.

Even after the cause of the disease was firmly established, the reason for the outbreak was never subjected to careful scrutiny to determine whether it was the result of a phenomenon that might recur. My own investigation into the subject reveals that such a possibility exists. The cause of the pellagra epidemic was similar to that now known to have occurred with other outbreaks of epidemic nutritional deficiency disease, especially beriberi.

THE STRUGGLE TO IDENTIFY THE CAUSE OF PELLAGRA. Dr. James Babcock and his co-worker, Dr. Joseph J. Watson organized a Conference on Pellagra with the support of South Carolina's Governor Martin Ansell and Senator Benjamin R. Tillman. The conference, which convened in Columbia on December 9, 1908, became known as the first National Conference on Pellagra. It generated press reports documenting the existence of a new, spreading, and possibly infectious, disease. Public concern was aroused—panic might better describe the public reaction to news of increasing cases.

On November 3, 1909, a Second National Conference on Pellagra followed and, during that conference, the National Association for the Study of Pellagra was formed. The Association met again in 1912 and 1915. Physicians from all over the country attended these meetings and reported their experience with the disease. They noted the association of the disease with poverty, and that severe outbreaks occurred in prisons and in "insane asylums" as mental hospitals were called then. A paper on "Aspects of the Pellagra Problem in Illinois," by Siler and Nichols, noted that the disease was not limited to the southeast, and they also noted that in the institution in which they worked, The Peoria State Hospital, "no nurses, attendants, or employees have shown the disease," thus duplicating Searcy's original observation.

The epidemic of pellagra became a source of embarrassment to the South, because it emphasized the existence of poverty and because it was thought to be contagious and, therefore, dangerous. Pellagra was a "social stigma," but its existence was undeniable; many believed it was more acceptable for pellagra to be caused by an infectious agent than to be in some way a direct result of poverty. Because pellagra was known to be common in Italy, an influx of Italian immigrants into the South was blamed for the new plague. No one seemed to notice that those Italians living in the southeastern United States did not have pellagra—undoubtedly because they did not favor the classic cornbread and molasses diet that led to the disease in that part of the country.

In 1908, when Dr. Babcock brought national attention to the outbreak of a new disease, he was considered a hero, complimented and honored publicly by the governor of South Carolina. But attitudes changed and, by 1914, he was forced to resign as superintendent of the State Hospital for the Insane in Columbia on the grounds that he had "brought injury" to the state by calling attention to the existence of pellagra. It was clearly unacceptable to consider the suggestion by Dr. Joseph Goldberger, a physician who was both a northerner and an immigrant himself, that social and economic factors were responsible for the disease because of the effect they had on the diet of the poor. Editorial pages and speeches by congressmen criticized and condemned such insulting inferences concerning the contentment and well-being of the people of the South. Besides, the suggested remedy—improving the diet of the impoverished citizens—was clearly impractical. Congressman James F. Byrnes (later Secretary of State, and Supreme Court Justice) called the news reports of "famine and plague" in South Carolina an "utter absurdity." Byrnes demanded the rejection of offers of aid from the Red Cross. A Georgia city wired U.S. Senator Tom Watson, "When this part of Georgia suffers from famine, the rest of the world will be dead!" (Unfortunately, contemporary examples of similar political influences on the acceptability of medical and scientific theory could also be cited.)

The characteristic "three D's" of pellagra—dermatitis, diarrhea, and dementia—make it relatively easy to diagnose. Unfortunately, the rapidity with which the number of cases reached epidemic proportions pointed to an infectious cause and prejudiced thinking about the etiology.

Public alarm continued to mount as scare headlines and news reports of its increasing frequency sold newspapers. The concern about the mounting epidemic led two philanthropists, Col. Robert M. Thompson of New York, and J.H. McFadden of Philadelphia, to donate $15,000 to establish a private commission to investigate the cause and make suggestions concerning how to stop the contagion. The Thompson–McFadden Pellagra Commission then studied cases in the cotton mill districts around Spartanburg, South Carolina, an area with a particularly high incidence of pellagra. After conducting a house-to-house survey, the commission concluded that the spread of the disease seemed most rapid where sanitary disposal of waste was poorest, and that it occurred almost exclusively in people who lived in or next to the house of another person with pellagra. Proponents of the infection theory of pellagra's etiology found support in their findings, and continued to quote the commission's report for decades. The commission did not note the association of the disease with the poverty that caused areas with poor housing and sanitary facilities, nor did they note any relationship between the disease and diet.

These events occurred during an era when dramatic advances in medical science, particularly bacteriology and pathology, had provided a true scientific basis for modern medicine. The causative agents for major deadly diseases—including typhoid fever, lobar pneumonia, tuberculosis, cerebrospinal meningitis, syphilis, Asiatic cholera, malaria, amebic dysentery, scarlet fever, tetanus, and diphtheria—were being discovered at the rate of about a disease a year. From vague concepts about toxic miasmas and mystical theorizing, medicine moved into the light of science during those years. Because infectious microbial agents were identified for so many diseases, it seemed obvious that all epidemic disease would eventually be found to have a microbial cause.

Therefore, in 1914, Dr. Rupert Blue, the Surgeon General of the U.S. Public Health Service, assigned Dr. Claude H. Lavinder, an experienced investigator of epidemic infectious disease, to find the etiologic agent and perhaps the insect vector causing the epidemic of pellagra. He was instructed to find if reports of isolation of a "*Streptobacillus pellagrae*" were valid.

Assisted by Dr. Edward Francis, Lavinder toured those areas of the country having the highest incidence of pellagra and established a laboratory at the Marine Hospital in Savannah to study the disease. Researchers there attempted to transmit a causative agent to monkeys. Lavinder was highly regarded by others in the field and, in 1912, he was elected president of the National Association for the Study of Pellagra at its second meeting in Columbia, South Carolina.

ENTER DR. JOSEPH GOLDBERGER. In 1914, Lavinder asked to be assigned other responsibilities, and the Surgeon General substituted Dr. Joseph H. Goldberger, another Public Health Service officer experienced in the study of epidemic infectious disease. Pellagra was still rampant, and national concern about the epidemic was increasing. Goldberger had earlier determined the nature of several outbreaks of infectious disease by careful epidemiologic investigations. Having acquired yellow fever during one of his assignments, and being thus immune to that disease, he was considered particularly valuable when outbreaks of yellow fever needed to be studied. He also caught dengue fever while studying an epidemic in Texas, which helped him convince local authorities of the infectious nature of the problem then affecting the port of Brownsville. His experience and "constitution" (i.e., his ability to survive these diseases) made him the ideal investigator to find the etiologic agent of pellagra.

Goldberger had immigrated to the United States from Hungary at the age of six, and his parents had managed to send him to the Bellevue–New York University School of Medicine. He graduated before he was 21 and served an 18-month internship at that hospital during 1896 and 1897. After an unsuccessful attempt to earn a living in private practice, he attempted to join the U.S. Navy at the beginning of the Spanish-American War but, according to one biographer, the Navy already had one officer with a Jewish name, and politely turned him down. Entry into the Public Health Service did not take religion into account, being based instead on a competitive examination, and Goldberger scored highest in the country. He spent the rest of his career in that service.

He began his assignment with a three-week tour of southern institutions having a high incidence of pellagra, including orphanages in Jackson, Mississippi, the Georgia State Asylum for the Insane in Milledgeville, and a hospital for pellagrins in Spartanburg, South Carolina. He confirmed earlier reports that staff members in intimate contact with inmates never got pellagra, and immediately dismissed the concept that pellagra was a communicable, infectious disease.

Goldberger was struck by the limited, monotonous diet served at those institutions, and he quickly focused on it as a likely factor in the cause of the disease. He had some difficulty explaining the absence of the disease in staff members, since they usually ate the same meals as the patients, in the same dining rooms. However, he noted, that the staff ate first, taking the leanest portions of the very fatty meat and whatever variety was available, and that they could supplement their diet with food obtained outside the institution. Inmates were left with cornmeal mush, cane syrup, molasses, gravy, and biscuits—the ubiquitous diet of the poor Southerner. This diet became known as the "Three M's": meat, meal, and molasses. The meat was mostly pork fat ("fatback" or "streak-o-lean," referring to the tiny strands of actual meat within the fat), and the meal was cornmeal.

In orphanages, the disease was most prevalent among the younger children, but rarely affected infants or older children. These gaps in the distribution of the disease would not have been expected if the disease were infectious. Goldberger later realized that infants and very young children were given whatever milk was available, and that older children took all the meat on the food platters by intimidating the smaller ones. All that was left for the youngest children was cornbread and molasses.

His certainty that the disease was not infectious was reinforced by the studies of Dr. Edward Francis, who, working with Lavinder, had failed to transmit the disease to monkeys in the research being done in Savannah. (Francis had caught every other disease he had worked on, but had not caught pellagra.)

Using federal funds to test his hypothesis that dietary inadequacy was the cause of the disease, Goldberger attempted to treat it in two orphanages in Jackson by providing a more varied diet, including purchasing fresh meat and abundant milk with his research funds. He also began a similar program among the inmates in one building of the asylum at Milledgeville in Georgia. With the diet he provided, cases of pellagra in these institutions cleared. By the spring of 1915, when new cases usually appeared, no new cases appeared in the studied institutions and no relapses were observed. Goldberger's report to the Public Health Service revealed his elation with the results and his optimism that the disease could be controlled. However, as soon as the federal research funds ran out, the old diet was restored and pellagra returned; during the spring of 1916, 40 percent of the children in the orphanages had the disease.

On the basis of his reports, Goldberger was asked to give the Cutter lecture on preventive medicine at Harvard University, where he was well received and congratulated; he was also invited to speak at the Southern Medical Association and the Association for the Study of Pellagra, but there he was attacked and vilified. His conclusion that a more varied diet was needed, one that included other sources of vegetable protein, was considered an absurdity. Proponents of the theory of an infectious etiology dominated those meetings and dismissed the concept of a dietary deficiency.

Goldberger reasoned that inducing pellagra experimentally would convince the skeptics. Earl Brewer, the Governor of Mississippi, cooperated by offering pardons to inmates of the Rankin Prison Farm who participated in the experiment. Twelve members of a "pellagra squad" were housed separately in clean quarters, to isolate them from the possible spread of infectious material from other inmates. They were fed biscuits, gravy, cornbread, grits, rice, syrup, collard greens, and yams, while the rest of the prisoners were given a more varied diet. The experiment began on February 4, 1915 and was terminated on October 31, when classic manifestations of pellagra were present in six of the eleven volunteers. Several prisoners were so miserable that they tried to end the experiment before the scheduled date of completion. One said, "I have been through a thousand hells!" while others pleaded for a quick death from a bullet. Goldberger was accused of torture, and Governor Brewer was accused of having arranged the experiment to be able to pardon two of the prisoners, who were his friends and convicted of embezzlement. Skeptics remained unconvinced that pellagra was not infectious.

In another attempt to establish that pellagra was not communicable and could not be transmitted in the fashion of known infections, Goldberger conducted "filth parties." He had himself, his wife, and his associates injected with blood from pellagrins, and he and his male colleagues wrapped skin scales, feces, dried urine, and other dirt from pellagrins in dough and swallowed repeated doses. Mrs. Goldberger was a devoted colleague and assistant, but she did not (or would not) participate in this phase of the experiment. None of the researchers got pellagra, or anything worse than nausea and mild diarrhea (*mirabile dictu*). However, these experiments were also dismissed because pellagra usually was more common in women, and thus his male staff were considered "constitutionally resistant" to the disease.

Goldberger could not explain why pellagra was twenty times more common in women than men between the ages of 20 and 50. In retrospect, it seems that the explanation lies in the fact that women gave whatever meat and other supplementary foods that were available to the men, who did more strenuous work in the fields. In addition, it is worth noting that, during the childbearing years, women had increased nutritional requirements, and they usually worked in the fields, too.

Goldberger eventually stopped trying to convince stubborn adherents to the concept of an infectious etiology of pellagra and devoted the remainder of his life to an attempt to identify the nutritional factor he was sure prevented or cured pellagra. Vitamins had been discovered by this time, and various names were suggested for the pellagra preventive factor or PPF, as he called it, including vitamin G for Goldberger. His dietary approaches cured thousands of patients before nicotinic acid was eventually identified in the laboratory of Elvehjem at the University of Wisconsin, in 1937. Goldberger's last project, before he died of cancer in January 1929, was an attempt to develop a table comparing the PPF content of various foods. Earlier, he had been nominated for a Nobel Prize (never given posthumously), and his work is still quoted as the most important nutritional research done by an American investigator.

EXPERIMENTAL PELLAGRA IN DOGS. The studies of PPF were aided by the recognition that a nutritional deficiency disease that could be induced in dogs, "black tongue," was actually a canine form of pellagra. Nutritional investigators at Yale University originally observed black tongue in 1916, when they fed dogs a poor but varied diet. The relationship of the deficiency syndrome in the dogs to human pellagra was suspected, since the sores and hemorrhages in the mouth that led to the name of the disease were similar to the oral manifestations of pellagra. In the South, a similar disease in dogs was called "canine plague." It was known to be very difficult to raise healthy dogs in those areas of the southeast where pellagra was most common, but this only reinforced the thinking that it was an infectious disease.

Establishing that black tongue was the same deficiency disease as pellagra was a major step in expediting studies of the disease. By using dogs instead of humans, the laborious dietary studies analyzing the content of "pellagra preventive factor" in a variety of foods could be done much more quickly and safely.

No papers on this subject explain how Goldberger and his associates knew that black tongue was analogous to human pellagra. An elderly physician I met on an occasion when I spoke on pellagra to the County Medical Society at Milledgeville told me that he had worked at the state mental hospital there, during the period when Goldberger's team was conducting its studies at that institution. He related the following story:

A laboratory assistant working with the Public Health Service team at the hospital also raised hunting dogs. Someone told him that the dogs would perform much better when the hunting season opened if he would feed them only cornbread and molasses for a few weeks beforehand. He did just that, but it rained very heavily that spring, and the ground was too muddy to allow hunting for several weeks after the season was scheduled to open. He kept the dogs on the same diet, expecting to be able to hunt any day, but when the ground was finally dry enough for hunting, the dogs were too weak to participate. He told his problem to Dr. Charles Tanner, the head of the PHS research team in Milledgeville, who went to see the dogs, immediately recognized that they had black tongue, and that it had developed while they ate the classic diet that produces pellagra in humans. Tanner notified Goldberger, who was working primarily in the Public Health Service laboratories in Washington. Goldberger used the pellagrogenic diet to confirm the observation and began to study black tongue in dogs.

This experimental model quickly led to a discovery that both expedited the research and quickly improved treatment for humans. The dogs on the experimental diet would not eat, and they were not very keen about the meat-free diet in any case. As occurred in human cases, the sore mouth made them unwilling to swallow anything. Goldberger asked a veterinarian how he could get the dogs to eat his test foods. The vet suggested stimulating their appetite with brewer's yeast, a veterinary panacea at the time. (At that time, packages of yeast came in a wrapper depicting a horse, a cow, and a pig, to reflect its most common use.) To get the dogs with very sore mouths to swallow the yeast, on the advice of the veterinarian, Goldberger rolled it into tiny balls and pushed it down their throats. Given the yeast, the dogs showed signs of recovery from black tongue before they started to eat much of his experimental diet, and Goldberger realized that yeast had PPF in it. He went on to show that yeast could reverse the disease after it was fully developed, and he began use yeast in the treatment of human pellagra. As with the dogs, it was particularly valuable for patients whose mouths were too sore to eat foods known to be therapeutic, and it saved many lives before injectable treatment became available in the late 1930s.

Yeast also saved many lives when the Great Flood of 1927, a massive human disaster, occurred along the Mississippi River. Goldberger arranged to have the Red Cross ship large quantities of brewer's yeast into flood–stricken areas. The expected outbreak of pellagra did not occur and, instead of an epidemic of the disease, its incidence fell below the usual level for that time of year. However, after the emergency, the yeast was no longer provided, and the accustomed level of pellagra returned to the area.

The final, virtually complete elimination of pellagra dates to the early years of World War II. Elvehjem and his coworkers showed that nicotinic acid was the specific micronutrient deficiency responsible for the disease, and Sydenstricker and others showed that most patients with symptoms of pellagra actually had multiple nutritional deficiencies, particularly of members of the group of B vitamins, including riboflavin. The availability of cheap, synthetic forms of these various vitamins stimulated legislation requiring their addition as supplements to "enrich" commonly used foods in many states. A number of nutritional deficiency syndromes were virtually eliminated almost simultaneously by laws requiring the addition of iodine to table salt to reduce endemic goiter due to iodine-deficiency, vitamin D to milk to fight rickets, vitamin C to juices and other foods to prevent scurvy, and multiple B vitamins to flour to combat pellagra and beriberi. These "enriched" products substituted for the lack of micronutrients in the diet, and these syndromes almost vanished, except among alcoholics and food-faddists.

WHAT WERE THE REASONS FOR THE EPIDEMIC OF PELLAGRA?   Maize had been a dietary staple of the Native Americans, who did not suffer from pellagra, and no change occurred in the type of corn used, or in the method of planting and harvesting, that would account for the appearance of a pellagra epidemic in the United States. However, the Native Americans ground their corn into meal using limewater, and such alkaline solutions increase the extraction of the nicotinic acid that is present in corn, thus increasing the nutritional value of the resulting meal. This practice may account for the absence of any known pellagra among Native Americans, but it is more likely that a varied diet, especially the addition of beans and game meat, was the most important factor.

Because the three M diet of meat, meal, and molasses was common in the South for so long, especially among the poor, the diet itself cannot be the reason for the sudden appearance or marked increase in the frequency of the disease. However, the diet became most popular in the post-frontier era in the South, when game became less available. Farmers commonly raised corn and hogs: cornmeal, pounded and hand-ground, was made into the dietary staples of cornbread and grits, and the pigs were fed the surplus corn.

Epidemiologic investigations, including those conducted by Joseph Goldberger, noted an especially high incidence of pellagra in southern cotton-growing areas near textile mill towns. Goldberger noted that the disease did not occur uniformly in all such towns, and that mill towns with a low incidence of pellagra tended to be in those areas where, in addition to cotton, a variety of vegetables were grown, and meat and produce were for sale. Towns surrounded entirely by cotton fields, without truck farms and produce, had the highest incidence of pellagra. In more isolated areas, in the hills away from railroad lines, people were as poor or poorer in terms of cash income, but pellagra was less frequent because these people tended to raise a variety of vegetables for their own consumption. Therefore poverty alone was not the reason for the disease.

Casimir Funk, who helped to elucidate the role of thiamin in the etiology of beriberi, was also an early investigator of the problem of pellagra. Funk published his studies on pellagra in the 1913–1914 volume of the *Journal of Physiology*. He analyzed the nitrogen content of corn after various methods of milling and pointed out that "highly milled maize is deprived of some important constituents, such as phosphorus...and also fat." He was puzzled by the fact that the nitrogen concentration was not lowered by milling; he studied yeast to see how much of its nitrogen content could be accounted for as by the nitrogen in vitamins. It is fascinating to note that in this study, he specifically measured nicotinic acid, which he knew to be contained in the "vitamine-fraction," and found that it "yields only a very small part of the total nitrogen," which is not surprising since these compounds are present only in tiny quantities. He concluded that, "the amount of vitamine-N to the total-N must be a negligible quantity." Thus, milling maize could remove part of its nutritional value without a detectable decrease in total nitrogen, analogous to the effect of milling on rice in relation to the development of beriberi.

Because Funk knew that epidemic beriberi developed in the Far East during the 1880s following a change in the method of milling of rice, he suggested that the same mechanism might be responsible for pellagra, and he was probably right. Unfortunately, his report was ignored. Although much has been written about the cause and cure of pellagra, I have found no other papers addressing the reason why the disease appeared when it did. It is possible that the fact that pellagra existed for almost two centuries in Europe, whereas beriberi was a completely new disease in most areas, prevented people from seeing the analogy.

In attempting to determine what changes occurred in corn milling methods at the turn of the last century, which might have resulted in the outbreak of pellagra, I learned that the "germ" or embryo in the corn kernel contains a high proportion of the lipid, enzymes, and cofactors, including nicotinic acid. Degerminating corn during milling removes the embryo along with its lipid and enzymes; without these enzymes, the resulting cornmeal does not spoil readily, exactly the same phenomenon that occurs when rice is finely milled. (The separated corn germ, with its high lipid content, is used to produce corn oil.) An investigation of agricultural and technologic history, and consultation with a number of curators of agricultural history at the Smithsonian Institution and historians in the Department of Agriculture in Washington, led me to Dr. O.L. Brekke, a retired professor of agriculture at Purdue University. He sent me an article, written by E.P. Stimmel, which appeared in *The American Miller* in 1941(vol. 69, pages 30–33). The article opens with the following statement: "The present method of milling corn got its start when the Beall degerminator was first introduced in the years 1900 and 1901."

With that information in hand, I think it is possible to explain many of the observations of the epidemiology of pellagra that remained puzzling for a long time. The disease was most prevalent in orphanages, mental hospitals, and prisons—institutions in which people existed for long periods on a restricted, monotonous diet. In the South, cornmeal was a main source of calories in these institutional diets but, despite its restricted nutritional value, pellagra was rare or nonexistent until after 1900. After degermination began, these same foods contained inadequate quantities of certain micronutrients, especially nicotinic acid. In the textile mill towns, surrounded by cotton-fields, food was shipped in by railroad; the cornmeal purchased in company stores was processed in the Midwest, where degermination was introduced. Very rural and impoverished areas had less pellagra: Being remote from railroads, they ground their own corn, mostly using old, water-driven stone mills, and this corn was not degerminated. (It is still a tradition in the South that "stone-ground" corn is healthier.) When the new method of degerminating corn was introduced, the precarious diet of the poor in the mill towns and institutions became worse and pellagra appeared.

CONCLUSION. Is pellagra a disease of the past? My own investigations into the subject reveal that a possibility of recurrence does exist. The "Three M" diet of meat, meal, and molasses had long been a favorite among the southern poor, and it can still lead to pellagra if other foods or good grades of meat are not combined with it. I have seen pellagra develop in elderly southern Alzheimer's patients who would eat only foods they preferred in childhood, namely cornbread and molasses.

If changes in food processing technology caused outbreaks of nutritional deficiency disease, could the same thing happen again? For example, the main source of vitamin C in our diets is orange juice but, in urban areas, where it is usually bought in cartons or bottles, pasteurization has destroyed most of that heat-labile vitamin. Might the almost total use of chemical fertilizer on agricultural lands result in the absence of certain trace minerals from foods that are our main source of such micronutrients? Such phenomena are at least possibilities and therefore deserve careful monitoring.

Technological progress unintentionally caused the appearance of epidemic pellagra. The facts that such a major epidemic quietly disappeared thanks to preventive measures, and that most physicians and medical students have never seen the disease and are unaware of its frequency during the early part of the twentieth century, are themselves most remarkable.

(Addendum: Since my original work on this subject I have learned that Dr. Kenneth Carpenter, of the University of California, Berkeley, has done original research on this subject and come to a similar conclusion; he has published several short articles on the subject, listed below.)

ADDITIONAL READING

Babcock JW. How long has pellagra existed in South Carolina? A study of local medical history. *Am J Insanity* 1912–3;69:185.

Bollet AJ. Politics and pellagra: the epidemic of pellagra in the U.S. in the early twentieth century. *Yale J Biol Med* 1992;65:211.

Bollet AJ. *Civil War Medicine: Challenges and Triumphs.* Tucson, AZ: Galen Press, 2002.

Carmichael EB. The pellagra story in the U.S. *J Med Assoc State Ala.* 1980;49:23.

Carpenter KJ. Contribution of the dog to the science of nutrition. *J Nutr* 1991;*121*(11 suppl):S1–7

Carpenter KJ, Lewin WJ. A reexamination of the diets associated with pellagra. *J Nutr* 1985;*115*:543.

Carpenter KJ. Effects of different methods of processing maize on its pellagrogenic activity. *Federation Proceedings* 1981;*40*:1531.

Casal G. The natural and medical history of the principality of the Asturias. In: Major RH, ed. *Classic Descriptions of Disease* Springfield, IL: Chas C. Thomas, 1932.

Davenport CB. The hereditary factor in pellagra. *Arch Intern Med* 1916;*18*:4.

Elmore JG, Feinstein AR. Joseph Goldberger: An unsung hero of American clinical epidemiology. *Ann Intern Med* 1994;*121*:372.

Etheridge EW. *The Butterfly Caste: A Social History of Pellagra in the South.* Westport, CT: Greenwood Pub Co, 1972.

Goldberger JH, Wheeler GA. Experimental pellagra in the human subject brought about by a restricted diet. *Public Health Reports* 1915;*30*:3336.

Goldberger JH. The cause and prevention of pellagra. *Public Health Reports* 1914;*29*:2355.

Green ERR. The great famine (1845–1850). In: Moody TW, Martin FX, eds. *The Course of Irish History.* Cork, Ireland: The Mercier Press, 1967.

Lavinder GH. The prevalence and geographic distribution of pellagra in the United States. *Public Health Reports* 1912;*27*:2077 and 2087.

Major RH. Don Gaspar Casal, Francois Thiery and pellagra. *Bull Hist Med* 1944;*16*:351.

Muncey EB. A study of the heredity of pellagra in Spartanburg County, South Carolina. *Arch Intern Med* 1916;*18*:32.

Roe DA. Attempts at the eradication of pellagra: a historical review. *Henry E. Sigerist Supplement to the Bulletin of the History of Medicine* 1980;suppl. 5:62.

Roe DA. *A Plague of Corn; The Social History of Pellagra.* Ithaca, NY: Cornell Univ Press, 1973.

Searcy GH. An epidemic of acute pellagra. *JAMA* 1907;*49*:37.

Searcy, GH. An epidemic of acute pellagra. *Trans of the Med Assoc State Ala* 1907;307.

Sebrell WH Jr. The history of pellagra. *Fed Proc* 1981;*40*:1520.

Siler JF, Garrison PE, MacNeal WJ. Introduction to the third report of the Robert M. Thompson Pellagra Commission of the New York Post-Graduate Medical School and Hospital. *Arch Intern Med* 1916;*18*:1.

Siler JF, Garrison PE, MacNeal WJ. The relation of recurrent attacks of pellagra to race, sex and age of the patient and to treatment of the disease. *Arch Intern Med* 1916;*18*:652.

Stimmel EP. *The American Miller* 1941;*69*:30–33.

Sydenstricker VP. The history of pellagra, its recognition as a disorder of nutrition and its conquest. *Am J Clin Nutr* 1958 6:409.

Terris M, ed. *Goldberger on Pellagra.* Baton Rouge, LA: Louisiana State Univ Press, 1964.

Thiery F. Description of a malady called Mal de la Rosa. In: Major RH, ed. *Classic Descriptions of Disease,* Springfield, IL: Chas C. Thomas, 1932.

Vedder EB. Dietary deficiency as the etiologic factor in pellagra. *Arch Intern Med* 1916;*18*:137.

Wilder RM. A brief history of the enrichment of bread and flour. *JAMA* 1956;*166*:1539.

Wood EJ. The appearance of pellagra in the United States. *JAMA* 1909;*53*:274.

[1]Bollet, AJ. Civil War Medicine, Challenges and Triumphs. Tucson, AZ, Galen Press, 2002.
[2]Gen. H.B. Chapman, *The Tragedy of Andersonville,* p 139

CHAPTER 11

SCURVY

THE PURPUREA NAUTICA

Scurvy is a nutritional deficiency disease caused by a lack of vitamin C. It has occurred in epidemic form whenever people are deprived of adequate quantities of fresh vegetables. Because the stores of vitamin C in the body are relatively small compared to those of most other essential nutrients, scurvy has been a dominant feature and main cause of death during generalized famine, as well as during certain endeavors, when other food sources are adequate but the diet lacks fresh vegetables, such as long sea voyages. A prime example of scurvy during famine occurred in Ireland in the mid-nineteenth century, when a majority of the people who died of malnutrition had developed the specific symptoms of scurvy, as well as extreme weight loss and emaciation.[E1]

Until synthetic vitamins became available in the late 1930s, no substitute for the vitamin C in reasonably fresh vegetables existed. To support even moderate numbers of people, large amounts of fresh vegetables are needed. Unfortunately, vegetables are bulky, subject to spoilage, and their vitamin C content rapidly diminishes even at normal room temperatures. As a result, soldiers, whose food needs were always a major logistical problem, and sailors, who could not get fresh food unless they put into a port, were highly susceptible to scurvy. When army food supplies had to be brought by horse-drawn wagon over primitive roads, competing for transportation with arms, ammunition, and forage for the horses, generals considered vegetables impractical luxuries. The problem is illustrated by the Surgeon Generals' reports of the U.S. army stationed almost entirely at frontier posts in the pre-Civil War years. These reports reveal that scurvy was the most common disease diagnosed in those years. It appeared primarily in late winter and early spring, after winter-stored vegetables had been consumed or their antiscorbutic vitamin C content had decayed, and new crops had not yet grown.

Supplying vegetables to large armies, such as those mobilized for the major campaigns of the Civil War, was even more of a problem. Scurvy was kept under control when soldiers could forage to find sufficient quantities of fruits, vegetables, and herbs. But during a siege, or in areas where previous foraging had cleared out everything edible, soldiers could, within a few months, become severely weakened by symptoms of scurvy and entire armies made ineffective.

LAND SCURVY. Among the earliest descriptions of severe scurvy were outbreaks affecting medieval Crusaders, who sometimes were trapped for long periods without supplies of fresh food. For example, in December 1218, an army of Crusaders in Egypt, "suffered severely from scurvy," while besieging the Egyptian port of Damietta. Historians describe soldiers "... seized with violent pains in the feet and ankles, their gums became swollen, their teeth loose and useless, while their hips and shin bones first turn black and putrefied. Finally an easy and peaceful death, like a gentle sleep, put an end to their suffering. A sixth of the pilgrim army was carried away by this disease which no medicine could cure."

The French chronicler Jean de Joinville (1224?–1317) accompanied Louis IX (St. Louis) on the seventh crusade (1249 to 1254). He left eyewitness accounts of some of the epidemics that affected the Crusaders, including, in 1249, a good description of scurvy, although he did not name it. He described the extreme swelling of the gums characteristic of the disease: "The disorder I spoke of very soon increased so much in the army that the barbers were forced to cut away very large pieces of flesh from the gums, to enable their patients to eat. It was painful to hear the cries and groans of those on whom this operation was performed; they seemed like to the cries of women in labor...."

It has been suggested that military campaigns in classical times were limited to summer months to avoid scurvy. Men could forage during their marches through agricultural areas, and armies were small enough to subsist on the food available in this fashion. But during the winter, food had to be brought along and, not only was transportation a major problem, but fresh food was not available for transport in sufficient quantities.

Lack of vitamin C was also a problem for American colonists, whose food lost its antiscorbutic properties during winter storage, before new crops grew. The timing of the usual early symptoms of scurvy is thought to have led to the term "spring fever," originally a description of the lassitude of scurvy among early settlers.

Purpura Nautica. Scurvy became a disease of sailors during The Age of Discovery, since the first discovery of the age was the ability to make long sea voyages. The disease appeared when sailors were kept at sea without fresh provisions, such as when they were bringing spices and other products from the East Indies or India to Holland or Britain. Reserve stores of vitamin C in body tissues could sustain men on their usual diet for two to three months. However, men weakened during longer voyages; hemorrhages appeared in the skin; the gums thickened, grew sore, and bled easily; and teeth loosened and fell out. Later, weakness became prostration and death followed.

The Age of Discovery began when Prince Henry the Navigator of Portugal founded a school to teach navigation to sailors, hoping to stimulate exploration and thus enhance the acquisition of wealth that would be brought back to Lisbon. His school taught sailors the use of the astrolabe to determine latitude by taking a sighting on the North Star, thus enabling them to know their position when sailing along the coasts of Africa. Although most adventurers feared going too far south along the coast of Africa, with Henry's prodding, the range of his sailors grew until they could reach India, and on to even farther shores.

Long sea voyages became common once Columbus applied this new knowledge of navigation by sailing west to find the East Indies. Although sailors found that they did not fall off the edge of the earth, as some had feared, they began to perish from scurvy, a previously rare disease. After the time of Columbus, scurvy became as great a scourge for sailors as smallpox was for landlubbers. However, in contrast to smallpox, survival after developing scurvy did not result in immunity from future attacks. The disease was so pervasive that it occasionally wiped out entire crews: On one occasion a Spanish galleon was found floating at sea, all hands dead of scurvy.

The disease was often called *Purpura nautica,* based on the association with sailors and the purple blotches caused by the bruiselike hemorrhages occurring just under the skin. Some authors recorded the opinion that scurvy was a venereal disease, in view of the usual proclivities of sailors, but rather than being acquired (along with other venereal diseases) when they reached shore, scurvy appeared when they could not get to shore. In his textbook of medicine, Martin Lister, Physician to Queen Anne at the beginning of the eighteenth century, placed his chapter on scurvy adjacent to that on venereal disease, noting that both were new diseases that had appeared only after Columbus' voyages to the New World, and that both occurred frequently in sailors. Lister wrote that the two diseases "are so closely related and have so much in common that they are not readily distinguished from each other, except by an experienced physician."

Thus, a four-century epidemic of scurvy among sailors began as a result of changes in navigation and the development of long-distance seaborne commerce. The significance of scurvy in naval history, and the measures that led to its control, can be summarized by the biography of the Scottish physician James Lind.

Dr. James Lind and the Use of Lemon Juice to Fight Napoleon. In 1795, when the British Admiralty finally adopted the recommendation made by Dr. James Lind regarding the prevention of scurvy aboard their men-of-war, the manpower of the British Navy was effectively doubled. Lind is given major credit for making possible Admiral Nelson's many victories (most notably Trafalgar) and thus thwarting Napoleon's plans to invade Britain.

The value of Lind's contribution can be seen in some statistics from the main British naval hospital at Haslar, where he served as chief physician. During 1750, a typical year before Lind's treatise, 1,457 cases of scurvy were admitted to that hospital. In contrast, when the First Lord of the Admiralty, Earl Spencer, visited Haslar in 1797, and asked to see a case of scurvy, there were none to show him! Between 1806 and 1810, key years in the struggle against Napoleon, only two cases of scurvy were admitted to Haslar.

James Lind (1716–1794) grew up in Edinburgh, son of a merchant and brother of a naval officer. At the age of 23, after serving a brief apprenticeship to a surgeon, he joined the Royal Navy as a surgeon's mate. When Britain went to war with France and Spain in October 1739 ("The War of Jenkin's Ear," 1739–1743), Lind was assigned to HMS *Salisbury*, which joined the expedition under Captain (later Lord) George Anson. He received a thorough education in the medical problems of British sailors during Anson's 1740–1744 trip around the world to harass Spanish commerce and foment revolt against Spain by colonists in Chile and Panama. The fleet rounded Cape Horn early in 1741, and by May of that year sickness had caused the death of half of the company aboard Anson's flagship, the *Centurion*. There were similar problems aboard the other vessels. As Anson wrote on one occasion, "Out of 200 odd men which remained alive ... the lieutenant could number no more than two quartermasters and six fore-mast men capable of working."

After that war ended, Lind returned to Edinburgh, completed his education, and received his medical degree in May 1748. While practicing medicine in Edinburgh, he wrote and published both his *Treatise on Scurvy* and an essay on preserving the health of seamen in the Royal Navy that contained effective suggestions for the control of typhus and tropical fevers. In 1758, he left Edinburgh to become Physician-in-Charge of the Royal Naval Hospital at Haslar, where he remained for 25 years.

During Lind's first two years at Haslar, 5,743 sailors were admitted as patients, of whom 1,146 had scurvy. During the next large European War (The Seven Years' War, 1756–1763, called the French and Indian War in the American colonies), whenever the Channel fleet put into its base at Spithead, it usually sent between 1,000 and 2,000 men with scurvy to Haslar for treatment. Lind continued his efforts to convince naval officers of the need for preventive measures against the disease, and gradually individual officers began to pay increasing attention to his suggestions.

Although there is no evidence that Captain James Cook knew Lind personally, he was familiar with the principle that fresh food was essential to the health of sailors during long sea voyages. When he set out on his second voyage of exploration, a three-year trip around Cape Horn and into the Pacific that circumnavigated the globe (1772–1775), he insisted that his ships take every opportunity to touch land and obtain fresh supplies of vegetables and fruit. He believed in the antiscorbutic use of celery, "scurvy grass," and especially sauerkraut, which the Dutch Navy had found beneficial. "Scurvy grass" could have been one or more of several plants that were observed to be effective agents in treating scurvy, including the spoonwort (*Cochlearia curiosa* or *officinalis*) or cresses, such as species of *Cardamine*. During the voyage, any man showing signs of scurvy was given a malt brew and a portion of concentrated juice of oranges and lemons (a quantity called a "rob"). Although Cook failed to find the postulated huge southern continent (he may have been searching for Antarctica, based on sketchy reports of its existence), he did discover Easter Island and the Sandwich (Hawaiian) Islands, and he visited Alaska, seeking the "Northwest Passage." He entered what is now known as Cook's Inlet and reached the present site of the city of Anchorage before abandoning his quest and reversing his course in a body of water known ever since as "Turnagain Bay." On his return to London he was awarded the Copley Medal by the Royal Society, as much for achieving such a long sea voyage without losing a single man from scurvy as for his geographic discoveries.

"Scurvy grasses" were long known to be beneficial against scurvy. In his book, Lind quoted the outstanding seventeenth-century British physician Sydenham as having employed leaves of scurvy grass in the form of an extract, like tea, in the treatment of the disease in 1685. As one remedy, Lind proposed combining the juice of half an orange with the leaves and seeds of scurvy grass steeped in either wine or beer.

The Dutch were the first to build large cargo ships, and they dominated commerce with their imports from the East Indies. Like all sailors at sea for long periods, Dutch sailors engaged in this commerce suffered from scurvy. In his *Treatise*, Lind mentioned that the Dutch physician Ronsseus of Gonda had employed oranges and lemons as a cure for scurvy in 1564, and that Sir Richard Hawkins protected his crew aboard the *Dainty* in similar fashion. In 1600, Commodore James Lancaster of the East India Company also emphasized the value of lemon juice, as did the Dutch captain, Hakluyt, who added oranges to the list of antiscorbutic agents. Knowledge of these observations by the Dutch was a major reason why Lind tested oranges and lemons for antiscorbutic action in his famous 1740 controlled experiment.

While serving as surgeon aboard HMS *Salisbury* during his round-the-world trip with Captain Anson, Lind was faced with a great number of cases of scurvy and a high mortality rate. To test which of the many suggested remedies were truly useful, Lind designed the first carefully controlled therapeutic trials in history. Lind set up what would later be called a "clinical research unit" in a forward hold of the *Salisbury* to test the suggested cures. The following passage appears in his book, and was also reprinted verbatim in the first edition of the *Encyclopedia Britannica*, first published in Edinburgh, in 1771, by "A Society of Gentlemen in Scotland."

"Of the Prevention of Scurvy:
On the 20th of May 1747, I selected twelve patients in the scurvy, on board the Salisbury at sea. Their cases were as similar as I could have them. They all in general had putrid gums, the spots, and lassitude, with weakness of their knees. They lay together in one place, being a proper apartment for the sick in the fore-hold; and had one diet common to all, viz. water-gruel sweetened with sugar in the morning; fresh mutton-broth often times for dinner; at other times light puddings, boiled biscuit with sugar, etc. and for supper, barley and raisins, rice and currants, sago and wine, or the like. Two of these were ordered each a quart of cyder a day. Two others took twenty-five drops of elixir vitriol three times a day, upon an empty stomach; using a gargle of it for their mouths. Two others took two spoonfuls of vinegar three times a-day, upon an empty stomach, using a gargle of it for their mouths. Two others took two spoonfuls of vinegar three times a-day, upon an empty stomach; having their gruels and other foods sharpened with vinegar, and also the gargle for their mouth. Two of the worst patients, with the tendons in the ham quite rigid (a symptom none of the rest had) were put under a course of sea-water. Of this they drank half a pint every day, and sometimes more or less, as it operated by way of a gently physic. Two others had each two oranges and one lemon given them every day. These they ate with greediness, at different times,

upon an empty stomach. They continued but six days under this course, having consumed the quantity that could be spared, The two remaining patients took the bigness of a nutmeg three times a-day, of an electuary recommended by a hospital surgeon, made of garlic, mustard-seed, horse-radish, balsam of Peru, and gum myrrh; using for common drink, barley-water boiled with tamarinds; by which, with the addition of cream of tartar, they were gently purged three or four times during the course.

The consequence was that the most sudden and visible good effects were perceived from the use of oranges and lemons; one of these who had taken them being at the end of six days fit for duty. The spots were not indeed at that time quite off his body, but his gums were sound; but without any other medicine, than a gargle of it for his mouth, he became quite healthy before we came into Plymouth, which was on the 16th of June. The other was the best recovered of any in his condition; and being now pretty well, was appointed to attend the rest of the sick.

Next to the oranges, I thought the cyder had the best effects. It was indeed not very sound. However, those who had taken it, were in a fairer way of recovery than the others at the end of the fortnight, which was the length of time all these different courses were continued, except the oranges. The putrefaction of their gums, but especially their lassitude and weakness, were somewhat abated, and their appetite increased by it."

Lind died before his recommendations to stock ships with oranges or citrus juices were implemented, but he found a champion in Gilbert Blane, also a graduate of Edinburgh Medical School. Blane served at sea during the American War of Independence with Admiral Romney. In 1781, the British Fleet in the West Indies under Romney had nearly 3,000 cases of scurvy, but the opposing French fleet had an even greater incidence. Blane felt that the collection of accurate data was important, and recorded that scurvy was second only to infections (probably largely yellow fever) as the cause of 1,600 deaths in a fleet of 12,000, with only 60 deaths due to enemy action. After leaving the navy, Blane became a successful practitioner in London, but kept an interest in the health of sailors, publishing two editions of a book, *Observations on the Diseases of Seaman.* He was appointed by Admiral Romney to be a Commissioner of the Board of Sick and Wounded Sailors. Blane was an ardent advocate of Lind's principles, and much more articulate and influential than Lind had been. The Admiralty accepted the recommendation made by the Board, and authorized a daily allowance of three-quarters of an ounce of lemon juice in the navy. Admiralty records reveal that, between 1795 and 1814, 1.6 million ounces of lemon juice were issued.

Before this simple but epoch-making reform, a sea-going fleet had to be relieved every ten weeks, since by that time the crews were becoming weakened by scurvy. A fresh fleet of equal strength had to be sent to replace it so that the scurvy-ridden ships could return to their home ports for rehabilitation of the men, although naval historians usually refer only to refitting of the ships. During the symposium honoring Lind in 1953, a retired Director-General of the British Navy, Surgeon Vice Admiral Sir Sheldon Dudley, pointed out that "the application of Lind's recommendations suddenly killed naval scurvy in 1795... intelligent naval senior executive officers asserted that this event was the equivalent of doubling the fighting force of the navy.... It is no idle fancy to assert that Lind, as much as Nelson, broke the power of Napoleon."

Lind's efforts had not been entirely ignored during those 40 years following publication of his *Treatise*. During the Seven Years' War, Sir Edward Hawke was commanding a British fleet blockading the French fleet at Brest. Hawke, without authorization from the Admiralty, specifically followed the suggestions of Lind, insisting that fresh fruits and vegetables be sent to his ships regularly while on station during the blockade. They took their stations in May 1759, and remained at their posts without relief for seven months, when a decisive battle was fought at Quiberon Bay off the coast of Brittany. On the day of the battle, November 20, not more than 20 of the 14,000 sailors in Hawke's command were sick. His successful blockade prevented the French from reinforcing Montcalm in Quebec, and thus contributed significantly to the British conquest of Canada.

If Lind deserves some credit for the British victory in Canada, he gets none for the British efforts during the American Revolutionary war. That war began 22 years after his suggestions were published, but his proposals were ignored by the British commanders during the conflict. The personal experience of the future Lord Nelson, a junior officer at the time, typifies the problems faced by naval personnel before Lind's recommendations were adopted. In September of 1782, Nelson was serving aboard the *Albemarle*, blockading Boston harbor. The *Albemarle's* company had had their last fresh meal in Portsmouth, England, in April, before setting out to join the blockading fleet. While crossing the Atlantic, they had subsisted on the standard ration for ships at sea at the time: stale biscuits, rancid water, and salt beef. In September, Nelson and other members of the crew had "spongy gums, loose teeth, unnatural fatigue, and mental depression." The *Albemarle* was forced to abandon the blockade and set sail for Quebec to seek treatment for the men.

In 1803, Britain stood alone against France, and in 1804 Napoleon convinced Spain to declare war against Great Britain. He then started to gather his army near Boulogne for the invasion of Britain, calling the 100,000-man force "The Army of England." Some 2,000 boats and barges were gathered between

Brest and Antwerp to ferry the troops across the English Channel, but Napoleon knew he must have naval command of the Channel to successfully invade the British Isles. He boasted that if control of the channel could be obtained for six hours, "we shall be masters of the world."

Napoleon planned to gather the combined French and Spanish fleets, then lying at anchor in Atlantic and Mediterranean harbors, which were blockaded by the British. Admiral Nelson commanded the British fleet blockading the Mediterranean ports, and Napoleon tried to prevent him from joining the British Channel fleet. He instructed the commander of the French Mediterranean fleet to slip the blockade and draw Nelson in pursuit across the Atlantic, expecting to keep Nelson's crew at sea long enough for them to develop scurvy and be ineffective in reinforcing the channel fleet during the invasion.

Following Napoleon's orders, during the night of March 30, 1805, Admiral Villeneuve slipped out of Toulon with eleven ships of the line and eight frigates. It took some time for Nelson to decide which way the French had headed, but after receiving reports that Villaneuve had sailed past Gibraltar, he followed him westward into the Atlantic on what his biographers refer to as "The Long Chase."

When Villeneuve reached the West Indies on May 14, he landed 1,000 sick sailors, soldiers, and marines, and buried many others at Martinique. But, contrary to all past naval experience, the British fleet remained healthy. Nelson's ten ships of the line sailed across the Atlantic at an average speed of 5$\frac{1}{2}$ knots and made landfall at Barbados on June 4; there is no mention of illness among the men. Nelson, concerned about the health of his men, had obtained permission from the Admiralty to obtain 20,000 gallons of lemon juice locally for his fleet, supplementing the regular issue of 30,000 gallons. Judging from a letter he wrote to his friend, Lord Collingwood, Nelson knew of Napoleon's general strategy for weakening the crews of his ships: "Bonaparte has often made his boast that our fleet would be worn out by keeping the sea, and that his would be kept in order and increasing by staying in port; now I find, I fancy that his suffered more in a night than ours in a year."

When the news of Nelson's arrival reached Villeneuve, he quickly set sail eastward, leaving on June 8. Nelson immediately followed, believing the French were heading back to the Mediterranean. But instead, Villeneuve sailed to the English Channel. When Nelson reached Cadiz on July 18, he realized his error and departed for home waters on July 23, the same day that Napoleon arrived at Boulogne to begin final preparations for the invasion. Before leaving the area, Nelson went ashore at Gibraltar (July 20, 1805) and entered into his dairy, "went ashore for the first time since June 16, 1803, and from my foot out of the

Victory two years wanting ten days." Such a long stay at sea was impossible before James Lind.

Nelson joined the Channel fleet under Admiral Cornwallis, off Brest, on August 14, bringing the main fleet up to forty ships of the line. His men were ready to fight—not debilitated by scurvy as the French expected them to be after so long at sea. The French fleet under Villeneuve planned to link up with the fleet under Admiral Ganteaume at Brest, and then enter the channel in support of the invasion. But the large, fully manned British fleet blocked their entry into the channel, and Villeneuve turned back, heading for Cadiz. The threat of invasion was ended.

Nelson followed Villeneuve to Cadiz, and remained at sea while the French were in the port. When the French finally dared to leave Cadiz on October 21, 1805, Nelson engaged them immediately. The resulting action, the Battle of Trafalgar, destroyed so much of the French fleet that Napoleon permanently abandoned his plan to control the waters of the Channel and invade England. He turned instead to war with Austria and invasion of Russia.

Although Nelson did not follow the "Fighting Instructions" of the Admiralty at Trafalgar, preferring to invent his own plan of action, he did follow their instructions regarding the frequent provisioning of his ships with fresh fruits and vegetables and the ration of lime juice, as prescribed by Lind. It is somewhat surprising that Nelson obeyed these antiscorbutic orders, in view of the notes left by Dr. Beatty, his physician aboard the *Victory*, who was at his side when he died. Beatty recorded, "... early in his life, when he first went to sea, he left off the use of salt, which he believed to be the sole cause of scurvy, and he never took it afterward with his food." In retrospect, this view was not unreasonable: large amounts of salt were used to preserve the meat taken aboard ships during long voyages, and the sailors thus had a high salt intake during those periods when they had no fresh food. Analysis would have shown the association of scurvy with salt intake to be statistically significant and therefore a much more convincing hypothesis than the absence of something—vitamin C—whose existence was not known until over a century later.

When Lind's advice for the prevention of scurvy was finally implemented, the order from the Admiralty fixed an allowance of an ounce of lemon juice with one and a half ounces of sugar served daily to each sailor after two weeks at sea. The lemon juice was often called lime juice, and the British sailors were derisively called "lime-juicers," and then "Limeys" by American sailors. The interchangeable use of the name "lime" and "lemon" by the British led to tragedy well after the value of citrus juice in the prevention of scurvy was completely accepted. The term lime juice was used for both the Mediterranean lemon (*Citrus medical*, var. *limonum*) and the West Indian lime (*Citrus medica*, var.

acidum), but unfortunately, the latter is not an effective antiscorbutic. Some nineteenth and early twentieth expeditions to the Arctic and Antarctic carried the West Indian lime as their antiscorbutic, and thus suffered grievously from scurvy, whereas earlier expeditions, which had used lemons for this purpose, had been free of the disease.

SCURVY IN THE AMERICAN CIVIL WAR. Supplying armies with fresh vegetables to prevent scurvy was always difficult, and scurvy was as much a problem for soldiers as it was for sailors. Excellent records were collected during the American Civil War, and they were published by the Federal Surgeon General's office after the war in a monumental work called the *Medical and Surgical History of the War of the Rebellion*. These records are the most complete of any American war because the physicians at the time wanted their experiences to be available to others. The lessons they learned about scurvy are worth reviewing.

Even in the small, 15,000 man pre-Civil War United States army, scurvy was the most common disease reported from frontier posts. Providing fresh vegetables was an insurmountable problem because of the volume needed and the perishable nature of produce. As a result, the army devised a concoction to prevent scurvy called "desiccated compressed mixed vegetables," made by drying combinations of various vegetables and compressing them into cakes. Army regulations required preparing them for meals by boiling the desiccated vegetables in large volumes of water for five hours. These orders could be obeyed by professional soldiers on small army posts with designated cooks, but were impractical once large, volunteer armies were formed and men cooked individually or in small groups, or during strenuous training or campaigning. These unappetizing vegetable cakes probably had all the water soluble, heat-labile vitamin C cooked out of them. Refusing to eat the dried mass of roots, leaves, and stalks, troops called the cakes "desecrated vegetables."

Scurvy was reported in Union forces in the spring of 1862, but Army of the Potomac Medical Director Charles S. Tripler refused to believe the reports, since he knew that the troops had been issued the desiccated vegetables. When he checked, he found that the men were not eating them, and the reports of scurvy were correct. The disease became epidemic in the Army late in the Peninsula Campaign of 1862. Throughout the war, foraging was an important source of vegetables for campaigning troops, but in Virginia, fields were devastated by the war, and foraging was of no benefit when troops were immobilized during a siege, such as at Petersburg, or when fighting almost daily battles, as in Sherman's campaign.

Scurvy and night blindness, both later shown to be nutritional deficiency diseases, were included in the monthly reports sent in by field surgeons to the Surgeon General's office. The total numbers of diagnosed cases of these illnesses are relatively small, since diagnoses required fully developed syndromes and milder cases went undetected. Nevertheless, the data give us a good idea about the frequency and significance of malnutrition during the Civil War.

Army physicians noted that when some men had diagnosable scurvy, the entire unit was affected by less severe disease. The clinical manifestations of "florid scurvy" were described in impressive detail; the first manifestations observed were usually lassitude, an apparent laziness, and an indisposition to do assigned tasks. Terms such as "muscular debility and depression of the spirit" were recorded. Soon physical abnormalities became apparent in many men, such as "sallow appearance, puffy, tender, and bleeding state of the gums, with a tendency for the teeth to become loose." Small hemorrhages in the skin also were described, and some surgeons observed excessive bleeding from wounds. Scurvy was particularly common in Sherman's army during the Atlanta campaign of 1864, since all supplies were brought along a single-track railroad and vegetables were not a priority. One surgeon observed during this campaign that wounds "required a larger number of sutures than usual during surgery"—a prime manifestation of scurvy. Very few deaths of soldiers in the field were attributed directly to scurvy, but in prison camps the story was quite different. For example, about 25 percent of the deaths at Andersonville were attributed to scurvy by Confederate surgeon Joseph Jones, who was sent to study the reasons for the camp's high mortality rate.

Night blindness caused by vitamin A deficiency was observed frequently, but few men were relieved from duty because of it and, therefore, the number of cases in the official reports was low. It was considered a bizarre form of malingering, since the men could see well and were able to go into battle with their units after dawn. One Confederate physician, Dr. Robert J. Hicks, mentioned a dietary factor in the cause of night blindness in the Army of Northern Virginia. He recorded: "A man who could see well during the day complained at nightfall that he could not see, and like a blind man, walked holding the arm of a comrade.... It was considered . . . due to the meager diet, the want of vegetables." Some Union physicians recorded that furloughs cured night blindness, probably as a result of an improved diet at home, but other Civil War physicians felt that it supported the concept that night blindness was feigned for the purpose of obtaining a furlough.

The incidence of scurvy and night blindness rose almost continuously during the course of the war. The available data show the correlations between malnutrition, infectious diseases, and wound treatment. The case fatality rates for all major diseases, such as typhoid fever, pneumonia, smallpox, and tuberculosis, rose progressively throughout the war, despite decreases in the incidence of these disease (except for the 1863 smallpox epidemic) and considerable improvements in the overall quality of the medical care, efficient hospitals, and better nursing. No explanation for this phenomenon is obvious, but the increase in case fatality rates may relate to the increasing frequency of malnutrition as documented by an increasing incidence of diagnosed scurvy and night blindness.

Civil War physicians and nurses thought that malnutrition affected recovery from illness or wounds. For example, famed Confederate nurse Phoebe Pember, who served as a matron (essentially a charge nurse who supervised a large hospital ward or a group of wards) at Chimborazo Hospital in Richmond, wrote of the high mortality rate following late, secondary amputations. ("Secondary" amputations were done in a hospital long after the initial wound, to treat complications such as continued inflammation, infection, or repeated hemorrhage.) She believed the high mortality was mostly caused by the soldiers' nutritional state: "Poor food and great exposure," she wrote, "had thinned the blood and broken down the system so entirely that secondary amputations performed in the hospital almost invariably resulted in death, after the second year of the war. [The] only cases under my observation that survived were two Irishmen, and it was really so difficult to kill an Irishman that there really was little cause for boasting on the part of the officiating surgeon."

Analysis of the mortality rate among the wounded in Sherman's Union army during the Atlanta campaign provides additional support for the concept that malnutrition affected the fatality rate following wounds. During the Atlanta campaign, scurvy and night blindness progressively increased in incidence in Sherman's troops as his army fought frequent battles against General Joe Johnston's defending Confederate forces. In his memoirs, Sherman recalled "the extreme anxiety of my medical director, Dr. Kittoe, about the scurvy, which he reported at one time to be spreading and imperiling the army. This occurred at a crisis about Kennesaw [June 1864], when the [single-track] railroad was taxed to its utmost capacity to provide the necessary ammunition, food, and forage, and could not possibly bring us an adequate supply of potatoes and cabbage, the usual antiscorbutics." After the fall of Atlanta on September 1, the railroad brought in fresh vegetables for the troops. The mortality rate of the wounded rose in parallel with the incidence of diagnosed scurvy until September; then both fell and continued to parallel each other remarkably during the subsequent months of 1864.

Years after the war, Dr. Joseph Jones reflected on possible explanations for the increase in the frequency of wound complications over its course. He wrote, "Secondary hemorrhage, massive bleeding occurring several days or weeks after the surgery, as well as pyemia and hospital gangrene[E2] progressively increased with the progress of the war, and after the great battles of the expiring Confederacy...[in 1864–1865] it was of daily, and at times, almost hourly occurrence in the hospitals ....

"The great increase in secondary hemorrhage appeared to be referable to the prolonged use of salt meat, and to the consequent scorbutic condition of the blood, although active symptoms of scurvy were not manifested, the increase of pyemia and hospital gangrene, may in like manner, have been connected, in a measure at least, with the physical and chemical changes of the blood and organs, dependent upon imperfect nutrition and sameness of diet."

Civilians in the War Against Scurvy. Civilians as well as army surgeons knew that fresh vegetables were needed by the troops. Most women who contributed to the war effort were mothers who knew the importance of diet to health. They formed innumerable Ladies' Aid Societies, many of which became affiliated with the U.S. or the Western Sanitary Commission or the Christian Commission. Once scurvy appeared in epidemic form during the Peninsula campaign (June 1862), Sanitary Commission members focused some of their efforts on obtaining the vegetables that the army could not supply. Lemons and oranges were known to be most effective in combating scurvy, but could not be provided in sufficient quantities and spoiled too readily.

Mary Livermore, president of one of the dozen aid societies of Chicago and later a leader of the Western Sanitary Commission, focused her efforts on getting sufficient amounts of potatoes and onions, the most practical antiscorbutics, to the troops. Livermore arranged for local aid societies to give talent shows in which the charge for admission was a potato or an onion. School children competed to bring in the most potatoes. Signs and slogans appeared: "Don't send your sweetheart a love letter. Send him an onion."

Aid societies sent wagons door-to-door gathering potatoes and onions from storekeepers, farmers, and housewives, and ensured that the supplies collected would begin their journey towards the troops. For example, Livermore arranged for General Grant to provide the shipping if the women would see that the boats were manned; one of her associates, a Mrs. Hoge, became commander of the "potato fleet."

Livermore also arranged a huge Sanitary Fair in Chicago to raise money for the efforts of the commission and to provide shipments of vegetables for the troops. The day of the fair, October 27, 1863, the entire city of Chicago (population 110,000) shut down; banks closed, courts adjourned, and schools were dismissed. Parades included 100 wagons laden with potatoes, onions, cabbage, and beets, plus barrels of cider and kegs of beer. Spectators cheered and helped unload the produce into Sanitary Commission storage rooms. Newspapers printed daily human-interest stories, such as the gift of five barrels of potatoes by six young girls who had raised the vegetables themselves. For fourteen days, similar parades of foodstuffs arrived containing chickens, calves, loads of hay, apples, bags of beans, pots of butter, bundles of socks, mechanical products, and other gifts for soldiers or items to be sold to raise money. Similar fairs were held in many cities throughout the Union states.

These efforts helped minimize the frequency of scurvy, at least in camps and among garrison troops. However, the difficulty in transporting vegetables to campaigning troops resulted in an increase in the frequency of scurvy in the last year of the fighting. The experience of the Civil War was typical of the problems of malnutrition in general, and scurvy in particular, in armies before that time and for at least another half-century afterward.

HOW AN END TO WET-NURSING CAUSED AN OUTBREAK OF INFANTILE SCURVY. Because infants were exclusively breast-fed in the era before bottled milk, and breast milk contains enough vitamin C to prevent scurvy, this disease was not seen in infants until late in the nineteenth century. This epidemic of infantile scurvy was an unfortunate side effect of modern public health measures; public concern about germs changed many daily customs, including those associated with child rearing.

Before the twentieth century, well-to-do women rarely breast-fed their own children. Wet nurses were widely used for this purpose, and wet-nursing was a common way in which single women could obtain a livelihood. A poor, unmarried women would get pregnant, put her baby in a foundling home (where it usually died), and rent herself out to nurse other children until she stopped lactating, when she would repeat the process.

This centuries-old practice suddenly changed when the public became concerned about the spread of disease-causing germs. The discovery of the tubercle bacillus in 1882 and knowledge of the way tuberculosis spread brought wet-nursing to an end. Tuberculosis was a common causes of death at that time, "the white plague of the nineteenth century," and the possibility that a coughing nurse could infect a baby (as often happened) led people to seek a substitute. Physicians found that newborn infants could be successfully fed diluted cow's milk, but concerns were raised about germs in cow's milk due to the filthy conditions under which the cows were kept, and how the milk was collected and handled. To make the milk germ-free, it was pasteurized or boiled, but because vitamin C is heat-labile, the pasteurized cow's milk was devoid of vitamin C.

Bottle-fed infants received adequate calories and protein, but not enough vitamin C.

Infantile scurvy first appeared in 1877, when Dr. Walter Cheadle (1836–1910), a British expert on rickets, diagnosed scurvy as well as rickets in a sixteen-month-old boy. Although Cheadle was the first to describe the disease, Dr. Thomas Barlow of London wrote about it in 1884, reporting a large number of cases, including three at autopsy. Thus, it became known as Barlow's disease. Reports of infantile scurvy began appearing in the United States about 1891, when eleven cases were observed, and attention was focused on the problem in 1894, when 116 cases were reported at the New York Academy of Medicine.

A puzzling feature of infantile scurvy at the time was the occurrence of the disease in relatively well-to-do families, but not in the poor, the opposite of most of the other diseases. In retrospect, it is clear that poor women breast-fed their own babies, and thus these children did not develop scurvy. Wealthier women, who had eschewed the use of wet nurses, fed their infants boiled or "condensed" cow's milk, thus denying their children adequate amounts of vitamin C. The discovery of the role of vitamins in the diet and the importance of substitute sources of vitamin C for infants, usually in orange juice, brought the disease under control in about 1917.

ADDITIONAL READING

Adams GW. *Doctors in Blue; The Medical History of the Union Army in the Civil War.* New York: H. Schuman, 1952.

Alcott LM. *Hospital Sketches.* Chester, CT: Applewood Books, Distributed by Globe Pequot Press, 1993.

Bollet AJ. *Civil War Medicine: Challenges and Triumphs.* Tucson, AZ: Galen Press, 2002.

Carpenter KJ. *The History of Scurvy and Vitamin C.* New York: Cambridge Univ Press, 1986.

Confederate States Medical and Surgical Journal, With an Introduction By William D. Sharpe, M.D. Metuchen, NJ: Scarecrow Press, 1976.

Crandon JH, Lund CC, Dill DB. Human experimental scurvy. *N Engl J Med* 1940;223:353.

Creighton C. *A History of Epidemics in Britain.* London: Cass, 1965.

Dudley SF. James Lind: laudatory address. *Proc Nutr Soc* 1953;12:202.

Duffy J. *Epidemics in Colonial America.* Baton Rouge, LA: Louisiana State Univ Press, 1966.

Encyclopedia Britannica (First edition), Scurvy, vol III: 106. Edinburgh: Bell and MacFarquar, 1771.

Follis RH Jr. *Deficiency Disease.* Springfield, IL: Charles C. Thomas, 1958.

Hodges RE, Baker EM, et al. Experimental scurvy in man. *Am J Clin Nutr* 1969;22:535.

Holst A. Discussion on the causation and treatment of scurvy. *BMJ* 1908,ii:725.

Holt LE. *Diseases of Infancy and Childhood.* New York: D. Appleton & Co, 1897.

Hughes RE. James Lind and the cure of scurvy: an experimental approach. *Medical History* 1975;19:342.

Lewis HE. Medical aspects of polar exploration: sixtieth anniversary of Scott's last expedition. State of knowledge about scurvy in 1911. *Proc R Soc Med* 1972;65:17–25.

Lind J. *A Treatise on the Scurvy. In three parts. Containing an inquiry into the nature, causes, and cure, of that disease. Together with a critical and chronological view of what has been published on the subject.* London: A. Miller, 1757

Lorenz AJ. Some pre-Lind writers on scurvy *Proc Nutr Soc* 1953;12:306–24.

Wyatt HV. James Lind and the prevention of scurvy. *Medical History* 1976;20:433.

[E1]Although the initiating cause of the Irish "potato famine" was a fungal blight, conditions were exacerbated by human actions—namely, the enforced requirement that crops raised in Ireland that could have supported the population were demanded as payment by landlords and exported to England.

[E2]Hospital gangrene was a form of necrotizing fasciitis that spread primarily among hospitalized patients. It was often associated with erysipelas. It was probably caused by Streptococci.

CHAPTER 12

RICKETS

THE ENGLISH DISEASE

R ICKETS RESULTS FROM THE INADEQUATE MINERALIZA-
tion of bone. Especially during infancy and childhood, when it is forming,
the abnormally soft bone bends and curves during weight bearing and from other
stresses. If rickets occurs after growth is complete, the result is a softening of the
bone, known as osteomalacia. Because bones are always remodeling and reform-
ing, even adults can suffer rickets-caused deformities from prolonged physical
stresses.

The bony changes of rickets are particularly characteristic on x-ray examina-
tions. Osteomalacia is also diagnosable by x-ray or by bone density measure-
ments, but often cannot be distinguished from osteoporosis, the more frequent
cause of thinning bone, which is primarily the result of lack of bone matrix.

Rickets or osteomalacia occurs when the necessary minerals—calcium and
phosphorus, in particular—and vitamin D are not available. Humans can rarely
acquire sufficient amounts of vitamin D from dietary sources alone; however, we
can synthesize vitamin D through the skin, using ubiquitous precursors that are
activated by the ultraviolet rays of sunlight. Lack of sunlight is therefore a major
factor in the etiology of rickets. Human activities that limit exposure to sunlight
are important as a cause of rickets, especially in northern zones where sunlight
is marginal at best.

A normal individual synthesizes 7-dehydrocholesterol, which is converted to
calciferol in the skin by ultraviolet irradiation; subsequent hydroxylation (addition of -OH) in the liver, gut, and kidney completes the synthesis of all the
active forms of the vitamin. If humans do not get enough sunlight, they must
have dietary sources of Vitamin D as a substitute. Fully active forms of the vita-

min, which do not need exposure to ultraviolet light, have been synthesized and provided as a dietary supplement, especially in "vitamin-D fortified milk."

Paleontologic bone specimens reveal that rickets is clearly an ancient disease, one that existed in many long-extinct animal species. For example, a bowed femur and an unusually curved long bone of a small hawk, characteristic changes of rickets, were found in a Pleistocene wolf from the La Brea asphalt pits of the Los Angeles area. Cave-bear bones from Belgium show evidence of rickets. These bones were described by the famous German pathologist, Rudolph Virchow, who referred to the disease as "cave-rickets." Unmistakable examples of rickets have also been found among the skeletons of captive baboons from the dynastic tombs of Ancient Egypt.

Some medical authorities have suggested that people described as "crook-backed" in the Bible (e.g., in Leviticus) had spinal curvature caused by rickets, but spinal tuberculosis (Pott's disease) is also a possibility. Many mummies have been found showing evidence typical of Pott's disease, including a priest of the 21st dynasty, who lived about the same time as the period of the Exodus. Moreover, rickets is an unlikely occurrence in the sunny climate of Palestine and Egypt, and no mummies with confirmed findings of rickets or osteomalacia have been described. Those pet baboons must have been kept caged indoors.

Except for a few examples found in Scandinavia, bony evidence of rickets is scarce or nonexistent in ancient human skeletal remains until the late Middle Ages. During that time, the disease suddenly became frequent in cities across northern and central Europe. At Fazekasboda, Hungary, specimens of human bone dating from Roman times through the Middle Ages chronicle a steady increase in the frequency of rickets in that region during the Middle Ages. For example, in one area, Zalavar, rickets is three times as common in remains from the twelfth century as in those from the ninth. Very little evidence exists of rickets outside Europe, with the exception of cases seen recently in China, and in Pakistan among Moslem women who were kept in strict purdah.

In texts from about 130 CE, the noted physician Soranus of Ephesus referred to a disease that caused "backbone bending" and twisted thighs. Ephesus is situated along the western coast of present-day Turkey and has a very sunny climate but it was a crowded, busy seaport and commercial center from early Greek times. Soranus noted that the disease was less common in the countryside than in the smoky city, where numerous fires were kept going for warmth, cooking, and industrial purposes. In northern Europe, the coming of the Industrial Age and its accompanying air pollution decreased the small amount of ultraviolet radiation available from sunlight and duplicated the observations made by Soranus 1,800 years earlier.

The modern medical history of rickets began on October 18, 1645, when a 25-year-old English medical student from Oxford, Daniel Whistler (1619–1684), read a thesis for his doctorate degree at the celebrated Dutch medical school at Leiden. The title of his thesis "Concerning a Disease of English Children Which Is Popularly Called the Rickets," indicates that the name "rickets" was apparently in popular use before that time. Once the disease was medically recognized through Whistler's thesis, diagnoses of rickets increased rapidly, and many practitioners believed it was a new disease. Its outbreak quickly became of sufficient concern that the Royal College of Physicians in London formed a three-member commission to look into the problem. In 1651, the committee, which included three of the most prominent physicians of the time (Francis Glisson, George Bate, and Ahaseurus Regemorter), reported that, "He, who will accurately contemplate the signs of this affect... may most easily persuade himself that this is an absolutely new disease."

New or not, the disease clearly was rapidly increasing in frequency at about this time, on the continent as well as in Britain. Following the reports of Whistler and that of Glisson's committee, rickets became known elsewhere in Europe as the "English Disease" ("Die Englisher Krankheit"). John Graunt, a Fellow of the Royal Society of Medicine, began recording "Bills of Mortality" in London; these records mention significant numbers of deaths from rickets in the middle of the seventeenth century. Graunt, a professional statistician who is considered one of the fathers of modern epidemiology, wrote in 1676, "It is also to be observed that the rickets were never more numerous than now, and they are still increasing."

The frequency of rickets in the Low Countries is reflected in some Flemish paintings dating to the sixteenth century, which show infants having the characteristic bowed limbs of the disease. The extent of the problem in eighteenth-century Germany is shown in an early nineteenth-century publication by G. Wendelstadt on "The Endemic Disease of Wezler." Wezler was a German town of 8,000 that was infamous because of the frequency of the disease there, "with entire streets where, in house after house, individuals crippled by rickets could be found."

An analysis of the incidence of rickets in Britain showed it to be most common in urban settings, particularly in towns with a great deal of air pollution caused by the burning of soft coal. According to data collected by the British Medical Association in 1889, the areas around London, Cardiff, Birmingham, Manchester, Liverpool, Newcastle, Glasgow, and Edinburgh were particularly affected. The good physicians were surprised that the incidence of rickets was lower in rural areas, in which poverty was more severe and people subsisted on a poorer diet.

Lack of exposure to sunlight thus seemed to be a more important determinant of the occurrence of rickets than economic status and diet. Rickets was rare in sunny climates, except among people who remain strictly indoors, such as women and infants in strict Moslem households, where customary seclusion forbids them from venturing uncovered outside the home. (The Eskimo and Inuit people are an exception; although they are exposed to little sunlight, they subsist primarily on fish, the livers of which are rich sources of vitamin D.)

The role of smoke pollution in influencing the environment of English cities is well described by James Leasor in *The Plague and the Fire*. Describing London during the great bubonic plague epidemics of 1665 and 1666, the same period as that in which the frequency of rickets was rapidly increasing, he emphasized, "the fearful smoke pollution. Nearly all manufacturers—the iron smelters, the makers of soap, the brewers, and others who day and night burned great quantities of coal—had their factories within the City walls. Dense choking clouds of thick black smoke hung over the rooftops, making the air foul and adding to the grime. In places the smoke became so thick (for even the chimney stacks of the furnaces were no higher than the roofs) that people could scarcely see one another in the streets, and stumbled about coughing and sputtering, as though walking in a never-lifting fog."

Mining coal has long been a major industry in areas of Britain, particularly since 1560, when, as a consequence of the Reformation, coal mines were removed from the control of monasteries and passed into private hands. With thousands of households using coal for heating and cooking, it was not surprising that John Evelyn, a middle-aged government official with a habit of making notes on everything he saw, should write a pamphlet on the subject. "This horrid smoke obscures our churches and makes our palaces look old," he wrote. "It fouls our clothes and corrupts the waters ... with its black and tenacious quality, spots and contaminates whatever is exposed to it."

It is interesting to note that when people from equatorial latitudes, in which their normally darkly pigmented skin provides protection against too much ultraviolet light, migrate to more sparsely lighted northern latitudes, modern outbreaks of rickets occur in northern cities. Dietary supplementation eliminated rickets from Scottish children in Glasgow, for example, but dark-skinned Asian immigrants to that city still suffer from the disease.

The need for sunlight explains the observation that children born during northern European winters had a higher incidence of rickets in the first year of life than those born in the spring. The custom of June marriages may have arisen from such experience, since these marriages resulted in more children being born in the spring. Other child-rearing customs may relate to the high incidences of rickets. For example, the wives of American servicemen living in

Germany have been criticized by German women for allowing an infant to sit up while being strolled in their baby-carriages; German mothers traditionally do not allow young infants to sit or stand for fear that soft spinal bones may bend, resulting in permanent curvature (scoliosis), even though the use of supplementary vitamin D eliminated rickets in Germany long ago.

The high incidence of rickets-caused scoliosis in children in the eighteenth century led to the development of surgical procedures to correct the deformity. The first surgeon to attempt to correct scoliosis was a Parisian doctor, Nicolas André. In 1741, at the age of 83, André wrote a treatise on the art of preventing and correcting bodily deformities in children. Considered the founder of the field of orthopedics, since he coined the term *orthopedics* to describe the objective of his new type of surgery: from *ortho*, Greek for straight or proper (as in orthodox) and *pedon*, child (as in pediatrics). Thus, orthopedists originally were child straighteners.

In contrast to such linguistic logic, the origin of the word "rickets" troubles etymologists. The suggestion that it is derived from the Greek *rachitis*, meaning spinal disease, is widely accepted; however, although the term was in use among the English population before Whistler's thesis and the report by the Glisson commission in 1650, it seems unlikely that a lay term would have its basis in a Greek word. David LeVay, a British orthopedist, has suggested that the term is derived from an old Scandinavian root, *rykk*, meaning twist, tug, or pull, a reference to the twisted limbs and spine characteristic of the disease. The same root is responsible for the word *rack*, a torture device used to cause stretching, twisting, or dislocation.

Rickets, then, is primarily a disease caused by air pollution. The industrial use of coal for heat and industry brought on the disease primarily in geographic areas with marginal amounts of sunlight.

ADDITIONAL READING

Arneil GC. Nutritional rickets in the children of Glasgow. *Proc Nutri Soc* 1975;34:101.

Bollet AJ. Twisted spines and child straighteners. *Resid Staff Physician* 1980;26:31.

Chick H. The discovery of vitamins. *Progr Food Nutr Sci* 1975;1:1.

Cone TE Jr. The treatment of rickets, as suggested by Boerhaave and Glisson and interpreted by Dr. John Theobald of Londin in 1764. *Pediatrics* 1970;46:619.

Cone TE Jr. A rachitic infant painted by Burgkman 126 years before Whistler described rickets. *Clin Pediatr* 1980;19:194.

DeLuca HF. The vitamin D story: a collaborative effort of basic science and clinical medicine. *Fed Am Soc Am Biol J* 1988;2:224.

Glisson F. A *Treatise on Rickets Being a Disease Common in Children*. London: Peter Cole, 1651.

Glisson F. The signs of rachitis. In: Clendening L. *Source Book of Medical History*. New York: Dover Pub, 1942.

Holick MF. Photosynthesis of vitamin D in the skin: effect of environmental and life-style variables. *Fed Proc* 1987;46:1876.

Holt LE. *Diseases of Infancy and Childhood*. New York: D. Appleton & Co, 1897.

Le Vay D. On the derivation of the name 'rickets.' *Proc R Soc Med* 1975;68:46–50.

Loomis WF. Rickets. *Sci Am* 1970; 223:76.

CHAPTER 13

GOUT

THE DISEASE OF GOOD LIVING

URING THE MID-SEVENTEENTH CENTURY IN ENGLAND, an epidemic of a metabolic disease developed that seems to have resulted from political and economic measures, as well as an unquenchable thirst for port wine.

During the War of Spanish Succession (1701–1714), Portugal became an ally of the British and Austrians under a treaty signed by King Dom Pedro II and the British ambassador, Paul Methuen, on May 16, 1703. The treaty gave Portugal naval protection and assistance in the event that France or Spain attacked her. Portugal actually fought with the British, and the war gave the British control of Gibraltar. The improved relationship between Portugal and Great Britain culminated on December 27, 1703, with the signing of a commercial treaty between the two countries, negotiated by a special British envoy, John Methuen, the ambassador's father and a former Chancellor of Ireland. The terms of the Treaty of Methuen, as it became known, were responsible for an epidemic of gout in eighteenth-century Britain; the same form of gout that has long been endemic in parts of the United States today.

The treaty of Methuen stated:

"Article I. His Sacred Royal Majesty of Portugal promises, both in his own name and that of his successors, to admit hereafter into Portugal the woolen cloths and the rest of the woolen manufactures of the Britons, as was accustomed till they were prohibited by the Laws: nevertheless upon this condition;

Article II. That is to say, that her Sacred Royal Majesty of Great Britain [Queen Anne] shall in her own name and that of her successors, be

obliged forever after to admit the wines of Portugal into Britain; so that at
no time... anything more shall be demanded for these wines, by name of
Custom or Duty...than what shall be demanded from the like quantity of
French wine, deducting or abating a third part of the Custom or Duty...."

Entrepreneurs rapidly moved in to take advantage of the lower tariff and
organize the wine exporting business in Portugal, and English names are still
attached to the finest brands of port and sherry. After 1788, the amount of
Portuguese wines exported to Britain often exceeded 20,000 tuns (a liquid measure), reflecting its premier position in the British market.

However, transportation in the eighteenth century so slow that the wine
often spoiled before it could be sold in England. To enable it to "travel better,"
that is, to prevent spoilage and to make it more fitting to a British palate recently
introduced to gin, the wine was "fortified," meaning that its alcohol content was
increased by the addition of Portuguese brandy. This brandy was routinely stored
in lead casks, and since lead is soluble in alcohol, the addition of the brandy to
the port resulted in rather high lead concentrations. Some of the port and
Madeira wines from that era are still extant and have been analyzed for their
lead content. A bottle of 1805 port was found to have 830 micrograms of lead
per liter, and some Canary Island wine from the period of 1770–1810 contained
1,900 mcg/L.; in contrast, modern wine has about 160 mcg of lead per liter.
(Using modern methods in their analyses, the investigators who performed them
needed very little wine for the chemical determinations. They recorded that the
rest of the wine was delicious.)

According to Andre Simon in *Wines of the World*, "...Port became what it is
still today, the most popular wine in England, one might even say the national
wine of England." The popularity of port in England is also illustrated by an
anecdote that appeared in *The Times*, on February 19, 1708: "To which
University," said a lady... to the sagacious Dr. Warren, "shall I send my son?"
"Madam," replied he, "they all drink, I believe, near the same quantity of port
in each of them."

Gout was well known in Britain before the Treaty of Methuen. Perhaps the
best description of the disease was provided by Sydenham, the leading physician
of his time, in his "Treatise on Gout and Dropsy," dated May 21, 1683. It is
detailed and accurate, since Sydenham had the disease himself; in his dedication
to Dr. Thomas Short of London, Sydenham explained why the tract was briefer
than he had planned. "By applying my mind...to the utmost," he wrote, "I
brought on a fit of gout such as I had never before suffered from...." Perhaps
Sydenham applied himself so strenuously that he required a great deal of wine
to sustain his efforts.

After Britain began to be flooded with port wines, gout became a high-profile condition. Treatises on the subject proliferated, popular health manuals devoted pages to it, physicians began to specialize in it, and quack remedies proliferated. It is clearly recorded that well-to-do Englishmen were the group most commonly afflicted with gout. Lord Chesterfield is quoted as saying, "Gout is the distemper of gentlemen, whereas the rheumatism is the distemper of a hackney coachman." Upper class Englishmen were such prodigious eaters and drinkers that the term "Aldermanic gout" has been applied to the attacks following ingestion of huge quantities of the purine-rich foods that characterized their meals. Huge quantities of liquid were needed just to accompany that volume of food. It is worth keeping in mind that India was not yet exporting tea, and the water was rarely potable and even dangerous, since it was mostly from the Thames River where the sewage was discharged. The intake of wine, and consequently of lead, was therefore considerable. Purines are components of nucleic acids and are metabolized mainly to uric acid. Many so called "rich" foods contain a lot of purines, but all meats, especially organ meats, are particularly rich in purines.

In discussing gout in affluent Englishmen, one has to be careful about the use of the term. Sydenham and others described typical *podagra* (acute, severe attacks of painful inflammation of the big toe) and the inflammation of other joints, which is typical of the disease we still see. Gout was so strongly associated with the wealthy that the term was used for almost any disease afflicting well-to-do or aristocratic Englishmen. Thus, in the English literature of the time, we read of gout of the liver, gout of the intestine, as well as the true, typical arthritic gout depicted in cartoons of the same period. Lead poisoning also causes intestinal colic, and there is evidence that colic, the "dry gripes," was a common problem in Britain at this time; it was often called "visceral gout."

Gout was known in ancient Egypt, and mummies have been found to have the characteristic tophaceous (uric acid) deposits of gout. The Ebers papyrus, dating from the reign of Amen-Hotep I, about 1550 BCE, recorded the effectiveness of extracts of the autumn crocus (the source of colchicine) for treating arthritis. Since colchicine is effective almost exclusively in the treatment of gout, that disease probably was one of the major forms of arthritis seen during this period. Similarly, we know that gout was common in ancient Greece during the fifth century BCE, since it is well described in the works attributed to Hippocrates. Both Ancient Egypt and Classical Greece were known for their high wine consumption.

The eighteenth and nineteenth century view of the relationship between gout and alcohol consumption is recorded in many famous cartoons and in the literature of the time. For example, cartoons by Gilray usually show the obviously well-off, painfully afflicted man with his flannel-wrapped, gouty extremity carefully raised on a pillow or on the T-shaped support known as a "gout stool." The treatment for gout at the time was "flannel and patience," reflecting the fact that attacks usually subsided spontaneously in a week or two. Always obvious in these cartoons was the nearby bottle of wine, apparently port, indicating that the association with wine was clear in the public mind at that time.

On the other hand, it was known that not all alcoholic beverages were equally potent as causes of gout. Sydenham pointed out that native London "small beer" was not harmful and might even be beneficial to his gout, possibly because of its diuretic effect. At least the London beer did not contain Portuguese lead. The first edition of the Encyclopedia Brittanica (1771) also reported that small beer was therapeutic. And punch, made with whiskey, was not considered to cause gout; in fact, one cartoon shows a corpulent carouser with both feet elevated and wrapped in flannel, along with a gaunt consumptive-looking man and a dyspeptic-appearing woman clutching her abdomen, all raising their glasses over a prominent punch bowl and saying, "Punch cures the gout...and the 'tisick...(and) the colic." Only the fortified wines, port and sack (sherry), were associated in the popular mind with attacks of gout, and the analyses of the lead content of those wines confirm that this association was correct.

The epidemic of gout in eighteenth-century England was thus, at least in large part, saturnine gout (gout resulting from lead deposition in the kidneys, impairing the ability of these organs to excrete uric acid) due to the importation of the fortified Iberian wines. The frequency of gout seems to have decreased markedly in England after the cost of other wines became comparable and tea became popular.

Saturnine gout still exists, as a recent outbreak in the southeastern United States illustrates, although not to the extent that it did in eighteenth century England. The reason for saturnine gout in the United States is similar to the reason for its existence in England, although it was not wine that contained the lead, but rather "moonshine" whiskey, which is much cheaper than taxed, store-bought whiskey. Authorities recently estimated that, in at least two or three states, more moonshine was consumed than legal liquor. Much of the moonshine contained lead, because the alcohol is usually distilled using old automobile radiators as condensers; the connections on these homemade stills are made with lead solder—and lead is still soluble in alcohol. In addition, special materials may be added to the brew during fermentation to increase its "piquant" flavor, as one connoisseur advised me; automobile batteries with lead plates are favored by some palates. Analyses of confiscated moonshine have revealed very high lead concentrations, and saturnine gout is being diagnosed frequently in addition to other complications of lead poisoning.

ADDITIONAL READING

Ball GV, Sorenson LB. Pathogenesis of hyperuricemia in saturnine gout *N Eng J Med* 1980;*280*:1199.

Copeman WSC. *A Short History of the Gout and the Rheumatic Diseases.* Berkeley, CA: Univ of California Press, 1964.

Dequeker J. Arthritis in Flemish paintings (1400–1700). *BMJ* 1977;*1*:1203.

Dequeker J. Rheumatism in the art of the late middle ages. *Organorama* 1979;*16*:9.

Drummond JC. *The Englishman's Food; A History of Five Centuries of English Diet.* London: J. Cape, 1939.

Healey LA. Port wine and gout. *Arthritis Rheum* 1975;*18*;659.

Porter R. *Gout, the Patrician Malady.* New Haven, CT: Yale Univ Press, 1998.

Simon A. *Wines of the World.* New York: McGraw-Hill, 1962.

Sydenham T. A treatise on gout. In: Major RH, ed. *Classic Descriptions of Disease.* Springfield, IL: Chas C. Thomas, 1932.

Sydenham T. *The Works of Thomas Sydenham.* Birmingham, AL: Classics of Medicine Library, 1979 (reprint).

Valaer PJ. *Wines of the World.* New York: Abelard Press, 1950.

PART THREE

Intentionally Induced and Newly Emerging Diseases

CHAPTER 14

ANTHRAX

FROM WOOLSORTER'S DISEASE
TO TERRORISM

THE FIRST BIOLOGICAL TERRORIST ATTACK ON U.S. SOIL
was made using anthrax. As of this writing, the responsible persons or groups have not been identified, and no evidence shows that the attack was from a foreign source. However, the attack demonstrated how easily a major outbreak of a disease with a high fatality rate can be induced by terrorists, domestic or foreign, and how widespread the panic that follows such an attack can be.

HISTORY OF ANTHRAX. Anthrax has long been known as a disease of domestic animals, most commonly herbivores, which are infected after the ingestion of soil-borne spores contaminating the grass they eat. Large epizootics have occurred, including one that killed a million sheep in Iran in 1945. Anthrax spores are found in soil samples throughout the world, and because they resist drying or weather extremes, and therefore can persist for decades, they infect some animals every year.

In humans, naturally occurring anthrax occurs from contact with infected animals or animal products contaminated with anthrax spores. Most infections occur in special risk groups: people who work with animal skins, or with goat hair, or with wool contaminated by anthrax spores that the animals picked up in the fields where they fed.

The disease was sometimes called "woolsorter's disease," since the most commonly infected people were workers handling wool from sheep that had picked up spores from the fields. These workers usually acquired skin or cutaneous anthrax, a relatively benign form of the disease. Pneumonia caused by anthrax was quite rare until the agent began to be used as a biological weapon.

Human infection can occur via three routes: inhalation, through the skin, and through the gastrointestinal system following swallowing of organisms. Cutaneous disease is the most common form of naturally occurring anthrax, causing an estimated 2,000 cases per year worldwide. In the United States, 224 cases of cutaneous anthrax were reported between 1944 and 1994. The largest anthrax epidemic occurred in Zimbabwe, between 1979 and 1985, when more than 10,000 human cases were reported, nearly all of them cutaneous infections. Gastrointestinal anthrax has been reported following the ingestion of insufficiently cooked meat contaminated with spores. However, little information is available on this rare form of anthrax. The third form of infection, inhalational anthrax, occurs after exposure to an aerosolized preparation of spores, such as those prepared as a biological weapon.

Historically, anthrax is a disease of considerable interest. It is believed to have been one of the Biblical plagues of Egypt. The study of anthrax spores was the first project the young Dr. Robert Koch initiated when he decided to convert from being a general practitioner to a research scientist. He showed that spores could become full-fledged, multiplying bacteria that cause disease and were infectious for animals. His study is considered the beginning of experimental microbiology.

INFECTIONS STARTING IN THE LUNG. Inhalational anthrax occurs when spores are in the inspired air. The spores tend to clump and deposit on the wall of larger bronchi and bronchioles, where they are caught up in the mucus and removed from the lungs by normal defense mechanisms. If the spores are dispersed into tiny particles, in the 1 to 5 micron (μm) range, when inhaled they can be carried all the way to the alveolar spaces of the lungs where gas exchange normally occurs. Once they are deposited in the pulmonary alveoli, phagocytic cells called macrophages ingest the spores, some of which survive the defense mechanisms of these cells. These spores and the phagocytic cells are then transported via the lymphatics to the mediastinal lymph nodes in the center of the chest. Here, the spores germinate, multiplying and becoming mature, functioning, toxin-producing bacteria. After a variable period of time, they start producing disease. In accidental cases, in which the time of exposure was known, symptoms began after 2 to 43 days; in experimental exposure of monkeys, fatal disease began as late as 58 to 98 days after the introduction of the spores.

Clinical symptoms develop rapidly once the spores begin to germinate. The bacteria release toxins that cause hemorrhage, edema, and tissue necrosis. When toxin production has reached a critical threshold, death occurs even if the blood-stream is then sterilized by the administration of antibiotics. It is believed that the 50 percent lethal dose (LD_{50}) for humans is between 2,500 and 55,000 inhaled anthrax spores. Primate data suggests that as few as one to three spores may be sufficient to cause infections, and it is believed that the two cases of fatal inhalational anthrax that occurred in New York City and Connecticut, following the anthrax attack of 2001, developed after inhalation of very few organisms.

The term "anthrax pneumonia" is somewhat misleading, because the disease in the lung is neither full-blown lobar pneumonia nor even patchy bronchopneumonia. It consists primarily of a hemorrhagic inflammation of thoracic lymph nodes, with surrounding mediastinal inflammation, usually associated with hemorrhagic pleural effusions.

In April, 1979, an outbreak of anthrax occurred in the former Soviet Union, following the accidental release of spores from a research facility. The ensuing cases were well studied and documented; initial symptoms were nonspecific, including fever, cough, some shortness of breath, headache, vomiting, chills, weakness, abdominal pain, and chest pain. This stage of illness, sometimes called flulike, lasted from hours to a few days. A period of improvement was sometimes seen before the second, fulminating stage of the illness developed. Focal hemorrhagic inflammation did occur in the areas of the lung where the infection began, with extensive necrosis of pulmonary tissues. Characteristically, focal pneumonia and regional lymph node enlargement occurs. This is analogous to a syndrome seen in primary pulmonary tuberculosis, called the Ghon complex, which consists of an area of pneumonia accompanied by enlargement of regional lymph nodes.

Anthrax also causes inflammation of arteries in the area of the infection, and rupture of affected arteries occurred in many cases. About half the patients in this outbreak developed hemorrhagic meningitis. Organisms were recovered in blood and spinal fluid in concentrations of up to 100 million colony forming units per milliliter. (A colony forming unit means that a recognizable colony of organisms grew out in culture medium, usually the result of the multiplication of a single organism.) The toxins affected the function of those brain centers controlling respiration and circulation, causing low blood pressure and poor respiratory function. Treatment included correction of electrolyte disturbances and acid-base imbalance, glucose infusion because of low blood sugar, agents to try to maintain blood pressure, and the early institution of mechanical ventilation to substitute for the impaired function caused by depression of the respiratory center of the brain.

This epidemic of anthrax spread among people who lived or worked in a narrow zone downwind and within four km of the Soviet military microbiology facility in Sverdlovsk (now Katerinberg) in what is now Russia. In addition, livestock died of anthrax to a distance of 50 km along an extension of the epidemic zone. At the time, the Soviets denied that this epidemic was caused by release of agents from their biological weapons program; however, in 1992, then President Boris Yeltsin admitted that the epidemic had been caused by the accidental release of anthrax spores on the morning of April 3. At least 77 human cases occurred from inhalation of anthrax, resulting in 66 deaths, the largest documented epidemic of inhalational anthrax in history. Sverdlovsk patients who had onset of disease 30 or more days after the release of organisms had a higher reported survival rate than those with earlier disease onset. Antibiotics, antianthrax globulin, corticosteroids, mechanical ventilation, and vaccine were used to treat some residents in the affected area after the accident, but it is unknown how effective these agents were. A community-wide intervention about the 15th day after exposure did appear to diminish the projected attack rate. In fatal cases, the interval between onset of symptoms and death averaged three days.

CASES OF ANTHRAX IN THE UNITED STATES. In the early twentieth century, the mortality of occupationally acquired inhalational anthrax cases in the United States was 89 percent. These cases occurred before the development of critical care units and mostly before the advent of antibiotics. The 2001 terrorist attacks in the United States caused eleven cases of inhalational anthrax, with five deaths. Malaise and fever were initial symptoms in all eleven cases; cough, nausea and vomiting were also prominent. In a majority of cases, drenching sweats, shortness of breath, chest pain, and headache also occurred. Chest x-rays, which were abnormal in all the cases, revealed mediastinal widening, pulmonary infiltrates, and pleural effusions. For those patients from whom the information was available, the interval between time of exposure and onset of symptoms ranged from four to six days, and patients sought care within 3.5 days after symptoms began; all four patients who exhibited signs of fulminant illness prior to being given antibiotics died.

CUTANEOUS ANTHRAX. Cutaneous anthrax was reported in the Sverdlovsk outbreak in the Soviet Union. Evidence of the infection appeared early, within 12 days after the original exposure. No reports were made of cutaneous cases appearing after a period of prolonged latency.

Anthrax skin lesions usually begin with an itchy patch or papule that develops an ulcer by the second day. Subsequently, tiny (one to three mm in diameter) vesicles usually appear and discharge clear or bloody fluid containing numerous anthrax organisms. A black crust typically forms, with extensive associated local swelling. The crust dries and falls off in the next one to two weeks. Inflammation of lymphatic channels draining the area of the lesion can usually be detected, and a painful lymph node swelling may occur, with associated fever and symptoms of systemic illness. Antibiotics do not seem to change the course of the skin lesions, but do decrease the likelihood of systemic disease. Without antibiotic therapy, the mortality rate has been reported to be as high as 20 percent, but death reportedly is rare when antibiotics are administered. In the 2001 terrorist attacks in the United States, eleven confirmed or probable cases of cutaneous anthrax occurred, with incubation periods varying from one to ten days (averaging five days) after exposure. Cutaneous lesions were seen on the forearm, neck, chest and fingers. In a seven-month-old child, the disease was extremely severe and almost fatal, but all patients with solely cutaneous lesions recovered.

TREATING AND PREVENTING ANTHRAX. Inhalational anthrax is often fatal once the organism has multiplied, since by then it has started to produce large amounts of toxin. Although antibiotics may kill or suppress the growth of the bacteria, it is the toxin that eventually kills the patient. Thus, five people died in the bioterrorism incident in the United States after inhaling spores of *B. anthracis,* although they were hospitalized and treated with antibiotics.

The potential for person-to-person spread of pulmonary anthrax is limited, therefore the antibiotic prophylaxis of people who have been exposed to patients with this disease is not recommended. This is different from prophylaxis following exposure to spores, for which post-exposure prophylaxis is recommended and should be continued for 60 days.

Efforts being made to develop antibodies to the toxins (antitoxin antibodies) include a high binding affinity antibody that will bind to the toxin, neutralize it, and remove it from the circulation. Some concern exists that antibiotic-resistant anthrax organisms might be developed and used as a bioweapon; under such circumstances, an antitoxin antibody might not be sufficiently protective, because the bacteria would continue to proliferate unchecked and produce large amounts of toxin that would eventually overwhelm the antiserum.

Vaccines to protect against anthrax are also under development, but initial forms of the vaccine were associated with adverse reactions. At present, these vaccines are not recommended for use in the general public in the absence of an immediate threat. One advantage of the antitoxin antibody is that it could be administered only to people showing symptoms of anthrax or suspected of having been exposed to anthrax; the general population would not need to receive it. The development of such antibodies is currently one of the main objectives of the biotechnology industry. However, the high cost of research, coupled with the legal and patent difficulties, and the small market for the antibody, may delay its development.

A live attenuated vaccine has been produced and used in other countries, but safety concerns have precluded its licensing for use in the United States. The vaccine that is currently licensed in the U. S. needs to be given in a six-dose series, and active duty military personnel have been receiving it. The principal antigen responsible for inducing immunity is called the PA *antigen*. The vaccine has not been associated with long-term sequelae, although headache, nausea, sweating, itching, and similar symptoms have been reported transiently. The Institute of Medicine has concluded that the vaccine is acceptably safe and effective against inhalational anthrax and, if given with appropriate antibiotic therapy, it should be helpful.

Vaccine supplies at the present time are limited and production capacity modest. The vaccine was not given immediately to persons believed to have been exposed to anthrax during the 2001 attacks. It was obtained later and given to the public health authorities who were investigating the outbreak and testing various areas for the presence of anthrax spores, since they were considered at high risk. It was administered as a series of three inoculations at 2-week intervals along with prolonged antibiotic prophylaxis. New recombinant vaccines currently are being developed.

Recommendations for anthrax infection therapy and possible therapeutic strategies for the treatment of large numbers of casualties are under constant reconsideration. Early antibiotic administration is essential, because it is necessary to stop the proliferation of the organism before large amounts of toxin have been produced. Given the difficulty of rapid microbiologic diagnosis of anthrax, all persons considered to have been at high risk of having been exposed to the agent, and who develop fever or evidence of systemic disease, should start receiving therapy for possible anthrax infection as soon as possible while awaiting the results of laboratory studies. No controlled clinical trials are available.

Most naturally occurring anthrax strains are sensitive to penicillin, which historically has been the preferred anthrax therapy. Doxycycline is the preferred option among the tetracycline class of agents, because it has been proved efficacious in monkey studies. Other members of this class of antibiotics are suitable, and animal studies suggest that such prophylaxis should be effective. The floroquinolone antibiotics (such as ciprofloxacin [Cipro®]) should have equivalent efficacy, but no data are available. Penicillin, doxycycline, and ciprofloxacin prophylaxis are the approved treatment for inhalational anthrax infection, and other antibiotics are under study. At present, it is recommended that prophylaxis with antibiotics should extend for 60 days.

There have been reports of anthrax strains engineered to resist the tetracycline and penicillin classes of antibiotics. For that reason ciprofloxacin or other floroquinalone agents should be initiated in adults with suspected inhalational anthrax infection. It is advised that resistance to penicillin- and tetracycline-class antibiotics should be assumed following a terrorist attack until laboratory testing demonstrates that the organisms are sensitive to those antibiotics. Because studies show in vitro resistance to all floxacins, the CDC guidelines advocate the use of two or three antibiotics in combination in those persons thought to have developed inhalational anthrax, with the choice of drug based on susceptibility testing of the epidemic strains. (Ciprofloxacin was used extensively during the 2001 attacks because of fears that the anthrax strains used might have been bioengineered to be resistant to older antibiotics, this turned out not to be true.)

Central nervous system disease presents another problem, because doxycycline or floroquinolone alone may not reach therapeutic levels in the cerebrospinal fluid. At present, some infectious disease experts recommend the preferential use of ciprofloxacin over doxycycline, with augmentation by chloramphenicol, rifampin, or penicillin when meningitis is suspected or established.

The 2001 isolates show a rapid ability to produce B-lactamase, the enzyme that neutralizes penicillin. Therefore, the CDC recommends that patients not be treated using penicillin or amoxicillin as single-therapy agents, and that ciprofloxacin or doxycycline be considered the standards based on in vitro activity. It is recommended that antibiotics be given intravenously, unless the number of patients needing treatment is overwhelming. With mass casualties, combination drug therapy and intravenous therapy may not be possible and, in such circumstances, oral therapy may be the only feasible option.

The early antibiotic treatment of cutaneous anthrax prevents the development of antibodies and immunity. Previous guidelines suggested treating cutaneous anthrax for 7 to 10 days, but the present recommendations call for 60 days of treatment after known exposure in a bioterrorism situation, given the presumed likelihood of concurrent inhalational exposure to the agent. The treatment of cutaneous anthrax generally prevents progression to systemic disease. Topical therapy is not useful.

ANTHRAX AS A BIOLOGICAL WEAPON. As many as thirteen countries may have offensive biological weapons programs, including the former Soviet Union, which is known to have had a large anthrax production program. In October

2002, Iraq acknowledged to the United Nations special commission that it was working on anthrax and botulism. The Iraqis admitted to having used imported chemicals and other media to produce large stockpiles of biologic agents, including 19,000 liters of concentrated botulinum poison and 8,500 liters of concentrated anthrax spores. Iraq had produced and weaponized anthrax, and at one point it had 200 missiles and bombs carrying anthrax.

In 1948, the United States built a test chamber at Fort Detrick, in Maryland, to test how anthrax spores spread and how long they stay alive. They also the studied a variety of other diseases and found that anthrax was the most powerful. In testing the potency of anthrax against various species, they exposed 2,000 monkeys and found it took about 3,000 spores each to kill 50 percent of them, but it took 50,000 spores each to kill 50 percent of guinea pigs. Rats could not be killed with anthrax, but mice were very susceptible.

Weapons-grade anthrax has a high spore concentration, uniform particle size, and low electrostatic charge, and it is treated to reduce clumping. Reports state that the Japanese Aum Shiriko cult that released sarin gas in a Tokyo subway station in 1995 also disbursed aerosols of anthrax and botulism throughout Tokyo at least eight times. However, forensic analysis of the anthrax strain used in these attacks revealed that it closely matched the strain that is routinely used for animal vaccination purposes and thus was not of significant risk to humans. It is possible that the cult attacks produced no illnesses for this and other technical reasons.

In the anthrax attacks of 2001, spores were sent in at least five letters to Florida, New York City, and Washington D.C. Twenty-two confirmed or suspected cases resulted. The spores were of the Ames strain, but could not be more precisely identified because of the common features in the DNA of anthrax strains from different laboratories. The letter mailed to Sen. Thomas Daschle reportedly had two grams of powder and contained between 100 billion and a trillion spores per gram. Many methods are possible for spore delivery in buildings or over large outdoor areas.

Aerosol-released anthrax is odorless and invisible and has a great potential to travel in the air for long distances. Tests of the release of anthrax in this fashion have been conducted by Iraq and the former Soviet Union, and by the U.S. military in the South Pacific. In 1970, the World Health Organization (WHO) estimated that 50 kg of anthrax spores released over an urban population of 5 million would sicken 250,000 people and kill 100,000. In 1993, a U.S. Congressional Office of Technology Assessment estimated that the release of 100 kg of anthrax would have a lethality matching that of the hydrogen bomb.

Anthrax spores intended for weapons use are finely milled, highly purified, and easily aerosolized. Weapons-grade anthrax spores may persist in the environment, as the natural spores do, or be easily carried and dispersed mechanically in mail sorting machines or by mail handlers who come in contact with spore-contaminated mail.

ADDITIONAL READING

Atlas RM. Bioterrorism before and after September 11. *Crit Rev Microbiol* 2001;27:355.

Bell JH, Fee E, Brown TM. Anthrax and the wool trade, 1902. *Am J Public Health* 2002;92:705.

Bray RS. *Armies of Pestilence, The Impact of Disease on History.* New York: Barnes and Noble, 2000.

Christopher GW, Cieslak TJ, et al. Biological warfare, A historical perspective. *JAMA* 1997;278:412.

Dennis DT, Inglesby TV, et al. Tularemia as a biological weapon: medical and public health management. *JAMA* 2002;287:452.

Dubois RJ, ed. *Bacterial and Mycotic Infections of Man.* Philadelphia: JB Lippincott Co, 1848.

Franz DR, Jahrling PB, et al. Clinical recognition and management of patients exposed to biological warfare agents. *JAMA* 1997;278:399.

Guillemin J. The 1979 anthrax epidemic in the USSR: applied science and political controversy. *Proc Am Philos Assoc* 2002;146:18.

Henderson DA, Inglesby TV, O'Toole T, eds. *Bioterrorism; Guidelines for Medical and Public Health Management.* Chicago: JAMA and Archives Journals (AMA Press), 2002.

Huerta M, Leventhal A. The epidemiological pyramid of bioterrorism *Israel Med Assoc J* 2002;4:498.

Ingelsby TV, O'Toole T, et al. Anthrax as a biological weapon, 2002: updated recommendations for management. *JAMA* 2002;287:2236.

Kasten FH. Biological weapons, war crimes and World War-I. *Science* 2002;296:1235.

Penn CC, Klotz SA. Anthrax pneumonia *Semin Respir Infect* 1997;12:28.

Pittman PR, Gibbs PH, et al. Anthrax vaccination: short-term safety experience in humans. *Vaccine* 2001;20: 972.

Plotkin SA, Brachman PS, et al. An epidemic of inhalation anthrax, the first in the twentieth century, I: Clinical features. *Am J Med* 2002;112:4.

Sato PA, Ryan M, et al. Surveillance for adverse events associated with anthrax vaccination, US Department of Defense, 1998–2000. *MMWR Morb Mort Wkly Rep* 2000;49:341.

Sidel V, Cohen HW, Gould RM. From woolsorters to mail sorters: anthrax, past, present and future. *Am J Public Health* 2002;92:754.

Sotos JG. Botulinum toxin in biowarfare. Editorial. *JAMA* 2001;285:2716.

Swanson-Bierman B, Krenselok EP. Delayed life-threatening reaction to anthrax vaccine. *J Clin Toxicol* 2001;39:81.

Turnbull PC. Introduction: anthrax history, disease and ecology. *Curr Top Microbiol Immunol* 2002;271:1.

Wilson TM, Gregg DA, et al. Agroterrorism, biological crimes, and biowarfare targeting animal agriculture. The clinical, pathologic, diagnostic and epidemiologic features of some important animal diseases. *Clin Lab Med* 2001;21:549.

Zilinskas RA. Iraq's biological weapons. The past as future? *JAMA* 1997;278:418.

CHAPTER 15

BOTULISM

FROM BAD FOOD TO BIOTERRORISM

BOTULINUM TOXIN IS ONE OF THE MOST POISONOUS SUB-stances known. A single gram, evenly disbursed and inhaled, could kill more than one million people. Botulinum toxin is an enzyme that breaks down the proteins that allow nerve cells to release acetylcholine, the agent that transmits motor nerve impulses to muscle fibers. It causes muscular paralysis that is so rapid that the inability to breathe is lethal in only a few minutes.

All forms of botulism result from the absorption of botulinum toxin into the circulation, either through the lungs, intestines, or wounds in the skin. The toxin does not penetrate intact skin. Botulism is traditionally associated almost exclusively with the accidental contamination of home-preserved food or contaminated unpreserved foods in public eating places. Because the toxin is relatively stable, contaminated food in preservation jars can remain toxic at room temperature for months or longer. The organism responsible for botulism, *Clostridium botulinum*, is a spore-forming bacterium that is widely found in soil, from which it can be isolated with relative ease. Because it is a ubiquitous organism, it can accidentally contaminate food prepared at home, and most known cases have occurred in this fashion.

The toxin is colorless, odorless, and tasteless. It is rapidly inactivated by heat ≥ 85 degrees C for five minutes, and thus most cases have been transmitted by foods that were not heated thoroughly before preservation or before eating. The most common of these have been contaminated potato salad, condiments, or uncooked or lightly heated foods allowed to stand long enough for the organisms to grow and produce toxin. Approximately nine outbreaks of foodborne botulism occur annually in United States, usually averaging 2.5 cases each, but in at

215

least one, which occurred in Michigan in 1970, 59 cases were caused by home-preserved jalapeno peppers.

The speed of onset and severity of botulism depends on the rate and amount of toxin absorbed. Symptoms of food-borne botulism may begin as early as 2 hours or as long as 8 days after ingestion of toxin, but typically most cases become symptomatic and seek treatment within 12 to 72 hours after ingestion of the contaminated meal. It is not known how long inhalation botulism takes to develop, because there are so few cases on record. However, monkeys exposed to airborne botulinum toxin showed signs of botulism 12 to 80 hours after exposure. The three known cases of inhalational botulism in humans had onset of symptoms approximately 72 hours after exposure to small amounts of aerosolized toxin.

A therapeutic form of botulinum toxin, known as Botox®, is approved as a drug for the treatment of human disease, including unrelievable stiffness of the neck muscles (cervical dystonia or spasmodic torticollis), spasm of muscles that move the eye causing intractable double vision (strabismus), and eye-lid muscle spasm (blepherospasm). Botox® is widely used as an unapproved or "off label" treatment for a variety of problems, including the removal of facial wrinkles, which it accomplishes by temporarily paralyzing the muscles that cause the wrinkles.

The toxin produces an acute, symmetric, descending flaccid paralysis that almost always begins in the upper musculature, the area innervated by the cranial nerves. The paralysis proceeds symmetrically, descending from the cranial nerve areas to the chest muscles and the muscles of the extremities. The clinical findings of botulism include weakness of the eyelids (ptosis), double vision, blurred vision, difficulty speaking, difficulty swallowing, and dry mouth; more generalized muscle weakness soon develops. Death results from airway obstruction or decreased action of the muscles of breathing. Weakness of the respiratory muscles frequently results in aspiration pneumonia. Patients remain completely clear mentally, aware of their state until lack of oxygen causes them to lose consciousness. If the individual survives the acute episode, recovery occurs when new twigs sprout from the motor nerves to reinervate paralyzed muscle fibers, a process that, in adults, may take weeks or months.

Because it is the toxin that causes the disease, not the microorganism, botulism is not contagious, and the toxin cannot be transmitted from person to person. However, using modern techniques, a microbe that does not ordinarily produce the toxin, but that can spread from person to person, might be intentionally modified to produce botulinum toxin. The development of such an agent is a matter of concern.

No instances of waterborne botulism have ever been reported, but it is possible that this potent toxin could be used to contaminate a municipal water supply. However, the toxin is rapidly inactivated by standard water treatments, such as chlorination or aeration and, because of the slow turnover time of large-capacity reservoirs, it would require a very large amount to be effective.

BOTULINUM AND BIOTERRORISM. The botulinum organism is widespread in soil and easily cultured; thus, it is not difficult to prepare purified toxin.

Aerosols of botulinum toxin were released by the Japanese Aum Shiriko terrorist cult at multiple sites in downtown Tokyo and at U.S. military installations on at least three occasions between 1990 and 1995. The attacks caused no casualties, apparently because of faulty microbiological technique, poor aerosol-generating equipment, or other factors.

During the occupation of Manchuria in the 1930s, the Japanese biological warfare group (Unit 731) fed cultures of C. botulinum to Chinese prisoners of war with a lethal effect. Because of fear that Germany had weaponized botulinum toxin, more than one million doses of botulinum toxoid vaccine were ready for Allied troops about to invade Normandy on D-day in 1944.

Later in the twentieth century, the Soviet Union produced botulinum toxin for use as a weapon. The Soviets tested it on an island in the Aral Sea and also tried to insert the gene that makes botulinum toxin into other bacteria. This program was discontinued after the demise of the Soviet Union, but thousands of scientists formerly employed in their biological weapons program have been recruited by nations attempting to develop such weapons. Four countries listed by the U.S. government as "state sponsors of terrorism" in 2002 (Iraq, Iran, North Korea, and Syria) have developed or were believed to be developing botulinum toxin as a weapon.

In 1991, after the Persian Gulf War, Iraq admitted to the United Nations inspection team that it had produced 19,000 liters of concentrated botulinum toxin, of which approximately 10,000 were loaded into military weapons. As of this writing, these 19,000 liters of concentrated toxin have not been fully accounted for and constitute approximately three times the amount needed to kill the entire current human population of the earth through inhalation. In 1990, Iraq deployed specially designed missiles with a 600 km range; thirteen of them were filled with botulinum toxin, ten with aflatoxin, and two with anthrax spores.

Although technical difficulties are associated with using botulinum toxin as a bioweapon, it is estimated that a point-source aerosol release of botulinum toxin could incapacitate or kill 10 percent of people within a 0.5 km distance downwind. The terroristic use of botulinum toxin might include the deliberate contamination of food, either in single attacks or as widely separated outbreaks. Estimates from primate studies show the lethal amount of toxin for a 70 kg human is approximately 0.09 to 0.15 micrograms intravenously or intramuscularly, 0.7 to 0.9 micrograms by inhalation, or 70 micrograms orally. (The therapeutic type A Botox® currently licensed in the United States contains only 0.3 percent of the estimated human lethal inhalation dose or 0.005 percent of the estimated lethal oral dose.)

TREATMENT AND PREVENTION OF POISONING WITH BOTULINUM TOXIN. Therapy for botulism consists of supportive care and, if available, passive immunization with a neutralizing equine antitoxin. The neutralizing antibody prevents the toxin from causing further nerve damage, but does not reverse existing paralysis. Seven distinct antigenic types of toxin exist; although all types of toxin produce the same clinical manifestations, the antibodies are specific for each individual toxin, thus complicating the problem of antitoxin production. Currently available antitoxin neutralizes toxin types A, B, and E, which are the most common causes of human botulism. An investigational heptavelent antitoxin against toxins A, B, C, D, E, F, and G is available on a limited basis.

The equine antitoxin may cause serum sickness syndrome, which includes a rash, joint inflammation, and sometimes a very severe anaphylactic reaction within 10 minutes of its administration.

Botulism patients may require parenteral nutrition, hospitalization in an intensive care unit, mechanical ventilation, and treatment for secondary infections, which occur primarily because of poor gag and cough reflexes that result in aspiration pneumonia. In a large outbreak of botulism, the need for mechanical ventilators, critical care beds, and skilled personnel may far exceed capacity. The United States is developing a reserve stock of mechanical ventilators. Human botulism immune globulin for intravenous use, which would prevent serum sickness reaction, is also being developed.

After a bioterrorist attack with botulinum toxin, the only effective preventive measure is the treatment of exposed individuals by intravenous injection with the equine botulinum antitoxin. The serum must be administered immediately, before nerve damage appears. The availability of adequate quantities of antiserum and means of administering it could present an insurmountable problem without a long, extensive period of preparation.

Pentavalent botulinum toxoid, a modified form of the toxin that stimulates the production of neutralizing antibodies without causing any harm, is investigational and is considered for use in laboratory workers at high risk of exposure, and by military personnel. But because of the scarcity of the spontaneous disease, mass immunization is neither feasible nor desirable, and such immunization would prevent the medicinal effects of Botox®. Immunization would be ineffective as post-exposure prophylaxis, since it takes several months to develop immunity after starting administration of the toxoid.

Decontamination is possible: The botulinum toxin is easily destroyed by heating. An internal temperature of 85 degrees C for at least five minutes will detoxify contaminated food or fluid; extremes of temperature and humidity will degrade aerosolized botulinum toxin, and fine aerosols will dissipate into the atmosphere. Depending on weather, aerosolized toxin has been estimated to decay at between less than one percent to four percent per minute. At a decay rate of one percent per minute, substantial inactivation of toxin occurs by two days after aerosolization. If the release of aerosolized botulinum toxin is suspected, some protection may be conferred by covering the mouth and nose with clothing such as an undershirt, shirt, scarf, or handkerchief. Intact skin does not need to be protected.

ADDITIONAL READING

Atlas RM. Bioterrorism before and after September 11. *Critl Rev Microbiol* 2001;27:355.

Bell JH, Fee E, Brown TM. Anthrax and the wool trade, 1902. *Am J Public Health* 2002;92:705.

Bray RS. *Armies of Pestilence, The Impact of Disease on History.* New York: Barnes and Noble, 2000.

Christopher GW, Cieslak TJ, et al. Biological warfare, A historical perspective. *JAMA* 1997;278:412.

Dennis DT, Inglesby TV, et al. Tularemia as a biological weapon: medical and public health management. *JAMA* 2002;287:452.

Dubois RJ, ed. *Bacterial and Mycotic Infections of Man.* Philadelphia: JB Lippincott Co, 1848.

Franz DR, Jahrling PB, et al. Clinical recognition and management of patients exposed to biological warfare agents. *JAMA* 1997;278:399.

Guillemin J. The 1979 anthrax epidemic in the USSR: applied science and political controversy. *Proc Am Philosc Assoc* 2002;146:18.

Henderson DA, Inglesby TV, O'Toole T, eds. *Bioterrorism; Guidelines for Medical and Public Health Management.* Chicago: JAMA and Archives Journals (AMA Press), 2002.

Huerta M, Leventhal A. The epidemiological pyramid of bioterrorism. *Israel Med Assoc J* 2002;4:498.

Ingelsby TV, O'Toole T, et al. Anthrax as a biological weapon, 2002: updated recommendations for management. JAMA 2002;287:2236.

Kasten FH. Biological weapons, war crimes and World War-I. Science 2002;296:1235.

Penn CC, Klotz SA. Anthrax pneumonia. Semin Respir Infect 1997;12:28.

Pittman PR, Gibbs PH, et al. Anthrax vaccination: short-term safety experience in humans. Vaccine 2001;20:972.

Plotkin SA, Brachman PS, et al. An epidemic of inhalation anthrax, the first in the twentieth century, I: clinical features. Am J Med 2002;112:4.

Sato PA, Ryan M, et al. Surveillance for adverse events associated with anthrax vaccination, US Department of Defense, 1998–2000. MMWR Morb Mort Wkly Rev 2000;49:341.

Sidel V, Cohen HW, Gould RM. From woolsorters to mail sorters: anthrax, past, present and future. Am J Public Health 2002;92:754.

Sotos JG. Botulinum toxin in biowarfare. Editorial, JAMA 2001;285:2716.

Swanson-Bierman B, Krenselok EP. Delayed life-threatening reaction to anthrax vaccine. J Clin Toxicol 2001;39:81.

Turnbull PC. Introduction: anthrax history, disease and ecology. Curr Top Microbiol Immunol 2002;271:1.

Wilson TM, Gregg DA, et al. Agroterrorism, biological crimes, and biowarfare targeting animal agriculture. The clinical, pathologic, diagnostic and epidemiologic features of some important animal diseases. Clin Lab Med 2001;21:549.

Zilinskas RA. Iraq's biological weapons. The past as future? JAMA 1997;278:418.

CHAPTER 16

THE SARS EPIDEMIC

A NEW DISEASE RETRACES THE
EXPERIENCE WITH OLDER DISEASES

N EAR THE END OF 2002 A NEW DISEASE, A DEADLY FORM
of pneumonia, appeared in a province in southern China and quietly
spread. Civic and public health authorities initially ignored the evidence of its
presence for as long as they could, but ignorance of the nature of the infecting
agent and absence of preventive measures or effective therapy led to a mounting death toll that finally brought the existence of the epidemic to public notice.
By that time it had spread regionally and had begun to appear internationally.

The deadly nature of the infection led to it being named Severe Acute
Respiratory Syndrome (SARS), at least temporarily. The initial rapid spread and
high mortality among reported cases generated fears of a repetition of an
extremely high international death toll like that of the 1918 influenza epidemic.
A public reaction close to panic developed, but simultaneously this reaction
spurred an international effort to identify and understand the disease—an effort
that was rapidly successful and led to effective public health measures that limited its spread.

Widespread media attention to SARS helped to trigger an unprecedented
collaborative international scientific effort; the causative viral agent was quickly
identified and its genome delineated. Standard methods of preventing spread of
respiratory tract infections were successfully employed, and efforts to control the
disease by means of vaccination began to be developed within a month of its
identification. These rapid scientific developments led to measures that, as of
this writing, seem to have controlled the spread of the disease and minimized its
mortality thus far. However, many questions remain about SARS and its

causative agent, a little-studied microbe called a *coronavirus*, and the possibility of a recurrence remains strong.

This disease is too new at this time for a "history" to be written. Almost every statement in this chapter needs to be qualified with the phrase "according to present knowledge." Nevertheless, enough is known to allow us to describe how SARS began by spreading from animals to humans, repeating a phenomenon documented historically in earlier chapters, and to trace its spread from an area in Southern China to many parts of the world.

The pattern of spread of SARS differs from that of most of the great pandemics of the past in two ways that reflect technological progress and resulting changes in human activity: Earlier pandemics spread by ship and affected port cities predominantly; SARS spread by air travel, and cities with major international airports were primarily affected. In earlier pandemics, the predominant mode of spread was commercial travel; SARS was spread mainly by tourist travel and people on business trips living in different parts of the world.

In China, bureaucratic bungling and commercial concerns led to attempts to cover up the problem, as has happened everywhere almost routinely in past epidemics. Government authorities hoped it would just go away, but public reaction led to official recognition of the problem once effective international news coverage was generated and there were bans on travel to affected cities and even whole countries, again mimicking events seen during previous epidemics. Thus far this reaction has contained the disease successfully, and a true international medical disaster seems to have been averted.

AN EPIDEMIC BEGINS. The first cases of SARS appear to have occurred in November 2002, mostly among people involved in the culinary preparation of rare animals in restaurants, probably in or near Foshan in the Guangdong Province of China, 90 miles up the Pearl River from Hong Kong. When World Health Organization (W.H.O.) officials were finally able to investigate the disease they found an unusual preponderance of food handlers and chefs, about five percent of the first 900 patients, compared with less than one percent of such workers among patients with ordinary forms of pneumonia. Guangdong province (the name used to be anglicized as Canton) borders on Hong Kong; it is notable for exotic cuisine prepared with freshly killed animals. In restaurants animals are kept alive until selected by patrons for preparation as food, and workers in these crowded, dirty "zoos" are in close contact with the animals.

In December 2002, one of the earliest cases of this new form of severe pneumonia died in the First People's Hospital of Shunde. He was a seller of snakes and birds. His wife and several of the hospital staff also developed a pneumonia that was unresponsive to known therapeutic agents. Around the same time in December, a chef was admitted to the People's Hospital in Heyuan, 100 miles to the north, and eight doctors became infected there. On Jan. 2, another desperately ill chef was hospitalized in the city of Zhongshan, south of Shunde, setting off yet another local outbreak. Early in January, health departments in Shunde, Heyuan, and Zhongshan reported clusters of strange, atypical pneumonia to Guangdong provincial authorities, but it is doubtful that the information was transmitted to the Ministry of Health in Beijing, or ever reported to international health agencies. Local knowledge of the untreatable disease resulted in herbal medicine shops being besieged and, when provincial health officials publicly suggested that residents fumigate rooms with a vinegar-based steam wash, the price of white vinegar shot up 12-fold.

On February 21, Dr. Liu Jianlun, a 64-year-old pulmonary specialist from the Zhongshan Hospital in Guangdong province, attended a nephew's wedding in Hong Kong, although he had a fever. He stayed at the three-star Metropole Hotel, and apparently passed the disease to several other guests at that hotel, including two Canadians, an American businessman en route to Hanoi, and three young women from Singapore, as well as a resident of Hong Kong. Shortly later, the disease appeared in Hanoi, Singapore and Toronto and spread in Hong Kong.

When Dr. Liu's breathing became difficult, he hospitalized himself at the Kwang Wah Hospital in Hong Kong and advised the medical staff about the existence of the new form of pneumonia ravaging his hometown. One of the heroes of this story, Dr. Liu insisted that he be placed in an isolation unit and that the hospital staff don protective gear before entering his room; although in subsequent outbreaks hospital workers were especially frequent among the new cases seen, only one worker at that hospital became infected. Dr. Liu died a few days after admission, but his story was not told to other doctors in Hong Kong or the rest of the world.

When guests at the Metropole Hotel left Hong Kong, they took SARS, until then confined to the Chinese mainland, with them and it began a journey around the world, spread quickly by modern air travel. An Italian doctor, Dr. Carlo Urbani, working in Hanoi, Vietnam, as a member of an international program providing medical care to underserved areas, alerted the World Health Organization about a new form of pneumonia he was seeing there. His report immediately launched international efforts to identify and control the disease, but Dr. Urbani soon died of it himself. A woman from Toronto visiting in Hong Kong, Kwan Sui-chu, returned home, became very sick and, on March 5, died in a Toronto hospital. Since precautions against spread of respiratory infections were not considered necessary, she spread the disease to her son and at least five hospital workers. Within two months the outbreak in Canada spread to at least 140 other patients and caused 15 fatalities. Warnings about travel to Toronto from the W.H.O. seriously damaged the economy of that city before the subsidence of the outbreak allowed the sanctions to be lifted.

ROLE OF THE W.H.O. The World Health Organization responded amazingly quickly and fulfilled one of its intended functions admirably, initiating studies to identify the new disease, obtaining international cooperation among virologists to find the causative agent, and alerting health authorities worldwide about its dangers. This episode constitutes an encouraging and outstanding example of peaceful, beneficial functions on an international scale. The story of the role of the W.H.O. is not a simple one, however, since it began when it was watching for the usual forms of influenza virus that cause pandemics, such as bird flu, in the area where SARS was just appearing. On Nov. 20, 2002, a W.H.O. official, Dr. Klaus Stöhr, was in Beijing meeting with China's health authorities to discuss China's flu vaccination policy. Dr. Stöhr, the head of the W.H.O. flu program, was looking for the likely cause of the next year's epidemic in time to prepare an effective vaccine against that specific strain. This extremely important program includes 111 laboratories around the world that annually scan 200,000 samples from flu victims, and the vaccines that are prepared each year thus far have contained the annual influenza outbreaks successfully.

Later it became clear that, while Dr. Stöhr was in Beijing, the first cases of SARS had emerged in Guangdong. During the meeting he attended in Beijing, Guangdong's representative described a small flu outbreak that had killed several people in one hospital. In retrospect, Dr. Stöhr subsequently said, "I think that was SARS." At the time, though, there was no particular reason to suspect that the outbreak was anything other than severe flu. In epidemiologic terms, he pointed out, "one or three or five deaths in a province of 55 million is nothing." He decided to get samples of the virus from Guangdong; they were tested at the Communicable Disease Control Center (the CDC) in Atlanta and at a cooperating Japanese laboratory, but they contained only the usual flu strains.

W.H.O. Investigators were particularly on the alert for bird flu, especially in southern China, since an outbreak there in 1997 had infected 18 people, 6 of whom died, a frighteningly high case fatality rate comparable to that of smallpox. As a result, 1.4 million birds were slaughtered, a considerable economic blow, but the outbreak was quickly stopped. In December 2002, an unusually powerful strain of influenza killed many wild birds in the Hong Kong Botanic Gardens. Although most strains that infect humans cause nothing worse than conjunctivitis and usually affect only poultry farmers, mutating bird flus spreading to humans remain a fearsome possibility.

As early as February 11, W.H.O. officials were suspicious about the reports of a new severe form of flu in southern China, but Beijing health authorities responded to an official inquiry saying only that an unidentified pneumonia in Guangdong had hospitalized 300 people and killed five. Guangdong's Communist Party secretary added, in an announcement to the news media, that "the illness has been effectively treated and controlled." However, at the same time, the provincial health officials publicly urged anyone with fever or cough to seek immediate medical help and suggested that residents fumigate rooms with vinegar-based steam, wear gauze masks, and stay away from shopping centers and train stations.

Despite the terse, uninformative, official replies, in mid-February a flu lab in Hong Kong, affiliated with the agency, was asked by the W.H.O. to get some samples from fatal cases in Guandong. The lab's doctors had friends and relatives working in hospitals in southern China and, traveling by bus or train, they quietly got samples from patients who died. However, since they were primarily seeking bird flu, they found nothing unusual. On February 18, the Chinese disease center announced that chlamydia bacteria, organisms that usually cause either conjunctivitis or venereal infection, had been found in the lungs of two patients. They attributed the outbreak of pneumonia in Guandong to that cause, but W.H.O. and CDC officials did not believe it.

Officials outside of China became increasinly concerned and tried another route to get specimens from affected patients. Dr. Keiji Fukuda of the C.D.C. and Dr. Hitoshi Oshitani of the W.H.O. were sent to Beijing with a plan to get to southern China, but Chinese officials remained uncooperative. For two weeks the two scientists got only routine briefings, and in early March they left in frustration.

That it was a form of pneumonia unresponsive to antibiotics and antivirals was not understood until March 11, when an American businessman named Johnny Chen, who had been in the Metropole Hotel in Hong Kong, had infected 7 employees at his garment business in Hanoi as well as 22 hospital workers, possibly including Dr. Carlo Urbani. When Dr. Urbani reported the alarming details of the outbreak he was fighting in Hanoi before he died of the disease himself, renewed efforts were made to investigate the outbreak. Tissue samples from fatal cases in Hanoi were flown to Bangkok on a plane chartered by the United States Embassy, because local airlines refused to carry them but, once again, influenza virus was not found. Meanwhile, workers in a Hong Kong hospital were falling sick; an airport worker, who had also been in the Metropole, had been given a jet nebulizer to clear his lungs in the hospital and his secretions infected 112 others. Again, a Hong Kong laboratory cultured specimens from some of these cases but found no flu virus.

On March 12, the W.H.O. issued a global health alert as a routine news release, but it was little noticed, since at that time the press was focused on the impending war in Iraq. However, Canadian health authorities read the announcement and realized that the pneumonias that occurred in one Toronto family, the one whose mother had been in Hong Kong, fit the pattern. When a doctor who had treated patients with the new, severe form of pneumonia in Singapore left for a medical conference in New York after telling relatives he was feeling sick, authorities there felt that they needed to find him and see that he was isolated to prevent further spread of the disease. During a stopover in Frankfurt he was found at the airport and safely isolated. That incident galvanized W.H.O. officials into issuing a much more urgent and detailed alert on March 15. They decided that a name was needed for the new disease to make it easy to concentrate attention on it. After several tries, Dr. David L. Heymann, Head of Infectious Diseases at the W.H.O., settled on a pronounceable acronym, SARS.

The W.H.O. obtained unprecedented cooperation from a group of laboratories around the world and sent them all specimens from infected cases. Within a few days they all had isolated the same virus, providing instantaneous confirmation and quickly establishing it as the causative agent. The viral particles visualized with the electron microscope showed little excrescences on the surface, giving it a crown-like appearance, hence the name "*coronavirus.*" It was a new form of this group of viruses; previously known coronaviruses had caused mild intestinal and respiratory diseases in humans and a sometimes more severe disease in a variety of animals including enteritis in pigs, infectious bronchitis in turkeys, respiratory disease in other birds, hepatitis in mice, encephalomyelitis in pigs, peritonitis in cats, and have also caused disease in dogs and horses. Two previously known coronaviruses that infected humans caused mild upper respiratory infections and perhaps as many as 30% of the "colds" in some years; they also caused a form of bowel inflammation that might sometimes have been labeled "intestinal flu."

By mid-April, two laboratories—the British Columbia Cancer Agency in Vancouver and the C.D.C. in Atlanta—had mapped the entire genome of the new virus. The SARS virus genome differed from any previously known coronavirus. It may have come from wild animals that had never been studied, or appeared as a mutation that enabled it to cause more severe disease and a higher fatality rate than did previously known human coronaviruses.

When the viral agent was identified it was sought in various animals sold in food markets in the originally affected areas, including snakes, chickens, cats, turtles, badgers, frogs, and rats. Microbiologists from Hong Kong University who bought 25 exotic animals in a food market found the SARS virus in six masked palm or Himalayan civets, a cat-size animal related to the mongoose that resembles a large weasel. In the wild the civet is a threatened species but as food it is obtained from special farms. The virus was found in the feces of some animals and was also found in single animals from two other species, including a raccoon dog. (The raccoon dog is a dog that resembles a raccoon, and it is also eaten in this area.) Antibody evidence of infection was also found in the blood of at least one badger in a wildlife market in Shenzen, in southern China. It should be noted that the virus might be spreading among various species and the ones initially identified as carrying the agent might not be the main reservoirs in the wild.

By the middle of March, Chinese officials admitted that an epidemic of SARS was affecting the country. Before this, unaware that patients diagnosed with pneumonia were infected with a new, virulent, highly contagious microbe, hospitals placed them in wards and treated them as they did other patients with the usual forms of pneumonia. Thus, the infection was passed on to others, and hundreds of health workers fell ill. In China and other parts of Asia, more than 30 percent of the initial SARS victims were hospital workers, pointing to the infectivity of the virus and the need for careful, thorough isolation of patients. Once such measures were finally adopted, the epidemic began to subside.

Some of the patients turned out to be "super-spreaders"—a small group of SARS patients who are highly infectious. The reason some patients are super-spreaders of the infection is unclear at this time. No special characteristics specific to the patients have been identified. Mutational variations that affect pathogenicity could explain the more efficient spreading of the disease by some patients.

If SARS reappears next winter, a vaccine may be available to prevent its spread. But developing a vaccine takes about eight months, so if a dangerous new flu is likely to hit the world by the next fall and winter—which was when suspicions arose this past year about the reports of pneumonia in southern China, time is already short; that is why W.H.O. officials have felt an urgent need to get the process in motion.

Respiratory infections occur predominantly in the winter, but the outbreak of SARS occurred in the spring and subsided as summer began in the regions affected. If SARS reappears, it is important to keep in mind that the virus is shed in intestinal secretions as well as from the respiratory tract, and that it is not delicate—it is capable of surviving on various surfaces and products for hours—perhaps as long as a few days. Although food workers handling exotic animals have been infected in large numbers, there is no evidence that the disease was transmitted by the ingestion of well-cooked meat from such animals.

It should be kept in mind that the outbreak of SARS occurred in the northern hemisphere, but it has appeared very close to the equator. If it spreads south of the equator, winter there will aid its spread. Other factors that can affect its spread and the likelihood of recurrences are the strong possibility that it exists in an animal reservoir, hence the possibility of spread from animal to animal, within species as well as from species to species. An animal reservoir for the virus also means that it might periodically disappear for a time and then be reintroduced to infect humans, making it difficult to control and impossible to eradicate. These factors add to the urgency for developing a vaccine as soon as possible.

ANOTHER ANIMAL DISEASE AFFECTING HUMANS. Present evidence points to SARS having begun as an animal disease transmitted to humans, like many others described in earlier chapters. Measles, smallpox, tuberculosis, whooping cough, some forms of malaria, ebola virus, and infection by dangerous strains of E. coli, are all thought to have originated as animal diseases. The most devastating pandemic disease of all time, AIDS, apparently began when a primate carrying a viral ancestor of AIDS infected humans, perhaps by means of a bite that penetrated the skin. Then it spread via human fluids directly from person-to-person, primarily by sexual transmission and through contaminated blood products or needles.

Diseases that primarily affect rodents, such as bubonic plague and hantavirus, a recently-discovered, devastating, systemic pulmonary infection, are other examples of animal to human transmission of disease. Most relevant to the tale of human infection from animal sources, however, is influenza, which has spread from pigs or poultry in the past to cause devastating human epidemics, especially the 1918 influenza pandemic described earlier.

LESSONS FROM THE SARS EPIDEMIC. As far as is known thus far, SARS remains a minipandemic. As of this writing there have been just under 9,000 known cases in at least eight countries. Reports of fatality rates have varied widely, with variations in the certainty of diagnosis. The fatality rate of reported cases overall has averaged about nine percent. This outbreak of SARS has reproduced many of the characteristics of severe plagues and epidemics that have affected mankind in the past as described in earlier chapters of this book.

Close proximity of humans to the animal reservoir is an important factor in spread of disease from animals to humans. In addition to the new experience with SARS, other examples previously discussed are the bubonic plague bacillus, spread from rats that live under or near human dwellings, and hantavirus, which is spread by exposure to small rodents or their droppings near human habitation and has occurred primarily in the rural US Southwest. In some of the known instances of animal diseases affecting humans, a mutational change or another mechanism of alteration of the genome of the infecting agent seems to have been responsible. In other instances, specifically influenza, the new agent may have gone from one animal, such as pigs, to another, such as chickens, and then to humans without genetic alteration.

Pets are another means of spreading animal infections to humans. Years ago we had a form of pneumonia called *psittacosis* that spread from pet parakeets and other exotic birds to humans. Most recently, early in the summer of 2003, a pox virus causing monkeypox, a disease similar to a mild form of smallpox, has been observed among people with unusual pets, especially prairie dogs. At least 33 cases were noted in reports of an initial outbreak in several midwestern states, including Wisconsin and Illinois.

Another disease that primarily affects animals appeared in humans in the 1970's. The new disease was first observed in Connecticut, causing a small but very unusual epidemic of chronic arthritis in children. An alert mother of one of the affected children realized there was a cluster of too many cases of disease thought to be non-infectious in a small town to be due to chance. Physicians at Yale University eventually identified the disease and named it after the town, Lyme. It took a few years to isolate the causative agent, a spirochete that was named *Borrelia burgdorferi*. It was found to be spreading from tiny ticks that usually fed on deer and small rodents, such as field mice, as well as on birds and dogs, but it took advantage of humans when they made themselves available. The disease may have resulted from the importation of deer carrying infected ticks from Europe. It spread to many areas of the country, especially near the east and west coasts, and continues to be a problem, causing a variety of illnesses. Unlike SARS, close human contact with infected animals is not necessary. Lyme disease is spread by infected parasitic insects—ticks—that usually affect other species when in infested areas, a phenomenon resembling the means of spread of bubonic plague.

In addition to its origin as an animal disease, SARS resembles many other major epidemic diseases in that, once people become infected, they spread it primarily by human travel. Speedy international air travel has been an important factor in this regard and likely will be so in any future epidemics. The SARS episode also differs from past epidemics in many important ways—especially in those factors that are the positive result of human intervention. Authorities denied its existence and tried to cover up the outbreak as a matter of national pride as well as for protection of commercial interests, as has happened repeatedly in the past. Once the seriousness of the problem became known, international cooperation identified the nature of the causative agent and instituted intelligent preventive measures that stopped its spread unbelievably quickly. This major triumph of international leadership and scientific cooperation, aided by public dissemination of important information by the media, apparently prevented a devastating pandemic, or at least limited it considerably. SARS serves as an important lesson and, hopefully, a model for future responses when outbreaks of threatening disease occur.

ADDITIONAL READING

Altman LK. The SARS enigma: cases are declining, but fears remain. *New York Times.* June 8, 2003

Altman LK. W.H.O. scientists say tactics to fight SARS are working. *New York Times.* May 18, 2003

Drosten C, Gunther S, et al. Identification of a novel coronavirus in patients with severe acute respiratory syndrome. *N Engl J Med* 2003 Apr 10; [epub ahead of print].

Emanuel EJ. Preventing the next SARS. *New York Times.* May 12, 2003.

Enserink M, Vogel G. Infectious Diseases: Deferring Competition, Global Net Closes In on SARS. *Science* 2003;300:224

Enserink M. Calling all coronavirologists. *Science* 2003;300:413–4.

Enserink M. Searching for a SARS Agenda. *Science* 2003;300:1487

Holmes LV, Enjuanes L. Perspective: The SARS Coronavirus: A Postgenomic Era. *Science* 2003;300:1377

Ksiazek TG, Erdman D, et al. A Novel Coronavirus Associated with Severe Acute Respiratory Syndrome. *N Engl J Med* 2003 Apr 16; [epub ahead of print].

Lee N, Hui D, et al. A Major Outbreak of Severe Acute Respiratory Syndrome in Hong Kong. *N Engl J Med* 2003 Apr 14; [epub ahead of print].

Marra MA, et al. The genome sequence of the SARS-associated coronavirus. *Science* 2003;300:1399

Poutanen SM, Low DE, et al. Identification of Severe Acute Respiratory Syndrome in Canada. *N Engl J Med* 2003 Apr 10; [epub ahead of print].

Rosenthal E. From China's Provinces, a Crafty Germ Spreads. *New York Times.* April 27, 2003

Rota PA, et al. Characterization of a novel coronavirus associated with severe acute respiratory syndrome. *Science* 2003;300:1394.

INDEX